Brooklyn Dodgers
Transactions,
1890–1957

ALSO BY LYLE SPATZ
AND FROM MCFARLAND

New York Yankees Openers: An Opening Day History of Baseball's Most Famous Team, 1903–2017, 2d ed. (2018)

Dixie Walker: A Life in Baseball (2011)

Yankees Coming, Yankees Going: New York Yankee Player Transactions, 1903 Through 1999 (2000; paperback 2009)

Bad Bill Dahlen: The Rollicking Life and Times of an Early Baseball Star (2004)

Brooklyn Dodgers Transactions, 1890–1957

A History and Analysis

Lyle Spatz

McFarland & Company, Inc., Publishers
Jefferson, North Carolina

Library of Congress Cataloging-in-Publication Data

Names: Spatz, Lyle, 1937– author.
Title: Brooklyn Dodgers transactions, 1890-1957 : a history and analysis / Lyle Spatz.
Description: Jefferson, North Carolina : McFarland & Company, Inc., Publishers, 2025 | Includes bibliographical references and index.
Identifiers: LCCN 2024055391 | ISBN 9781476693309 (paperback : acid free paper) ∞
ISBN 9781476655215 (ebook)
Subjects: LCSH: Brooklyn Dodgers (Baseball team)—History—19th century. | Brooklyn Dodgers (Baseball team)—History—20th century. | Baseball players—United States. | Baseball—United States—History—19th century. | Baseball—United States—History—20th century.
Classification: LCC GV875.B7 S63 2025 | DDC 796.357/640974723—dc23/eng/20241209
LC record available at https://lccn.loc.gov/2024055391

ISBN (print) 978-1-4766-9330-9
ISBN (ebook) 978-1-4766-5521-5

© 2025 Lyle Spatz. All rights reserved

No part of this book may be reproduced or transmitted in any form or by any means, electronic or mechanical, including photocopying or recording, or by any information storage and retrieval system, without permission in writing from the publisher.

Front cover: Brooklyn Dodgers players (highlighted from left to right—top row) Pee Wee Reese, Jackie Robinson, Roy Campanella; (second row) Bob Caruthers, Dolph Camilli, Doc Bushong, Dave Foutz; (third row) Jim Gilliam, Duke Snider, Preacher Roe; (fourth row) Al Burch, Bill Dahlen, Van Lingle Mungo, Pete Reiser

Printed in the United States of America

McFarland & Company, Inc., Publishers
 Box 611, Jefferson, North Carolina 28640
  www.mcfarlandpub.com

For all those who grew up with the joys
and sorrows of rooting for the Brooklyn Dodgers

Contents

Preface	1
ONE. 1890–1894	5
TWO. 1895–1899	17
THREE. 1900–1904	34
FOUR. 1905–1909	50
FIVE. 1910–1914	62
SIX. 1915–1919	76
SEVEN. 1920–1924	90
EIGHT. 1925–1929	102
NINE. 1930–1934	122
TEN. 1935–1939	145
ELEVEN. 1940–1944	169
TWELVE. 1945–1949	191
THIRTEEN. 1950–1954	209
FOURTEEN. 1955–1957	226
Chapter Notes	237
Bibliography	243
Index	249

Preface

The trading, drafting, buying, and selling of players has forever been a part of the quest to create better baseball teams. These transactions are also a major contributor to the game's history and folklore. But perhaps the most important role may be their ability to stir the interest and passion of fans. Whether it is the purchase of a veteran star during the heat of a pennant race, a multi-player trade made during the dead of winter, or the off-season scramble for desirable free agents, player transactions engender more interest and heated debate among fans than almost any other aspect of the game. In no other sport but baseball are the movements of players from one team to another so eagerly anticipated and analyzed. Additionally, baseball fans love trade rumors: they love to hear about them, to read about them, and to talk about them. They even love those that are rumored but don't get made.

Ostensibly, there is in every trade the assumption that the combination of current players, future players, or money a particular team is getting is approximately equal in value to what it is giving up. Of course, it rarely works out that way. Furthermore, some trades that seem one-sided when they are made often turn out to be so but not necessarily in favor of the team that appeared to have the advantage initially.

This book included the trades, drafts, sales, and purchases of the Brooklyn Dodgers from their entry into the National League in 1890 through the 1957 season, after which they moved to Los Angeles. Because it is space- and time-prohibitive to detail every transaction, each year includes a section called "Also in," which lists many of the other transactions made that year. I do not include deals where the Dodgers acquired a player who never played for them or was not part of a subsequent deal that did involve a Dodgers player. Some lifelong Dodgers appear in the narratives only in their relation to other transactions.

For those transactions I deem meaningful, I have attempted to put it and the players involved in historical perspective. I describe why the Dodgers and the other team(s) made the deal. Using the newspapers of the time, I quote the expectations that the owners, general managers, and managers of the respective teams had for their new players. I show what the players moving to and from Brooklyn thought about their old and new teams. The description and analysis of each transaction will vary from a few sentences to several paragraphs.

This book focuses primarily on the baseball aspects of these transactions; for the most part it deliberately excludes extensive discussions of money and length of contracts, including those details only when they were believed essential to the story. The business aspects of baseball transactions obviously are important, especially in the age of free agency; however, it is a subject adequately covered elsewhere.

The team names I use are the ones that were current at the time of the transaction. For minor league teams, the league in which they played will be identified, and often its classification. Mention of a player as a minor leaguer in the title of a transaction means that he has never before appeared in a major league game. And unless noted, the ending of a player's career refers specifically to his major league career. Many players in the time frame covered here would return to the minor leagues when their time in the major leagues ended.

Because this is primarily a reference book, each trade is treated as if the reader is looking at it without necessarily having read what came before. This makes it necessary to repeat certain facts pertaining to individual players and front office personnel, for which I beg your forbearance. For instance, within a chapter Leo Durocher might be called "Leo Durocher," "Durocher," "Dodgers manager Leo Durocher," "manager Leo Durocher," or "manager Durocher."

The basic building blocks for these transactions come from *Retrosheet* and the database built by the late and sorely missed Tom Ruane. During my research I came across several dates that differed from Tom's. Given that many newspapers often had multiple editions, some of the dates might be off by a day or so. Some perhaps even more, as the date the trade is made and the date a contract is signed may differ. This often occurs when a physical exam is required for one or more players. Sometimes I have used one and sometimes the other, as the specific date does not affect the analysis of the trade.

The primary source for information and quotes relating to these transactions was the newspapers of the day. Biographies from the SABR BioProject were also a valuable source of information for many players. The statistics I use are from three sources treasured by researchers: *Baseball-Reference*, founded by Sean Forman, *Baseball Almanac*, founded by Sean Holtz, and *Retrosheet*, founded by David Smith and currently under the direction of Tom Thress. While measures of performance, like batting average, runs batted in, won-lost records, and earned run average have come under attack in recent years, I believe they still tell a story, and so I use them.

I also use newer and perhaps more meaningful measures, like OPS+ for batters and ERA+ for pitchers. OPS+ is the player's OPS (the sum of his on-base average [OBA] and slugging percentage [SLG]) adjusted for that season's OPS league average and the player's home ballpark. ERA+ is a pitcher's earned run average (ERA) adjusted for that season's league average ERA and the pitcher's home ballpark.

Finally, I thank Gary Mitchem, McFarland's senior editor, for his encouragement, advice, and cooperation. As with my previous books, members of the Society for American Baseball Research were there to answer whatever obscure fact I asked them to verify. I thank Andy McCue for lending his expertise on the Dodgers ownership history. I thank Michael Spatz, who read and fact-checked some of the early chapters, but most of all I thank Maury Bouchard. Maury read and fact-checked the entire manuscript, saving me from numerous potential embarrassments. Any errors that slipped through are because I missed Maury's correction.

CHAPTER ONE

1890–1894

1890

The roster of the Brooklyn team that entered the National League in 1890 was much like the one that won the American Association (AA) pennant in 1889 and would win the National League pennant in 1890. They played their games at Washington Park. Bill McGunnigle was the manager, and these were the players on the roster for their first game in the new league, at Boston on April 19.

PITCHERS: Bob Caruthers, Mickey Hughes, Tom Lovett
CATCHERS: Doc Bushong, Bob Clark, Tom Daly, George Stallings
INFIELDERS: Hub Collins, Dave Foutz, George Pinkney, Germany Smith
OUTFIELDERS: Thomas Burns, John "Pop" Corkhill, Darby O'Brien, Adonis Terry (also a pitcher)

The following players from the 1890 team completed their careers with Brooklyn: Doc Bushong (1890), Hub Collins (1892), Darby O'Brien (1892), and Dave Foutz (1896).

Thomas Burns was released by Brooklyn early in 1895 and was signed a few days later by the New York Giants.

Bob Caruthers played for Brooklyn through the 1891 season and for the St. Louis Browns in 1892.

Tom Daly played for Brooklyn through 1901 (except for 1897) before "jumping" to the new American League's Chicago White Sox in 1902.

Mickey Hughes was released by Brooklyn in July 1890 and signed with the Philadelphia Athletics of the American Association later that month.

Tom Lovett was released by Brooklyn in March 1894 and signed with the Boston Beaneaters.

George Pinkney played for Brooklyn through the 1891 season. He was released in January 1892 and signed with the St. Louis Browns.

Adonis Terry played for Brooklyn in 1890 and 1891. He was released in June 1892 and signed with the Baltimore Orioles several days later.

July 7, 1890: Signed Free Agent Outfielder Patsy Donovan

The Brooklyn Bridegrooms, newly moved from the American Association to the National League, completed their first transaction on July 7, 1890. President Charles Byrne signed rookie outfielder Patsy Donovan, whom the Boston Beaneaters had released earlier that day. Donovan, a 25-year-old left-handed-hitter, batted .257 in 32 games for Boston. With Brooklyn outfielders Darby O'Brien and Pop Corkhill battling injuries, manager Bill McGunnigle said he would use Donovan in center field until one of them returned.

Donovan appeared in 28 games for Brooklyn. He showed great defense but batted just .219. He did much better in the postseason championship series between the Bridegrooms and the American Association champions, the Louisville Colonels. In the seven-game series, in which each team won three with one game ending in a tie, Donovan had eight hits in 17 at-bats for a .471 average. After Brooklyn failed to re-sign Donovan, manager Jack Chapman of the Colonels signed him in March 1891.

Also in 1890:
Released: Outfielder Pop Corkhill

1891

In 1891 the team moved from Washington Park to Eastern Park. For the 1891 season, John Ward replaced Bill McGunnigle as manager.

January 27, 1891: Signed Free Agent Pitcher George Hemming and Free Agent Catcher Tom Kinslow

The demise of the Players' League after one season had all the National League and American Association clubs eager to sign the best of that league's players. Number one on Brooklyn's list was John Ward, the longtime pitcher and shortstop for the National League teams in Providence and New York. Ward had played for and managed the Brooklyn Ward's Wonders of the Players' League in 1890, a league that he had been most responsible for creating.

On January 28, President Charles Byrne said he was almost certain Ward would be his manager this year. He revealed that Ward had met with pitcher George Hemming and catcher Tom Kinslow in New York and signed them for the 1891 season. Hemming, a 22-year-old right-hander, and the 25-year-old right-handed-hitting Kinslow had been teammates under Ward on the 1890 Wonders.

Hemming had an 8–15 record with a 4.96 earned run average in 1891, his only season with Brooklyn. Kinslow batted .271 in 267 games over four seasons with Brooklyn before being traded to the Pittsburgh Pirates in January 1895.

February 5, 1891: Signed Free Agent Shortstop John Ward

On February 5, John Ward made it official when he signed to manage and play for Brooklyn in 1891. "I am perfectly satisfied with the terms I signed under," Ward said. "I could have got more salary with some other club, but the reason I signed to play in Brooklyn is because I like that city."[1]

Ward served as the Grooms manager for two seasons with a .536 won-lost percentage. As the team's shortstop in 1891 and its second baseman in 1892, he batted .270 and stole 145 bases, including a league-leading 88 in 1892.

March 23, 1891: Signed Free Agent Outfielder Mike Griffin

After having spent the offseason in search of a center fielder, Charles Byrne announced he had signed 26-year-old Mike Griffin, a player with whom Brooklyn fans were familiar. They had seen the speedy left-handed-hitting Griffin as an opponent with the American Association's Baltimore Orioles (1887–1889) and with the Players' League Philadelphia Athletics (1890).

Manager Ward was leaving for a vacation in Europe when the signing took place but voiced his approval when he returned. "I was glad to learn the day I sailed that Mr. Byrne had signed Mike Griffin.... Mike is as fine an outfielder as can be found in the country, and is, besides, a good hitter and runner."[2]

March 24, 1891: Sold Catcher Bob Clark to the Cincinnati Reds

Bob Clark spent four years (1886–1889) with the Brooklyn club of the American Association and moved with the team to the National League in 1890. He had a combined .241 batting average, including a .219 mark in 1890. The addition of catcher Tom Kinslow in the offseason made Clark expendable.

The *Cincinnati Enquirer* applauded the deal. "Clark is a Covington [Kentucky] boy and is very popular on both sides of the [Ohio] river. He has a large following, and from a box-office standpoint, as well as in a playing sense, the local League club scored a big mark in securing him."[3]

April 9, 1891: Sold Shortstop Germany Smith to the Cincinnati Reds

When Brooklyn acquired John Ward in February 1891, to manage and play shortstop, the incumbent shortstop, Germany Smith, knew there would no place for him on the club. Smith said he preferred to play in Cincinnati, and Charles Byrne satisfied his wish by selling him to the Reds just before the season opened.

"Smith appreciated the justice of our move to secure a good captain and manager" Byrne said, "and while he would have liked to remain in Brooklyn, felt that there was no room for him on the team as long as we had Ward."[4]

"It will be a pleasure for me to play alongside Biddy McPhee and [Arlie] Latham," Smith said after reporting to manager Tom Loftus.[5]

December 1891: Were Assigned First Baseman Dan Brouthers by the National League

Dan Brouthers, one of the greatest sluggers of the nineteenth century, began his National League career with the Troy Trojans in 1879. He also played for the Buffalo Bisons, Detroit Wolverines, and Boston Beaneaters during his 11 seasons in the NL. "Big Dan," as he was called, was a left-handed batter who stood 6'2" and weighed more than 200 pounds. Brouthers led the league in batting average and on-base average three times, and slugging percentage and OPS (on-base average plus slugging percentage) six times. He played for the Boston Reds in the Players' League in 1890 and in the American Association in 1891. He led the AA in batting average, slugging percentage, and OPS in 1891.

"Brouthers really was a great hitter, one of the most powerful batters of all time.... I don't think I ever saw a stronger hitter," said John McGraw.[6]

The Reds disbanded after they were not among the four teams chosen when the AA merged with the National League in 1892. Despite his age—Brouthers would be 34 when the new season started—many clubs wanted him, but the National League assigned him to Brooklyn.

1892

February 21, 1892: Signed Free Agent Pitcher Ed Stein

Right-handed pitcher Ed Stein had an excellent 12–6 record as a 20-year-old rookie with the 1890 Chicago Colts. He was 7–6 in mid-July of 1891, but a recent spell of ineffectiveness led manager Cap Anson to sell him to Omaha of the Western Association. Brooklyn manager John Ward signed the 22-year-old Stein to pitch for the Grooms in 1892. Stein was an excellent addition. He won 90 games and lost 66 in his six seasons with Brooklyn, including 27, 19, 26, and 15 wins in his first four seasons.

March 15, 1892: Signed Free Agent Pitcher Bill Kennedy

President Charles Byrne returned from a trip to Bellaire, Ohio, with the signed contract of Bill Kennedy, a 24-year-old right-hander. Kennedy had come highly recommended by Bob Leadley, who managed the National League's Cleveland Spiders in the second half of 1890 and the first half of 1891.

"Kennedy looks like a promising man," Byrne said. "He carries himself well and seems to be endowed with great strength of character, a good quality for a pitcher. He has an excellent reputation in the West. He pitched for the Wheeling [WV] Club in 1889 and for Denver in 1890 and 1891. His work with both these organizations was eminently satisfactory."[7] Kennedy would join the Brooklyn club at their training camp in Ocala, Florida, Byrne added.

It was an outstanding signing by Byrne. Kennedy, known around the league as "Roaring Bill," would pitch for Brooklyn over the next ten years under six different managers. He was a four-time 20-game winner, winning 25 in 1893, 24 in 1894, and 22 and 20 for the 1899 and 1900 pennant-winning Superbas. But he pitched only 85 1/3 innings with a 3–5 record in 1901, and manager Ned Hanlon released him after the season.

Kennedy ranks at or near the top in several categories among Brooklyn pitchers. His 177 wins are second only to Dazzy Vance. He is the leader in games (382), innings pitched (2,866), losses (149), and walks (1,130).

May 16, 1892: Were Assigned Pitcher George Haddock by the National League

Right-hander George Haddock won 11 and lost 19 for the National League's Washington Nationals in 1889, his first full major league season. He joined the Buffalo Bisons of the Players' League in 1890, where he led that league in losses, with 26. Haddock made a complete turnaround in 1891, with a 34–11 record for the American Association's Boston Reds. The AA merged with the National League in 1892, when the eight-team NL added four AA teams—Baltimore, Louisville, St. Louis, and Washington.

The 25-year-old Haddock was assigned to Brooklyn but held out for the first month of the season over a salary dispute. He was Brooklyn's best pitcher in 1892, with a 29–13 record and a 3.14 earned run average. He was not nearly as effective in 1893, as a combination of arm problems and the increase in the pitching distance to 60 feet six inches resulted in an 8–9 record and a 5.60 ERA. Late in the season the club released him.

Also in 1892:
   Signed Free Agents: Outfielder Tommy Corcoran
   Released: Pitcher Bob Caruthers; Pitcher Adonis Terry

1893

For the 1893 season, Dave Foutz replaced John Ward as manager.

February 15, 1893: Sold Second Baseman John Ward to the New York Giants

In was not uncommon in this era for owners, and even players, to own stock in other teams. For one, Brooklyn's John Ward owned twenty shares of stock in the New York Giants. National League owners were worried about the failing franchise in New York and arranged for Brooklyn to sell Ward to the Giants. Ward batted .270 in 253 games in his two seasons with Brooklyn. He would play second base for New York and replace Pat Powers as the Giants manager.

February 18, 1893: Traded Third Baseman Bill Joyce and Cash to the Washington Senators for Infielder Danny Richardson

Brooklyn quickly replaced the departed John Ward at second base when they traded for Washington Senators infielder Danny Richardson. "Patrons of the game here," wrote the *Brooklyn Standard Union*, "regard the latest deal as being a decidedly one-sided affair, with all the odds in favor of Brooklyn."[8] In retrospect, it is hard to see why.

The 30-year-old Richardson had spent most of his nine-year career with the New York Giants. Playing for the Senators in 1892, he batted .240 in 142 games. The 25-year-old Joyce, batted .245 in 97 games in 1892, his only season in Brooklyn. But after holding out in 1893, Joyce had five successful seasons with Washington and the New York Giants.

April 20, 1893: Signed Free Agent Infielder-Outfielder George Shoch

George Shoch was a six-year veteran valued for his ability to play the infield and the outfield. While sharing the shortstop position with Tim O'Rourke for the 1892 Baltimore Orioles, he batted .276 with 50 runs batted in. A broken arm in August ended the 34-year-old Shoch's season early, and the Orioles released him. He signed with Brooklyn shortly before the start of the 1893 season.

May 25, 1893: Signed Free Agent Outfielder–First Baseman Harry Stovey

Right-handed-hitting Harry Stovey had been one of the top sluggers of the nineteenth century. Five times he led his league (the American Association or the National League) in home runs and extra-base hits; four times in triples and runs scored; and three times in total bases and slugging percentage. But at 36, Stovey's career was coming to an end. After batting a lowly .154 in eight games, the Baltimore Orioles released him on May 19. On the morning of May 25, he signed with Brooklyn, which was looking for a first baseman to fill in for the oft-injured Dan Brouthers. That afternoon, as the team's center fielder, Stovey had two hits, two walks, and stole two bases against his old team.

Stovey played his last game as a major-leaguer on July 29. Brooklyn released him on August 6. Appearing in 48 games, he hit .251 with one home run and 29 runs batted in. The home run, on June 8 against the St. Louis Browns, was the 122nd of his career, the major league-high at the time.

July 6, 1893: Signed Free Agent Pitcher Ed Crane

Ed Crane had pitched in the Union Association, the American Association, the Players' League, and the National League in his eight-year career. Years of overeating and excessive drinking left him terribly out of shape. Moreover, he had been a disruptive force wherever he played. Crane began the 1893 season with the New York Giants. He had a 2–4 record when the Giants released him on May 19. Brooklyn picked him up on July 6. In what would be the final appearances of his major-league career, he made two starts, both losses.

July 26, 1893: Purchased Third Baseman Willie Keeler from the New York Giants

In addition to being a left-handed batter, Willie Keeler was also a left-handed thrower. That did not prevent Giants manager John Ward from using him at third base in all 14 appearances of his rookie season,

1892. When the Giants traded for infielder George Davis before the 1893 season, they moved the 21-year-old Keeler to center field. He had a few poor performances there, and on May 10 he sprained an ankle that kept him out for five weeks.

There was no place for Keeler when he returned, and in a move that was unpopular with their fans, the Giants sold him to Brooklyn for $800. He played his first game for the Grooms the next day, playing third base and getting three hits before the home crowd at Eastern Park. "I am glad to be playing regularly. I dislike to be idle," Keeler said after the game.[9] "The Brooklyn club never made a better choice than this," wrote the *Brooklyn Citizen* about its new acquisition. "He is a ballplayer all the way through, in fielding and in batting."[10]

August 2, 1893: Signed Free Agent Pitcher Dan Daub

Dan Daub had shown promise in the four games he pitched as a rookie with the 1892 Cincinnati Reds. But Reds manager Charles Comiskey had too many seasoned pitchers on his club to retain the 25-year-old right-hander for 1893. Brooklyn signed Daub on August 2 of that year. He spent five seasons with them, pitching as a starter and a reliever, before arm trouble ended his career after the 1897 season. Daub had a won-lost record of 44–50 and an earned run average of 4.81 for Brooklyn.

December 29, 1893: Traded Third Baseman-Outfielder Willie Keeler and First Baseman Dan Brouthers to the Baltimore Orioles for Third Baseman Billy Shindle and Outfielder George Treadway

After purchasing Willie Keeler from the Giants in July 1893, Brooklyn's manager Dave Foutz used him the same way Giants manager John Ward had, as a fill-in at third base and in the outfield, though his defense was unsteady at both positions. Keeler's hitting, however, remained consistent; he batted .333 for the Giants and .313 for Brooklyn.

While Ward had no room for Keeler with the Giants, he had praised him to Ned Hanlon, who had just completed his first full season as the manager of the Baltimore Orioles. The Orioles had finished eighth in 1893, and Hanlon was intent on changing the makeup of the team. He approached Foutz and Charles Byrne about Dan Brouthers, Brooklyn's veteran first baseman. In 1892, his first season in Brooklyn, Brouthers led the league in batting average (.335), hits (197), and runs batted in (124), but injuries limited him to 77 games in 1893. Brouthers had been the game's greatest slugger, but he was now 35 years old and had lost favor with the Brooklyn fans.

In exchange for Brouthers, Hanlon offered 27-year-old right-fielder George Treadway, who batted .260 as a rookie and was reputed to have the best throwing arm in the league. Still, because of his looks, rumors spread that Treadway was black, and the fans in Baltimore, which was still very much a Southern city in its racial attitudes, had razzed him about it all season.

Foutz said he and Hanlon had been talking for several weeks about a Brouthers for Treadway trade. "In addition to his offer of Treadway for Brouthers," Foutz said, "Manager Hanlon also offered us Shindle for Keeler. This was also accepted."[11] Hanlon had suggested Billy Shindle because he knew of Brooklyn's need for a third baseman. The 33-year-old Shindle had openly expressed his desire to play elsewhere, which made Hanlon view him as a distraction. In addition, Hanlon already had decided to use Hughie Jennings at shortstop in 1894 and move John McGraw from shortstop to third base, making Shindle excess baggage. Brooklyn had wanted both Treadway and Shindle in exchange for Brouthers, but Hanlon, remembering Ward's recommendation of Keeler, held out for a two-for-two trade.

Shindle played five solid years for Brooklyn, batting .274 in 619 games. Treadway played two seasons for Brooklyn, the first of which, 1894, was sensational—a .330 batting average, 102 runs batted in, and an on-base average + slugging percentage (OPS) of .941.

Despite the contributions of Shindle and Treadway, the trade would prove to be one of the most lopsided ever, in favor of Baltimore. Yet at the time, some in Brooklyn felt it was they who had gotten the better of it. They had added two regulars in exchange for an over-the-hill Brouthers and the slightly built and unproven Keeler. Louisville Colonels manager Billy Barnie, a major league manager since 1883, was among them.

"Keeler is still an unknown quantity, and his work last year was not of the star order," Barnie said. "So, I can't see where Baltimore is going to profit by the deal. Brouthers is a good batter and Keeler may be, but good batting is not the only feature to be considered."[12] Keeler, of course, was about to launch his Hall-of-Fame career.

Also in 1893:

Released: Pitcher George Haddock

1894

March 15, 1894: Sold Second Baseman Danny Richardson to the Louisville Colonels

"One unfortunate and much regretted incident of the [1893] campaign," wrote the *Brooklyn Eagle*, "was the defection of Danny Richardson, a man who had achieved a reputation as being the best player in his position, to wit, second baseman of any ballplayer in the country."[13] The paper judged the outcome of Brooklyn's trade for Richardson as very detrimental to the club's interests. It had suspended Richardson for his bad habits, specifically his drinking, before the season reached its midpoint. He appeared in only 54 games and batted just .223. The second baseman's absence from the team required an almost daily change of players in the infield, costing the Brooklyn club several games and leading to a seventh-place finish.

Louisville manager Billy Barnie visited Richardson in Elmira, New York, and asked the player if he would be willing to play for the Colonels if Barnie could make a deal for him. Richardson said he would, and Barnie and President Byrne, of the Brooklyn club, met and negotiated the sale. Barnie offered $1,500 for the 31-year-old Richardson, while Byrne wanted $2,500. They finally agreed on $2,250, and Barnie handed over a check to complete the purchase. Richardson played just one season for Louisville, his final one.

April 27, 1894: Signed Free Agent Pitcher Hank Gastright

Hank Gastright, a 29-year-old right-hander, was a veteran of five major league seasons. His best was 1890, for the American Association's Columbus Solons, when he had a 30–14 record and a 2.94 earned run average. In 1893 he pitched for the Pittsburgh Pirates and Boston Beaneaters, where he won a combined 15 games and lost only five. His .750 winning percentage was the best in the National League.

Based on his 12–4 record with Boston, he wanted more money than the Beaneaters were willing to pay, so on April 13, they released him. Gastright met with Dave Foutz when the club was in Washington, and he accepted the Grooms' manager's offer. In 1894, his only season with Brooklyn, Gastright had a 2–6 record with a 6.39 earned run average in 16 games.

July 13, 1894: Signed Free Agent Catcher Billy Earle

Billy Earle had a .354 batting average in 21 games for the Louisville Colonels when manager Billy Barnie released him early in July. The Grooms signed him, and he batted .340 for them in 14 games before manager Dave Foutz released him on September 6. He was only 26, but he would never play in the major leagues again. Earle's ability to hypnotize his teammates, some of whom were convinced he had an "evil eye," caused too much disruption for any team to add him to their roster.

November 24, 1894: Purchased Catcher John Grim from the Louisville Colonels

While actively seeking to trade catcher Tom Kinslow, the Grooms purchased John Grim from the Louisville Colonels as his intended replacement. The price was $2,500 with $2,000 down and $500 when Grim signed with Brooklyn, which he did shortly before Christmas. Grim, a 6'2", 175-pound right-handed-hitter, batted .299 in 109 games for the 1894 Colonels. In five years with Brooklyn, he batted .268 in 322 games. He was released in July 1899 after Brooklyn traded for catcher Deacon McGuire.

Also in 1894:

Purchased: Outfielder John Anderson from the Haverhill (MA) club of the New England League
Released: Third Baseman Pete Gilbert

CHAPTER TWO

1895–1899

1895

January 25, 1895: Traded Catcher Tom Kinslow to the Pittsburgh Pirates for Pitcher Ad Gumbert

Ad Gumbert's departure from Pittsburgh seemed assured after his insubordination in St. Louis the previous July. Gumbert had criticized manager Connie Mack's trade of pitcher Red Ehret to the St. Louis Browns for pitcher Pink Hawley. The Pirates sent Gumbert, a right-handed pitcher, to Brooklyn for popular catcher Tom Kinslow. Mack tried to get Brooklyn to kick in an extra $500 as part of the deal, but Brooklyn president Charles Byrne refused.

Gumbert, had a 107–79 record for three teams in seven seasons, including a 15–14 mark for the 1894 Pirates. "I am very pleased over the deal," said Byrne. "He will do well with us as he has been eager to come here for some seasons."[1] Gumbert won 11 and lost 16 for the 1895 Grooms and was winless in four decisions in 1896 when he was released in July.

In his four seasons with the Grooms, Kinslow batted .271 in 267 games. John Grim, the catcher recently purchased from the Louisville Colonels, was expected to take his place.

June 24, 1895: Purchased Pitcher Bert Abbey from the Chicago Colts

On June 25 Charles Byrne verified the previous day's announcement from Chicago that the Colts had sold pitcher Bert Abbey to Brooklyn. The 25-year-old right-hander had a 9–30 career record, including a loss in his only appearance this season. Abbey won five of seven decisions for Brooklyn in the second half of the season and had an 8–8 record in 1896, his final major league season.

November 14, 1895: Drafted Outfielder Fielder Jones from the Springfield (MA) Maroons of the Eastern League

In 1895, 23-year-old Fielder Jones began the season, his third in the minor leagues, with the Binghamton Crickets of the Class B New York State League. When that league went out of business in midseason, Jones joined the Springfield Maroons of the Class A Eastern League. Playing 50 games for the Maroons, he batted a spectacular .399, with 57 runs scored and 29 stolen bases. As a Grooms rookie in 1896, he batted .354 with an OPS+ of 135 and team-high .427 on-base percentage.

Jones spent five years in Brooklyn, the first three as a right fielder and the final two as a center fielder. He batted above .300 in four of those seasons, with a combined batting average of .313 and a combined OPS+ of 112. Before the 1901 season Jones "jumped" to the Chicago White Sox of the new American League.

November 18, 1895: Purchased Outfielder Tommy McCarthy from the Boston Beaneaters

Tommy McCarthy, a 5'7" slap-hitting outfielder, had been a major leaguer for 12 years. His greatest success had come in the last four, as a member of the Boston Beaneaters. President Byrne purchased McCarthy from Boston for $6,000, ignoring the 32-year-old's mention of retirement. A week later Byrne traveled to Boston and persuaded him to sign.

McCarthy's OPS+ had slipped to 86 in 1895, which he blamed on a bad leg that had handicapped him all season. Together with the discord that existed on the Boston team made it a difficult year for him. For the last few seasons in Boston, McCarthy and his outfield partner, center fielder Hugh Duffy, often called the "heavenly twins," had been one of the best duos in the league.

McCarthy would be playing alongside a new center fielder in 1896, Brooklyn's very capable Mike Griffin. Byrne predicted that in Griffin and McCarthy the team would have two outfielders who are strong in every element of the game. Right field, he said, will be taken care of by either John Anderson or newcomer Fielder Jones.

Byrne expressed satisfaction at his success in securing McCarthy. "He is one of the most intelligent players in the National League ranks and will strengthen the team considerably. It took me a long time to bring him around, but I have succeeded to our mutual satisfaction."[2] In his only season in Brooklyn, McCarthy batted .249 in 104 games. A slight 145 pounds when he broke in, McCarthy was now in the 200-pound rage and wisely retired at the end of the season.

McCarthy's excellent 1893 and 1894 seasons and his consistent defense would lead eventually to an undeserved place in the Hall of Fame.

Also in 1895:
Chosen in Major League Rule 5 Draft: Infielder Frank Bonner
Released: Pitcher Jack Cronin

1896

Brooklyn finished in a ninth-place tie in 1896, and co-owner Ferdinand Abell was unhappy over Dave Foutz's inability to maintain order on the team. At season's end Abell declared, "Manager Foutz had very poor control over the men who did about what they pleased."[3] *Shortly thereafter, Billy Barnie replaced Foutz as the team's manager.*

November 13, 1896: Traded Shortstop Tommy Corcoran to the Cincinnati Reds for Shortstop Germany Smith, Pitcher Chauncey Fisher, and Cash

At the meeting of the National League owners in Chicago, Brooklyn's Charles Byrne and Cincinnati's John T. Brush swapped their longtime starting shortstops. Most observers believed the Reds had gotten the better of the deal that sent 37-year-old Germany Smith to Brooklyn in exchange for 27-year-old Tommy Corcoran. Brooklyn's newly named manager, Billy Barnie, and Cincinnati's manager, Buck Ewing, oversaw the negotiations. After much dickering, the Reds agreed to send right-handed pitcher Chauncey Fisher and $1,000 to Brooklyn to complete the deal. Brush and Ewing were jubilant after the trade. "I never felt better than I do right now," Brush said.[4]

Germany Smith had been with the Brooklyn club in 1890, their first season in the National League, after spending five years with them in the American Association. He was sold to Cincinnati in 1891, after the club hired John Ward to manage them and to play shortstop. Extremely popular in his six years with the Reds, Smith was an outstanding defensive player whose last two seasons had been his best on offense. Byrne, meanwhile, had never forgiven himself for letting Smith go. He considered him the most popular man to ever wear a Brooklyn uniform.

Tommy Corcoran began his career in 1890 with Pittsburgh of the Players' League. When that league went out of existence, he signed with the Philadelphia Athletics of the American Association for 1891. After the season that league folded, too, and in 1892 Corcoran signed with Brooklyn. Manager and shortstop John Ward recognized Corcoran's fielding ability and moved to second base so Corcoran could play shortstop. Like Smith, Corcoran was popular with the local fans, and he would be a better hitter, with a solid .273 average in his five seasons with Brooklyn.

Chauncey Fisher won ten games and lost seven, for the Reds in 1896. He would win nine and lose seven in 1897, his only season with Brooklyn.

Barnie tried to make another trade, this one with Louisville. It would send his veteran center fielder, Mike Griffin, to the Colonels for their sensational young left fielder, Fred Clarke. Not surprisingly, Colonels manager Bill McGunnigle wanted no part of such a deal.

1897

April 26, 1897: Signed Free Agent Pitcher Sadie McMahon

On April 17, 1897, the Baltimore Orioles released veteran right-hander Sadie McMahon. McMahon immediately received a generous offer to sign with the Louisville Colonels, but he turned it down. Manager Frank Selee of the Boston Beaneaters also tried to sign McMahon, with no success. On April 26, Brooklyn manager Bill Barnie was successful in signing him.

The 29-year-old McMahon had been a major leaguer since 1889, for the Philadelphia Athletics and the Baltimore Orioles in the American Association (AA) and then for the Orioles when they moved to the National League in 1892. He twice won more than 30 games in the AA and was a two-time 20-game winner for manager Ned Hanlon's NL Orioles.

When Barnie signed McMahon, he said he needed a pitcher and considered McMahon the best one available. But after he lost six games without a win, Barnie released him in July.

November 12, 1897: Traded Second Baseman George Shoch and Cash to the St. Louis Browns for Second Baseman Bill Hallman

Owners Charles Byrne and Ferdinand Abell of Brooklyn, and Benjamin Muckenfuss, secretary of the St. Louis Browns, completed a late-night deal that sent Brooklyn second baseman George Shoch to the Browns in exchange for their second baseman, Bill Hallman.

Shoch was already 34 years old when he signed with Brooklyn shortly before the start of the 1893 season. He spent the last five seasons with them, as an infielder and an outfielder, but primarily as a second baseman. Overall, he played 381 games for Brooklyn, with a .281 batting average and a 96 OPS+.

Hallman had worn a Philadelphia uniform—in the National League, the Players' League, and the American Association—from 1888 to June of 1897, when he was traded to St. Louis. He also served as the third of four managers the Browns had in 1897, with a 13–36–1 record for a team that went 29–102–2. In addition to his production declining, he clashed often with Browns owner Chis Von der Ahe, making his departure a foregone conclusion. In 1898, his one season in Brooklyn, Hallman batted .244 in 134 games.

Also in 1897:

Purchased: Outfielder Jimmy Sheckard from Brockton (MA) Shoemakers of New England League, Pitcher Ralph Miller from Fall River (MA) Indians of New England League; Catcher Jack Ryan from Syracuse Stars of Eastern League; Pitcher Joe Yeager from Lancaster (PA) Maroons of Atlantic League

Sold: Pitcher Jim Korwan to Chicago Colts

Signed Amateur Free Agents: John Brown

Released: Pitcher Dan Daub

1898

The Brooklyn club had three managers in 1898; Billy Barnie (15–20); Mike Griffin (1–3); and Charles Ebbets (38–68–4). Ebbets was now a co-owner with Ferdinand Abell and George Chauncey. Ebbets replaced Charles Byrne as president after Byrne passed away in January. In 1898 the team moved from Eastern Park to a new version of Washington Park.

March 6, 1898: Purchased First Baseman Tommy Tucker from the Washington Senators

George "Candy" LaChance had been Brooklyn's first baseman since 1894; nevertheless, the club sent $800 to the Washington Senators to obtain 34-year-old Tommy Tucker, an 11-year veteran. President Charles Ebbets gave his reasons for the purchase.

"I have secured Tucker for several reasons, the primary one being that LaChance has not yet signed a contract, and I do not propose to take any chances when the season begins. Should LaChance come to terms, and I do not wish to infer that he will not, we will have two first basemen, making us unusually strong in that position ... besides which, LaChance can cover the outfield and go behind the bat if that is necessary."[5] LaChance eventually signed and played 74 games at first base, mostly in the season's second half. Tucker had played first in 73 games before he was sold to the St. Louis Browns in July.

May 19, 1898: Traded Outfielder John Anderson to the Washington Senators for Third Baseman Al Wagner

Charles Ebbets announced he had sent outfielder John Anderson to the Washington Senators without indicating if Brooklyn would receive cash or a player in exchange. He did say he had refused offers for Anderson from the New York, Louisville and Baltimore clubs.

Former president Charles Byrne had purchased Anderson from the Haverhill, Massachusetts, club of the New England League in August 1894. Anderson, now 24, batted .288, .314, and .325 the past three seasons, but he had started slowly this year, with just three hits in 21 at-bats.

Anderson played 110 games for the Senators, with a .305 batting average, but on September 21 he was returned to Brooklyn. In 19 games with the Grooms, he batted .275, giving him a .294 batting average for the season. His combined slugging percentage of .494 and his 22 triples were both league highs. His final season with Brooklyn was 1899.

Ebbets needed a third baseman after releasing Billy Shindle, so Washington's third baseman Al Wagner was sent to Brooklyn to complete the trade. Wagner, the older brother of Honus, was a 26-year-old rookie who batted a combined .226 in 1898, his only major league season.

July 18, 1898: Sold First Baseman Tommy Tucker to the St. Louis Browns

Tommy Tucker contributed two hits in Brooklyn's 7–6 victory over the St. Louis Browns on July 18. After the game Browns manager Tim Hurst purchased Tucker from Brooklyn. When the Browns left for Boston after the series, Tucker went with them.

Tucker had played in 73 games at first base and had a .279 batting average, which led the *Brooklyn Standard Union* to call the sale unfathomable. "The team sadly needs strengthening," it wrote, "yet Tucker is one of the strongest players.... The release of Tucker will be a sad blow to the cranks of Brooklyn, who have admired his earnest ball playing all this season."[6]

The *Standard-Union* reported further that the Pittsburgh club, anxious to secure Tucker, had offered pitcher Frank Killen in an even trade, but their offer was turned down. Killen, the paper believed, would have greatly strengthened the team's pitching staff.

Also in 1898:

Purchased: Pitcher Harry Howell from the Meriden (CT) Bulldogs of the Connecticut State League

1899

In the weeks preceding the March 1899 National League's winter meetings, Brooklyn's co-owners, Ferdinand Abell and Charles Ebbets, and the Baltimore club's owners, Harry Von der Horst and manager Ned Hanlon, agreed to an exchange of stock and a merger of their operations. Called Syndicate Baseball, or cross-ownership, the owners each had the same percentage interest in both clubs. Attendance had been poor in both cities in 1898, but on the assumption that Brooklynites would turn out in far greater numbers for a strong team than Baltimoreans would, the syndicate chose to move the Orioles best players to the Grooms for the 1899 season, with Hanlon becoming Brooklyn's manager. (His new team would come to be known as the "Superbas," playing off a popular Broadway act called Hanlon's Superbas.)

A few days before Christmas 1898, Willie Keeler had said he knew the move from Baltimore to Brooklyn was coming, and he believed many of his teammates would prefer to be transferred as a group. On February 4, 1899, the deal was completed. Brooklyn received from Baltimore, "two thirds of the outfield, half the infield, and all three 20-game winners," wrote Baltimore historian James Bready. "In return, Baltimore got four .200-hitters, a 2–0 pitcher, a 1–7 pitcher, and a minor leaguer."[7] In all, nine players were assigned from Brooklyn to Baltimore, and seven players were assigned from Baltimore to Brooklyn. Orioles third baseman John McGraw and catcher Wilbert Robinson were also slated to go to Brooklyn, but both lived in Baltimore and were co-owners of the Diamond Café, a popular gathering spot in Baltimore. Both continued to play for the Orioles in 1899, with McGraw replacing Hanlon as the manager.

February 4, 1899: Assigned Pitcher Harry Howell from Brooklyn to the Baltimore Orioles

Harry Howell was the "2–0 pitcher" Orioles historian James Bready was referring to when he wrote about the lopsided transfer of players between Baltimore and Brooklyn. But Howell, a 22-year-old spitball pitcher, had appeared in only two games. He made his major league debut in October 1898, a few weeks after the Superbas purchased him from the Meriden (CT) Bulldogs of the Connecticut State League. The Brooklyn native appeared in two games within six days, both complete-game wins against the Philadelphia Phillies.

February 4, 1899: Assigned First Baseman Candy LaChance from Brooklyn to the Baltimore Orioles

George "Candy" LaChance, a 6'1" switch-hitter, had played first base for Brooklyn since 1894. He topped the .300 mark that season and again in 1895 and 1897. His normalized on-base average + slugging percentage (OPS+) exceeded the league average from 1894 through 1897. But LaChance had struggled in 1898; his batting average slipped to .247, and he led the league in strikeouts with 60. The Brooklyn fans turned on him, and he seemed to lose confidence. LaChance expressed his doubts to John McGraw, his new manager in Baltimore. "I don't know if I can make good or not after the way they roasted me in Brooklyn. It took all the starch out of me entirely."[8]

LaChance bounced back to have a successful 1899 season with the Orioles, but the syndicate sold him to the minor league Cleveland Blues of the newly named American League. In 1901 he was still with Cleveland when the American League was recognized as a major league.

February 4, 1899: Assigned Catcher Aleck Smith from Brooklyn to the Baltimore Orioles

Aleck Smith was 26 years old when he reached the major leagues with Brooklyn in 1897. He played in 66 games, batting .300 with 39 runs batted in and one home run, the only home run in his nine-year big-league career. Primarily a catcher, Smith also played the outfield. He spent part of 1898 in the minor leagues, but got into 52 games for the Grooms, with a .261 batting average.

February 4, 1899: Assigned Pitcher Kit McKenna from Brooklyn to the Baltimore Orioles

Twenty-five-year-old right-hander Kit McKenna spent only one season with Brooklyn, 1898. He appeared in 14 games, winning two and losing six, with an earned run average of 5.63. He was 2–3 with Baltimore in 1899, his final major league season.

February 4, 1899: Assigned Outfielder Jimmy Sheckard from Brooklyn to the Baltimore Orioles

Jimmy Sheckard, whom Brooklyn drafted from the Brockton (MA) Shoemakers of the New England League in August 1897, would prove to be the best player the Superbas lost in the exchange of players with Baltimore. In 105 games in 1898, his first full season, the 19-year-old Sheckard batted .277 with 64 runs batted in and an OPS+ of 112. The transfer to Baltimore was the first of several moves Sheckard would make between the two cities.

February 4, 1899: Assigned Catcher Jack Ryan from Brooklyn to the Baltimore Orioles

Jack Ryan had played three seasons with the Louisville Colonels of the American Association (1889–1891) and three with the National League's Boston Beaneaters (1894–1896) before the Superbas purchased him from the Syracuse Stars of the Eastern League in September 1897. A .189 batting average in 87 games in 1898 made him highly expendable. He played in two games for the 1899 Orioles but spent most of the season in the minor leagues.

February 4, 1899: Assigned Pitcher Ralph Miller from Brooklyn to the Baltimore Orioles

The Superbas purchased Ralph Miller in September 1897 from the Fall River (MA) Indians of the New England League. The now 25-year-old right-hander spent only one year with Brooklyn, 1898. He appeared in 23 games, 21 of which were starts. His record was 4–14, with an earned run average of 5.34. Miller was 1–3 with Baltimore in 1899, his final season.

February 4, 1899: Assigned Pitcher Jay Hughes from the Baltimore Orioles to Brooklyn

Pitcher Jay Hughes's performance against a team of barnstorming major leaguers in 1897 led Baltimore Orioles manager Ned Hanlon to sign the California native for the 1898 season. The 24-year-old rookie right-hander won 23 games, lost 12, and had a 3.20 earned run average for the second-place Orioles. Hughes did even better in 1899, his first year in Brooklyn, helping lead the Superbas to a pennant. He tied Joe McGinnity for the most wins in the league, with 28, and led the league in winning percentage (.824).

Homesick for the West Coast, Hughes played in the California League in 1900, before returning to Brooklyn in 1901, going 32–22 over the next two seasons. He left again for the West Coast in 1903, where he finished his career.

February 4, 1899: Assigned Shortstop Hughie Jennings from the Baltimore Orioles to Brooklyn

Before the swapping of players from Brooklyn and Baltimore, Hughie Jennings and several other of the key Orioles players being transferred to Brooklyn met in Baltimore. The purpose of the meeting was to form an alliance that would force the Brooklyn club to pay them a bonus. If Brooklyn were to be as monetarily successful as everyone was suggesting, they believed they deserved to share in the riches. They expected to be paid the league's top salary—$2,400—along with ten percent of the net profits.

"We believe we can play the game as well as ever and that we should be entitled to some of the profits which is the general belief will accrue from the change," said Jennings. "We like Baltimore, but we are dependent on the game for our livelihood and should be given a share of prosperity when it comes."[9]

Shortstop Jennings had been a major contributor to the Orioles great success from 1893 to 1898. He had a combined .359 batting average and an OPS of .918. But an early season arm injury kept him mostly sidelined until July, as Bill Dahlen replaced him at shortstop. Shortly after Jennings returned, on August 3, Ned Hanlon traded him back to Baltimore, for pitcher Jerry Nops and infielder Gene DeMontreville. Three days later the trade was canceled, and the players returned to their original teams. When Jennings returned to Brooklyn, Hanlon moved him to first base.

February 4, 1899: Assigned Outfielder Willie Keeler from the Baltimore Orioles to Brooklyn

Of all the players coming from Baltimore, the 5'4", 140-pound Keeler was the biggest prize. A Brooklyn-born left-handed batter, with the ability to find the open places on the field to direct his hits, he had thrived in Baltimore since being traded there by Brooklyn in January 1894.

In his five seasons with the Orioles, Keeler never batted below .371 or had fewer than 210 hits. He was the league's batting champion the past two seasons, with a .424 average in 1897 and a .385 average in 1898. He also led the league in hits in both those years, and he was still just a month short of his 27th birthday. Keeler was delighted to be coming to Brooklyn. "Well, I knew I had to go somewhere," he said, "and I can say frankly I would rather play in Brooklyn, my home, than anywhere else."[10]

February 4, 1899: Assigned Shortstop Bill Dahlen from the Baltimore Orioles to Brooklyn

Bill Dahlen never got to wear a Baltimore Orioles uniform. The Orioles had obtained him from the Chicago Orphans in exchange for shortstop second baseman Gene DeMontreville on January 25. Dahlen had been with Chicago since 1891, when he was a 21-year-old rookie. He was one of the best shortstops of his era, with a .299 batting average and an .834 OPS in his eight seasons. His 42-game hitting streak in 1894 is still the longest ever by a National League right-handed batter.

Dahlen was also someone who clashed often with Cap Anson, his manager for his first seven years in Chicago. Tom Burns who replaced Anson in 1898 had been trying for more than a year to work out a trade that would send him to Ned Hanlon's Orioles.

"But Hanlon did not have Dahlen in mind to be the shortstop in Baltimore. His plan was to bring him to Brooklyn to play third base. By stating his refusal to leave Baltimore for Brooklyn, John McGraw had created a potential vacancy there. It was that vacancy that Hanlon wanted Dahlen, rather than DeMontreville, to fill."[11]

February 4, 1899: Assigned Pitcher Al Maul from the Baltimore Orioles to Brooklyn

Al Maul's major league career began as an 18-year-old with the 1884 Philadelphia Keystones of the Union Association. In his only appearance, in August, the teenage right-hander pitched a complete game, allowing seven runs (only one earned) and lost. After two seasons in the minor leagues, he joined the National League's Philadelphia Quakers in 1887. Except for 1892, he had been a big-league pitcher since. But he had only two notable seasons—a league-leading 2.45 earned run average for the 1895 Washington Senators, and a 20–7 record with a 2.10 ERA for the 1898 Orioles. Maul was 2–0 for Brooklyn in 1899, when the club released him in August. He signed to play for the Philadelphia Phillies in 1900.

February 4, 1899: Assigned Outfielder Joe Kelley from the Baltimore Orioles to Brooklyn

In Joe Kelley Brooklyn was getting a 27-year-old outfielder who had been one of the "Big Four" that led the Baltimore Orioles dynasty of the mid–1890s. In seven seasons with the Orioles (six of them full seasons), the right-handed-hitting Kelley batted .351, drove in 653 runs, and had an OPS of .960. He also stole 290 bases, including 87 in 1896.

In a 1923 interview, Kelley's former teammate John McGraw told a reporter, "Joe had no prominent weakness. He was fast on the bases, could hit the ball hard and was as graceful an outfielder as one would care to see. He covered an immense amount of ground and had the necessary faculty, so prominent in [Tris] Speaker and others, of being able to place himself where the batter would likely hit the ball."[12]

February 4, 1899: Assigned First Baseman Dan McGann from the Baltimore Orioles to Brooklyn

Dan McGann was a 27-year-old switch-hitter who reached the major leagues with the Boston Beaneaters in August 1896. He batted .322 but committed 21 errors in 43 games at third base. Sent to the minor leagues in 1897, he switched to first base and was acquired by Baltimore in 1898 to replace veteran Jack Doyle. McGann batted .301 for the Orioles, with 106 runs batted in and a .404 on-base average.

February 4, 1899: Assigned Pitcher James McJames from the Baltimore Orioles to Brooklyn

James McJames earned the nickname "Doc" legitimately, having secured a medical degree before the start of the 1898 season. He was one of the three Brooklyn-bound Baltimore pitchers who were 20-game winners in 1898. His 27 wins were tops on the club, as were his 45 games and 40 complete games. It was McJames' first season in Baltimore, having been traded there by the Washington Senators along with Dan McGann and Gene DeMontreville.

McJames, 24, had a 19–15 record with a 3.50 earned run average for the champion Superbas in 1899, but struggled with physical problems. He sat out the 1900 season and was 5–6 in 1901 when the team released him in July.

March 11, 1899: Sold Outfielder Mike Griffin to the Cleveland Spiders

Mike Griffin lived up to the expectations owner Charles Byrnes and manager John Ward had for him when they acquired him as a free agent prior to the 1891 season. Griffin had a combined batting average of .305, a combined on-base average of .399, stole 264 bases, and scored more than 100 runs in six of his eight years in Brooklyn. His best two seasons were in 1894 and 1895.

Charles Ebbets had promised Griffin he would be the team's manager as well as a player in 1899, but that promise was broken when Ned Hanlon was named manager. An upset Griffin refused to play under Hanlon. He was sold to the Cleveland Spiders for $4,000, but refused to report and announced his retirement on April 7. He received a small settlement from the Superbas.

Griffin had been the team's finest and most popular player during his years in Brooklyn. According to the *Brooklyn Citizen,* "A sigh of intense regret will go up from the hearts of many Brooklyn baseball cranks when the news is conveyed to them that Mike Griffin, for many seasons a landmark with the Brooklyn team, and by long odds the slickest centerfielder that ever tore down a line drive is no longer connected with the team."[13]

April 2, 1899: Traded Shortstop George Magoon and Minor League Catcher Pat Crisham to the Baltimore Orioles for Catcher Aleck Smith

A day before the revamped Baltimore and Brooklyn clubs faced each other for the first time—a spring game in Augusta, Georgia—the teams negotiated a trade. Rookie George Magoon had been the Superbas primary shortstop in 1898, despite his .224 batting average and 45 errors. Hanlon had been pleased with the spring training play of newcomer Pete Cassidy and chose to trade Magoon.

Cassidy would play in six games before Hanlon included him in a multi-player trade later in the month. Pat Crisham played in 53 games for the 1899 Orioles—his only major league season—as a catcher and first baseman.

Aleck Smith was coming back to Brooklyn after being assigned to Baltimore in February. He batted .180 in 17 games and was traded to the Washington Senators in July.

April 23, 1899: Traded Pitcher Dan McFarlan, Infielder Pete Cassidy, Catcher Mike Heydon, and Cash to the Washington Senators for Catcher Duke Farrell, Third Baseman James Casey, and the rights to Minor League Pitcher Bill Donovan

Hopes were high for the revamped Superbas, but they had gotten off to a disappointing start, winning just three of their first seven games. Pete Cassidy had played well in spring training, leading manager

Hanlon to add him to the roster as a utility infielder. But he batted just .150 in three games at third base and two games at shortstop. The acquisition of James "Doc" Casey, an established third baseman, would allow Hanlon to move Bill Dahlen from third to shortstop, his natural position. Casey batted .269 as the full-time third baseman but lost his job to Lave Cross in 1900. He jumped to the Detroit Tigers in 1901.

Catcher Mike Heydon had yet to play a game for the Superbas and would play only three for the Senators this season. Pitcher Dan McFarlan, acquired from Baltimore, had appeared in only one game for Brooklyn. He was 8–18 for Washington.

In switch-hitting Duke Farrell, the Superbas were getting one of the best offensive and defensive catchers in the game. The 32-year-old veteran of 11 major league seasons was coming off consecutive seasons where he batted .322 and .314, but reportedly was unhappy in Washington. Farrell would bat .299 for Brooklyn in 1899 and have a combined .278 batting average for four seasons before jumping to the Boston Americans in 1903.

Hanlon was understandably pleased with the deal. "There will be a change for the better with Casey and Farrell on the team," he said. He was especially pleased by the addition of Farrell. "Farrell is an experienced catcher and will improve the backstopping wonderfully."[14]

Overlooked at the time was Bill Donovan, a 22-year-old right-hander who had a 1–6 record for Washington in 1898. He was currently with the Richmond (VA) Bluebirds of the Atlantic League. The Superbas purchased him at the end of July. After pitching briefly for Brooklyn in 1899 and 1900, he led the National League with 25 wins in 1901. Donovan won 17 in 1902 and then jumped to the Detroit Tigers of the American League.

July 13, 1899: Traded First Baseman Dan McGann and Catcher Aleck Smith to the Washington Senators for Catcher Deacon McGuire

"These negotiations for the trade have covered several days," Superbas manager Ned Hanlon said after completing the deal for Deacon McGuire. "I think we have made a good move, for our catching department has not been strong.... [Duke] Farrell and McGuire will alternate behind the bat from now on."[15]

The catcher Hanlon wanted to send to Washington was John Grim, but Senators manager Arthur Irwin would not make the trade unless he got Aleck Smith. Hanlon wanted McGuire badly and had to agree or risk losing the deal.

Smith, Farrell's backup, had played in only 17 games this season but was upset over the trade and said he would never play in Washington. He had nothing against Irwin and [owner J. Earl] Wagner, he said, but he did not care to leave New York, where he had a profitable business. The Brooklyn owners were not concerned about Smith's refusal to go to Washington. There were no restrictions in the deal and McGuire would come to Brooklyn whether Smith and McGann agreed to go to Washington or not. Smith did say he would be willing to go to Baltimore, and in early August the Orioles purchased him from Washington.

McGann took a more good-natured view of the matter. "I don't mind it a bit. I'd rather be playing regularly anywhere than warming a bench here."[16] After batting .243 in 63 games for Brooklyn, he batted .338 in 73 games for Washington. McGann played in the major leagues through the 1908 season, and he was the regular first baseman on the strong New York Giants teams of the early twentieth century.

Although McGuire was 35 and had been a major leaguer for 16 years, he was still a productive player. In his nine years with Washington (including one in the American Association), he had a .298 batting average and an OPS+ of 107. It was well-known McGuire was unhappy in Washington and was upset this past April when Hanlon traded for Farrell instead of him. McGuire batted .298 in 202 games over three years with the Superbas before jumping to the American League's Detroit Tigers in March 1902.

August 3, 1899: Traded First Baseman Hughie Jennings to the Baltimore Orioles for Infielder Gene DeMontreville and Pitcher Jerry Nops

This latest deal between Brooklyn and Baltimore solved two of Ned Hanlon's problems; it also sparked renewed criticism of syndicate baseball. Jerry Nops, a 23-year-old left-hander, who had a combined 36–15 record the past two seasons and was on his way to 17–11 mark this year, would be a significant addition to the Superbas pitching staff. Brooklyn's third base problem would be solved by moving Bill Dahlen from shortstop to third base, where he would replace James Casey, and installing the very capable Gene DeMontreville at shortstop. In return the Orioles were getting Hughie Jennings, whose bad throwing arm resulted in Hanlon moving him to first base.

The trade seemed extremely one-sided in favor of the Superbas, and the general reaction in the press was that "Brooklyn was being strengthened by their Baltimore farm team."[17] Within a few days the trade was canceled. Jennings had played two games for Baltimore, while Nops and DeMontreville played none for Brooklyn.

"I opposed the deal from the start, because I knew it would cause trouble," Hanlon said. "But Mr. Von der Horst had his heart set on getting Jennings, and it would have meant a loss of friendship to oppose him."[18]

August 12, 1899: Signed Free Agent Pitcher Bill Hill

On the evening of August 11, the first-place Superbas had a slim 1½-game lead over the Boston Beaneaters. Ned Hanlon was searching for pitchers who might help maintain or increase that lead over the season's final two months. The best he could land was left-hander Bill Hill, whom Baltimore had released a few days earlier. Hill had a reputation for being difficult to control, but an effective pitcher when in shape. Harry Von der Horst had recommended him to Hanlon believing he would pitch well under a disciplinarian.

Now 25, Hill began his league career by losing 28 games for Louisville in 1896 and 17 in 1897. He also pitched for Cincinnati and Cleveland, compiling a lifetime record of 35–69. Hill had a win and a save in his two appearances with Brooklyn, the final two games of his career.

Also in 1899:

Purchased: Infielder Erve Beck from Toledo Mud Hens of the Interstate League

Released: Catcher John Grim, Pitcher Al Maul

CHAPTER THREE

1900–1904

1900

At their winter meeting following the 1899 season, National League owners voted to reduce the 12-team league to eight teams. The four franchises eliminated were Baltimore, Cleveland, Louisville, and Washington. Brooklyn added several top players who had played for their syndicate partner, Baltimore, in 1899 to their roster for the 1900 season.

March 9, 1900: Received Outfielder Jimmy Sheckard, Infielder Gene DeMontreville, Pitcher Joe McGinnity, Catcher Aleck Smith and Pitcher Frank Kitson, from the Baltimore Orioles

Right-hander Joe McGinnity was the biggest prize of the five players coming to Brooklyn. As a 28-year-old Orioles' rookie in 1899, he won 28 games to lead the National League. He completed 38 of his 41 starts, had an earned run average of 2.68, and an ERA+ of 148. McGinnity had an even better season with the 1900 Superbas. He again led the league with 28 wins, which along with just eight losses gave him a league-leading .778 winning percentage. In 1902, he signed with the new Baltimore franchise in the American League.

Outfielder Jimmy Sheckard played in 13 games for Brooklyn as an 18-year-old rookie in 1897 and batted .277 as a regular in 1898. Sheckard was assigned to the Orioles in 1899 as part of the syndicated ownership of the two teams. He batted .295 that year, scored 104 runs, and led the league with 77 stolen bases. Sheckard also had 33 assists after Orioles manager John McGraw moved him from left field to right field.

Gene DeMontreville was a versatile infielder and a consistent hitter. In 1899 he batted .281 in 82 games at shortstop for the Chicago Orphans, and .279 in 60 games as Baltimore's second baseman.

Aleck Smith played for both teams in 1899, batting a combined .315 but with much greater success in Baltimore. He batted .383 in 41 games for the Orioles and just .180 in 17 games for the Superbas. Smith was sent to the minor leagues after appearing in seven games but continued his big-league career with the 1901 New York Giants.

Frank Kitson, a 30-year-old right-hander, reached the major leagues with Baltimore in 1898. The following season he won 22 games, with an earned run average of 2.78 and an ERA+ of 143. After a 15–13 season with Brooklyn in 1900, he won 19 games in 1901 and again in 1902, before jumping to the American League's Detroit Tigers in 1903.

March 1900: Signed Free Agent Pitcher Harry Howell

Former Orioles pitcher Harry Howell had gone unclaimed since this past winter, when the Baltimore franchise was eliminated from the National League. In mid–March the Superbas signed the 23-year-old Brooklyn native. It was Howell's second stint with the club, whom they signed out of the minor leagues in 1898. He joined the team in October that season and pitched two complete game victories over the Philadelphia Phillies.

The next year, as part of the syndicated ownership of the two teams, Howell was assigned to the Orioles. Under Orioles manager John McGraw in 1899, he won 13 and lost eight, with 21 complete games in 25 starts.

Howell went 6–5 for the 1900 Superbas, while leading the league with 11 games finished. He then left Brooklyn for Baltimore for the second time, but this time it was by choice. In 1901 he jumped to the Orioles of the American League, reuniting with its manager, John McGraw.

April 1900: Signed Free Agent Pitcher Jerry Nops

Over the past three seasons, Jerry Nops had won 53 games for the now disbanded Baltimore Orioles. On April 20 Ned Hanlon sent a representative to Baltimore to meet with Nops and urge him to sign with Brooklyn. Nops, who was running a restaurant in the city was reluctant to leave but eventually did sign. He split eight decisions before the Superbas released him in August.

May 14, 1900: Purchased Third Baseman Lave Cross from the St. Louis Cardinals

Three weeks into the 1900 season, Ned Hanlon announced he had purchased third baseman Lave Cross from the St. Louis Cardinals for $3,000. The news was surprising, as Brooklyn's infield seemed set. In addition, Cross had been expected to join the New York Giants, whose manager Buck Ewing was in serious negotiations with Cardinals owner Frank Robison regarding Cross. Ewing and Robison had reached an agreement, but Giants owner Andrew Freedman had the final say, and he would not agree to the asking price. "Managers do not hire ballplayers on their own authority nowadays," Ewing said.[1]

Cross, 34, was in his fourteenth major league season, and considered one of the game's best third baseman, especially defensively. He batted .293 in 117 games for the pennant-winning 1900 Superbas, before jumping to the American League's Philadelphia Athletics in 1901.

August 2, 1900: Signed Free Agent Pitcher Gus Weyhing

Gus Weyhing had been a major league pitcher in the American Association, the Players' League, and the National League since 1887. He had won 20 or more game in seven seasons, including three seasons of 30 or more wins. Overall, Weyhing had won 258 games, including 32 (with 47 losses) for the Washington Senators the past two seasons. When the Washington franchise was eliminated, the Superbas purchased his contract for $500.

Manager Ned Hanlon was unimpressed with Weyhing's work in spring training and released him. St. Louis signed him, and he had 3–2 record in seven games before the Cardinals released him in late July. Hanlon signed him a few days later in a move that perplexed the Brooklyn press. Weyhing had a 3–4 record for the Superbas and was released at the end of the season.

Also in 1900:

Purchased: Catcher Farmer Steelman from Louisville Colonels

Sold: Shortstop Zeke Wrigley to Syracuse Stars of Eastern League; First Baseman Candy LaChance, Catcher–First Baseman Pat Crisham, and Pitcher Kit McKenna to Cleveland Blues of the American League (then a minor league); John Anderson to Milwaukee Brewers of the American League (then a minor league)

Chapter Three: 1900–1904

Chosen in Major League Draft: Outfielder John Anderson
Released: Pitcher Jack Dunn

1901

February 17, 1901: Sold Infielder Gene DeMontreville to the Boston Beaneaters

Brooklyn's purchase of third baseman Lave Cross resulted in reduced playing time for Gene DeMontreville in the 1901 season. DeMontreville served as the team's utility infielder, mostly as a fill-in for second baseman Tom Daly. He appeared in 69 games—at all four infield positions—and batted just .244.

It was a disappointing season for DeMontreville, as he had been set on winning a regular position in 1900. He would become the regular second baseman in 1901, but it was for the Boston Beaneaters, to whom he was sold on February 17 of that year.

Because DeMontreville was popular with the fans in his one season in Brooklyn, many regretted his departure. So too did DeMontreville, particularly for the way the sale was conducted. He was not informed of it until it was an accomplished fact. "The elimination of this practice of buying and selling and farming players without their knowledge or consent is one of the demands made by the Players Protective Association," wrote the *Brooklyn Citizen*.[2]

March 31, 1901: Signed Free Agent Outfielder Tom McCreery

Switch-hitting outfielder Tom McCreery had spent six seasons in the National League, with Louisville, New York, and most recently with Pittsburgh. A .324-hitter with the Pirates in 1899, he slumped badly in 1900, with a .220 batting average in 43 games. The Pirates released him, but McCreery was only 26 years old, and several teams sought to sign him for the 1901 season. Connie Mack, manager of the American League's Philadelphia Athletics appeared to have the inside track, but Brooklyn's Ned Hanlon surprised by signing McCreery on March 31.

Hanlon had long thought highly of McCreery, who he believed would improve significantly under his tutelage. Fielder Jones had been an outfield fixture for Brooklyn these past five seasons, but Jones had jumped to the Chicago White Sox. Hanlon envisioned McCreery as his replacement, but McCreery was no Fielder Jones. He batted a combined .264 in three seasons before being released in September 1903.

June 14, 1901: Signed Free Agent Outfielder Cozy Dolan

Cozy Dolan, a 28-year-old outfielder, had played reasonably well for the Chicago Orphans this season, batting .263 in 43 games, primarily in right field. But Orphans manager Tom Loftus had to drop a player to comply with the 16-man roster limit that would go into effect on June 15, and he chose Dolan. Hanlon was expecting to use his new player as a backup for his outfield of Jimmy Sheckard, Tom McCreery, and Willie Keeler, but Dolan ended up replacing McCreery who moved to first base. He continued in that position in 1902, when he batted .280, while leading the league in games, plate appearances, and at-bats. Dolan went back to Chicago in 1903, jumping to the American League's White Sox.

June 20, 1901: Sold First Baseman Hughie Jennings to the Philadelphia Phillies

Hughie Jennings had done well after returning from an arm injury in 1899. Converted to first base because of the injury, he filled the position well and was a contributor to the pennant-winning Superbas of 1899 and 1900. Jennings had not played thus far in 1901, as several teams claimed ownership of him. One was the Philadelphia Phillies, who made it official on June 20, when they purchased him from Brooklyn for $3,000.

July 12, 1901: Signed Free Agent Third Baseman Charlie Irwin

On July 11 the Cincinnati Reds were in seventh place and very likely out of the pennant race. Owner John T. Brush chose this time to release Charlie Irwin, the Reds longtime third baseman. Irwin, a 32-year-old left-handed-hitter, had been with the Reds for six years, with a combined .265 batting average. He was struggling with a .238 average this season and had fallen out of favor with the local press and fans.

Nevertheless, Ned Hanlon saw Irwin as a big improvement over his own third baseman, Frank Gatins. Third base had been the Superbas weakest spot all season. Irwin played there the rest of 1901, batting .215.

(Gatins, who was released four days later, had a season average of .228.) In 1902, Irwin's final major league season, he improved to .273 in 131 games, with a 105 OPS+.

July 16, 1901: Signed Free Agent Pitcher Doc Newton

Four days after the Superbas signed third baseman Charlie Irwin, following his release by Cincinnati, they signed another recently released member of the Reds. Left-hander Doc Newton had a 9–15 record as a 22-year-old rookie in 1900. His earned run average was 4.12, and he walked 100 batters in 235 2/3 innings.

Newton blew late-inning leads in each of his first two starts this season and had a 4–13 record on a team destined for last place when new manager Bid McPhee released him on July 13. Hanlon thought Newton had the potential to be a good pitcher and signed him.

"I have pitched poor ball for the Reds, but I don't know how to account for it," Newton said after signing with Brooklyn. "Things have been breaking bad for me, and a change of teams may bring a change in my success."³

Newton was ineffective in his first start, but by mid–August, he began living up to Hanlon's expectations, producing a 6–5 record, with a 2.83 earned run average. In 1902 he accounted for 15 of Brooklyn's 75 wins, had a 2.42 ERA, and led the National League in fewest hits allowed per nine innings (7.1). When he and Hanlon could not agree on a contract for 1903, Hanlon released him.

Also in 1901:
Released: Catcher Farmer Steelman; Outfielder Lefty Davis; Pitcher James McJames

1902

July 21, 1902: Signed Free Agent Pitcher Roy Evans

In early July 1902, the National League delivered a significant blow to Ban Johnson and his American League when Baltimore Orioles manager John McGraw forced his release from the club and signed to manage the New York Giants. Shortly after he signed McGraw, Giants owner Andrew Freedman gained control of the Baltimore franchise. His first move was to release six Orioles players unconditionally. Four of them—pitchers Joe McGinnity and Jack Cronin, first baseman Dan McGann, and utilityman Roger Bresnahan—immediately signed with the Giants. To make room for the new additions, Freedman announced on July 16 the release of several current Giants, among them was right-handed pitcher Roy Evans, who had an 8–13 record.

Evans, 28, was a man with a shady past who had pitched previously for National League teams in St. Louis, Louisville, and Washington, in addition to the Giants. A few days after his release, Evans signed to pitch for Brooklyn. Ned Hanlon put him to use immediately, starting him the next day in the second game of a doubleheader against Philadelphia. He responded by pitching a shutout but lost six of his final ten decisions. Evans was 5–9 in 1903, when the Superbas released him on June 24.

August 21, 1902: Signed Free Agent Catcher Joe Wall

Joe Wall, a left-handed-hitting (and throwing) catcher batted a combined .409 in ten games for the Giants over the past two seasons. But new manager John McGraw had no place for Wall and released him on August 15. The Superbas signed the Brooklyn native on August 21. He had three hits in 18 at-bats, the final 18 at-bats of his career.

September 5, 1902: Signed Catcher Lew Ritter from the Binghamton Bingos of the New York State League

Lew Ritter had played in the minor leagues since 1896, including this season and last with the Binghamton Bingos of the New York State League. Ned Hanlon signed the 26-year-old Ritter, considered the best catcher in the league, to a Brooklyn contract on September 5, 1902. Ritter made his debut later that month and played for the Superbas through the 1908 season, catching 410 games and batting .219.

September 17, 1902: Signed Free Agent Pitcher Ned Garvin

At 6'3" Ned Garvin was among the tallest players in the major leagues. The 28-year-old right-hander was also one of the most traveled, having pitched for four different teams in his five major league seasons. In that time, Garvin had an undistinguished won-lost record of 37–62, but consistently impressive earned run averages. "He was pretty much the tough-luck pitcher of the year every year," wrote baseball historian Bill James.[4]

This season was much the same. Garvin had a 10–10 record and a 2.21 ERA for the Chicago White Sox when manager Clark Griffith released him on August 29. Griffith's decision was no doubt influenced by an incident earlier in the month when an intoxicated Garvin shot a Chicago bar owner and pistol-whipped a policeman. On September 17, with the season nearing its end, manager Hanlon signed him, reasoning that if the 28-year-old Garvin behaved himself, the Superbas had added a good pitcher for 1903.

December 11, 1902: Signed Free Agent Third Baseman Sammy Strang

In 1901, his first full major league season, Sammy Strang batted .282 for the New York Giants. He jumped to the American League's Chicago White Sox in 1902, where he had another strong season, batting .295. However, he made 62 errors at third base, an American League single-season record for third basemen that still stands. Owner Charles Comiskey berated Strang after one of those errors cost the White Sox a late-season victory. The two men came to blows, and after the American League season ended, Strang was released. The National League season was not yet over, and Strang played three games in October for the Chicago Orphans. On December 20, 1902, when Superbas owner Charles Ebbets gave out a list of players signed by Brooklyn for 1903, Strang's name was among them.

Strang had a good first season with the Superbas, batting .272 in 135 games, but fell off sharply in 1904, with a .192 average in 77 games. He was released at the end of the season and signed to play for the Giants again in 1905.

December 12, 1902: Purchased First Baseman Jack Doyle from the Washington Senators

President Charles Ebbets made a major upgrade for the 1903 season by signing veteran first baseman Jack Doyle. Tom McCreery filled the position in 1902 but batted just .244. The 33-year-old Doyle had spent 14 seasons in the major leagues and been successful wherever he played.

Nicknamed "Dirty Jack" for his aggressive style of play, he had been an important part of the swaggering, belligerent Baltimore Orioles dynasty for two seasons in the mid–1890s.

Doyle started the 1902 season with the New York Giants, but when his former Orioles teammate John McGraw, with whom he had never gotten along, became the Giants manager that year, he was released. Brooklyn fans called for the Superbas to sign him then, and criticized manager Ned Hanlon when he did not. Doyle signed instead with the American League Washington Senators.

Also in 1902:
Released: Pitcher Bill Kennedy

1903

On January 10, 1903, at the St. Nicholas Hotel in Cincinnati, the National and American Leagues reached an agreement that ended their two-year war. The two leagues had been battling over the ownership rights to players since 1901, when the Americans declared themselves a major league. A crucial feature of the peace agreement settled the question, with a few exceptions, of which players belonged to which teams.

February 11, 1903: Purchased Pitchers Rube Vickers and Henry Thielman from the Cincinnati Reds

Bill Donovan had been Brooklyn's best pitcher in 1901, with a league-leading 25 victories. He followed with 17 wins in 1902 and had an earned run average below 3.00 in both seasons. The peace agreement between the two leagues, signed in January 1903, for the most part ended the raiding of players by one league from the other. Donovan beat that agreement signing with the American League's Detroit Tigers shortly before it went into effect.

Cincinnati Reds president Garry Herrmann had relinquished his claim to Donovan, thereby making possible the pitcher's jump to the American League. As a sop to the Brooklyn organization, Herrmann made available several pitchers, two of whom he would sell to the

Superbas. Manager Ned Hanlon chose right-handers Rube Vickers and Henry Thielman.

Vickers, 23, appeared in three games for the Reds in 1902, all complete-game losses. He lost his only decision for the Superbas in 1904 and was released. Thielman, 22, was the more promising prospect. He was 9–16 in 1902, including one loss when he was a member of the Giants early in the season. After losing three games in his four appearances in 1903, Hanlon released him on May 18.

February 20, 1903: Signed Free Agent Catcher Fred Jacklitsch

Manager Hanlon was in Brooklyn to meet with Henry Chadwick regarding the proposed changes in the National League rules. Hanlon a member of the rules committee, was advocating several changes, including one to abolish the recording of errors on infield fumbles. While in Brooklyn, Hanlon announced he had released catcher Tacks Latimer and signed catcher Fred Jacklitsch, a 26-year-old Brooklyn native.

Latimer played in just eight games for the Superbas in 1902, batting .042. Jacklitsch had been the Philadelphia Phillies backup catcher to Red Dooin. He would split catching duties with Lew Ritter in 1903 and would be the backup to newly acquired Bill Bergen in 1904. In his two seasons with Brooklyn, Jacklitsch batted .257 in 86 games.

May 11, 1903: Signed Free Agent Outfielder John Dobbs

An injury to rookie outfielder Ed Householder forced Superbas manager Ned Hanlon to seek a replacement. He found one in John Dobbs, whom the Cubs had released following his slow start to the season. Dobbs batted .274 as a rookie for Cincinnati in 1901 and a combined .299 for the Reds and Cubs in 1902. A 27-year-old left-handed batter, Dobbs became Brooklyn's regular center fielder, a position he would occupy the rest of this season and for the next two. He was released in 1905, with a combined batting average of .247 in 335 games with the Superbas.

July 2, 1903: Signed Free Agent Outfielder Doc Gessler

Detroit Tigers rookie Doc Gessler hit a game-winning double on Opening Day, but he had struggled since. Gessler was batting .238 in late June when the Tigers tried to send the 22-year-old outfielder to the minor leagues. Several major league teams were interested in Gessler, but when Ned Hanlon offered $150 a month more than the Chicago Cubs, the next highest bidder, Gessler quickly accepted "for fear Ned might change his mind."[5]

July 15, 1903: Signed Free Agent Pitcher Jack Doscher

Finding his team short of pitchers, Ned Hanlon signed Jack Doscher, just released by manager Frank Selee of the Chicago Cubs. Doscher, a rookie left-hander two weeks short of his twenty-third birthday, had an 0–1 record in his four games with the Cubs. Hanlon said Doscher had been signed on a tryout basis. Doscher appeared in three games in 1903 and two in 1904, all in relief, with no decisions. He won one game in 1905 but had five losses. Doscher's final season was in 1906, when he pitched in two games with one loss. Doscher was the son of former major league third baseman Herm Doscher, making him the first second-generation major leaguer.

July 19, 1903: Signed Free Agent Pitcher Bill Reidy

Manager Hanlon continued his quest to strengthen his pitching staff by signing right-hander Bill Reidy, raising the number of pitchers on the Superbas roster to five. For the 29-year-old Reidy, recently released by the St. Louis Browns, it was his second stint with Brooklyn. He had appeared in two games, with one win, for the 1899 club.

Reidy jumped to the American League in 1901 and had a 16–20 record with the Milwaukee Brewers. In 1902 the Brewers moved to St. Louis, where Reidy had a 4–9 record over the past year and a half. He won six of 13 decisions for Brooklyn in the second half of 1903 and was 0–4 in 1904, his last major league season.

September 17, 1903: Signed Third Baseman Emil Batch from the Holyoke (MA) Paperweights of the Connecticut State League

The September 18, 1903, *Brooklyn Standard Union* reported that Brooklyn had signed Emil Batch, a 23-year-old third baseman whom they drafted from the Holyoke (MA) Paperweights. Batch had an outstanding offensive season for the Paperweights in 1903—a .336 batting average, a .501 slugging percentage, and a league-leading seven home runs. The Superbas called him up in September 1904. He played four seasons for Brooklyn, the first two at third base, where he was an awful fielder, and the last two in the outfield. Batch's batting averages ranged from .247 to .256, and his on-base average for the four seasons was just .290.

November 1903: Drafted Outfielder Harry Lumley from the Seattle Siwashes of the Pacific Coast League

In November 1903, the Superbas drafted Harry Lumley from the Seattle club of the Pacific Coast League (PCL). The husky, left-handed-hitting outfielder signed with Brooklyn the first week in December. Lumley led the PCL with a .383 batting average in 1903 and was considered a prize catch. In his first season with Brooklyn (1904), he led the National League in home runs (9) and triples (18). Lumley's best season was 1906—a .324 batting average and the league's highest slugging percentage (.477) and OPS+ (179). He played with Brooklyn through 1910, but never came close to his early success. In 1909 he managed the club to a sixth-place finish.

December 12, 1903: Traded Shortstop Bill Dahlen to the New York Giants for Shortstop Charlie Babb and Pitcher Jack Cronin

The strong likelihood that the New York Giants would be unable to keep shortstop George Davis in 1904 led manager John McGraw to look elsewhere. Aware that the acquisition of Honus Wagner was unlikely, McGraw decided to go after Brooklyn's Bill Dahlen, the league's second-best shortstop. In his thirteen years in the league, the last five with the Superbas, Dahlen had been a steady hitter and among the game's fastest and smartest base runners.

In exchange for Dahlen, Brooklyn was getting Jack Cronin, a journeyman right-handed pitcher, and Charlie Babb, a rookie shortstop. Cronin had been with six major league teams in six years and had a lifetime 31–35 record. Babb batted .248 in 1903 as a fill-in for Davis, who spent most of the season with the Chicago White Sox. A rumored $5,000 accompanied Babb and Cronin to Brooklyn, a rumor that both McGraw and Ned Hanlon denied. Even if it had, money in the team's treasury was irrelevant to the Brooklyn fans who were irate at losing yet another one of their favorites. Losing him to the hated Giants and getting what they perceived as so little in return, made the deal even more intolerable for them.

The exchange seemed so one-sided it led the *Brooklyn Eagle* to write, "To give up the best shortstop in the league and the most popular player of the Brooklyn team for one average fielder and a second-rate pitcher is apparently not upholding the reputation for cleverness maintained by Hanlon in the past."[6] But the writer cautioned his readers not to judge the trade too quickly. He suggested that Dahlen, who would turn 34 in a few weeks, was likely nearing the end of his career. Meanwhile, Hanlon was proclaiming that Babb would eventually be the equal of Dahlen, and although he was a mere three years younger, would be playing long after Dahlen was through.

As it turned out, this trade, which appeared so one-sided in favor of the Giants on the surface, was exactly that. Babb played only two seasons and Cronin one before they were gone from the major leagues. Meanwhile, Dahlen would have a most productive four-year stay with the Giants. McGraw would later call the trade the most successful deal of his managerial career.

Yet even after "stealing" Dahlen, McGraw was not completely satisfied. He then asked the Superbas about their one remaining high-priced player, outfielder Jimmy Sheckard. Feeling that the loss of Dahlen was just about all their fans would accept, Brooklyn chose to keep Sheckard.

Also in 1903:

Released: Pitcher Henry Thielman; Pitcher Roy Evans; Outfielder Tom McCreery; Catcher Tacks Latimer

1904

March 4, 1904: Purchased Catcher Bill Bergen and Pitcher Ed Poole from the Cincinnati Reds

Cincinnati catcher Bill Bergen did not get along with his manager, Joe Kelley. As a result, during the winter of 1903–1904 newspapers in Cincinnati printed stories of Bergen's likely trade; most had him going to the St. Louis Cardinals. But Bergen remained the property of the Reds until just before the start of spring training, when he and right-handed pitcher Ed Poole were sold to Brooklyn.

The right-handed hitting Bergen, 26, was an excellent defensive player with an accurate throwing arm. He was, however, a woeful hitter. In his three years in Cincinnati, Bergen played in 234 games with a combined batting average of .191. He would spend eight years with Brooklyn, in which he cemented both his positive defensive reputation and his negative offensive one, a .162 batting average in 713 games. Bergen's on-base average during those eight seasons was .184, and his slugging percentage was .187.

Poole, 29, was 12–4 for the Reds in 1902, but slipped to 7–13 in 1903. He was 8–14 for the Superbas in 1904, his last major league season.

April 26, 1904: Sold First Baseman Jack Doyle and Outfielder Deacon Van Buren to the Philadelphia Phillies

The Superbas reduced the average age of their roster by selling their two oldest players. Gone to Philadelphia were 34-year-old Jack Doyle and 33-year-old Deacon Van Buren. Despite his advanced age, Van Buren was a rookie who appeared in only one game, singling as a pinch-hitter.

Doyle, a major-leaguer since 1889, had a fine season in 1903, his first in Brooklyn, batting .313 with 91 runs batted in. But in addition to his slow start this season (5-for-30), his conduct on one Western trip last season had upset manager Ned Hanlon. The arrival of Frank Dillon to play first base and Doyle's wish to play in Philadelphia made this an easy decision for Hanlon.

Dillon, no youngster either, at 30, had played 177 major-league games for three different teams from 1899 through 1902. He was the player-manager of the Pacific Coast League's Los Angeles Angels in 1903, which led Hanlon to name him the team captain. "Never before has any player been brought into the big league and made captain of a team right from the jump," wrote the *Brooklyn Citizen*.[7] Dillon spent the one season in Brooklyn, batting .258 in 135 games, before returning to Los Angeles where he would play and manage through 1915.

August 1, 1904: Signed Free Agent Pitcher Doc Scanlan

Twenty-two-year-old left-hander William "Doc" Scanlan reached the major leagues with the Pittsburgh Pirates late in the 1903 season. He appeared in one game, a complete-game loss. Scanlan was 1–3 in 1904, when the Pirates released him in late June. Brooklyn signed him on August 1, and he did well for the sixth-place Superbas, splitting twelve decisions and throwing three shutouts.

Scanlan pitched six more seasons for Brooklyn (1905–1907, 1909–1911); he sat out the 1908 season. During these years, he attained a degree in medicine and began practicing surgery in the offseason. Overall, Scanlan had a 64–67 record with Brooklyn, including a 14-win season in 1905 and an 18-win season in 1906. After he went 3–10 in 1911, the Superbas traded him to the Philadelphia Phillies, but he refused to sign with them, ending his baseball career.

August 27, 1904: Signed Free Agent Pitcher Fred Mitchell

Right-handed pitcher Fred Mitchell began his major league career with the Boston Americans in 1901, moved to the Philadelphia Athletics in 1902, and to the Philadelphia Phillies in 1903. He was 11–16 for the Phillies that year but was struggling at 4–7 in 1904 when the Phillies released him in late August. The Superbas signed the 26-year-old Mitchell a few days later. He was 2–5 the rest of the season and 3–7 in 1905.

September 9, 1904: Sold Pitcher Ned Garvin to the New York Yankees

Ned Hanlon had signed right-hander Ned Garvin in September 1902 in the hope that if the then 28-year-old Garvin stayed out of trouble, he had added a good pitcher for 1903. That he had. Garvin won 15 games in 1903 (15–18) and was 5–15 this season for mediocre Brooklyn clubs. His 1.68 earned run average this season was second in the National League to the Giants' Joe McGinnity.

Staying out of trouble was another matter. Garvin was charged with insubordination during the Superbas last Western trip while Hanlon was absent. On hearing the news, Hanlon told Garvin he could accept a release or be indefinitely suspended. Garvin chose the release and tried to make a deal with the Pittsburgh Pirates that fell through. He was put on waivers and signed by the New York Yankees, for whom he pitched his final two major-league games.

September 1904: Drafted Pitcher Elmer Stricklett from the Milwaukee Brewers of the American Association

Elmer Stricklett started one early-season game for the 1904 Chicago White Sox (a loss) before they sold the 27-year-old righthander to the Milwaukee Brewers of the American Association. An early user of the spitball, Stricklett won 20 games (20–11) for the Brewers, including six shutouts. He pitched three seasons for the second-division Superbas (1905–1907), compiling a 35–50 record with ten shutouts. Stricklett jumped to the San Jose club of the independent California State League in 1908 and was barred from returning to Organized Baseball.

September 1904: Purchased Pitcher Mal Eason from the Jersey City Skeeters of the Eastern League

Mal Eason had little success in his four previous major-league seasons (1900–1903), winning 21 games and losing 35 for Chicago and Boston in the National League and Detroit in the American League. But the 25-year-old right-hander was very successful with the Jersey City Skeeters in 1904, leading the Eastern League with 26 wins. He reverted to form in his two seasons in Brooklyn, with a 5–21 record for the last-place Superbas in 1905, and a 10–17 mark in 1906.

Also in 1904:
Purchased: Infielder-Outfielder Charlie Malay from Amsterdam-Gloversville-Johnstown (NY) Jags of the New York State League; Pitcher Harry McIntire from Memphis Egyptians of the Southern Association; Pitcher Doc Reisling from Los Angeles Angels of the Pacific Coast League
Sold: Catcher Frank McManus to Detroit Tigers
Chosen in Major League Rule 5 Draft: Bull Durham
Released: Pitcher Rube Vickers; Third Baseman Sammy Strang

CHAPTER FOUR

1905–1909

1905

Charles Ebbets and Henry Medicus bought out Ferdinand Abell's and Ned Hanlon's remaining holdings.

June 14, 1905: Borrowed Infielder Bob Hall from the New York Giants

In the middle of June, the last-place Superbas found themselves short of players. They solved the problem by borrowing utility infielder Bob Hall from the New York Giants, a favor from manager John McGraw to manager Ned Hanlon. Through June 14, Hall had appeared in only one game for the Giants. He was Brooklyn's second baseman the next day and was a regular, mostly in the outfield, for the rest of the season, batting .236. Hall was returned to McGraw after the season, but never again played in the major leagues.

August 13, 1905: Signed Second Baseman John Hummel from the Holyoke (MA) Paperweights of the Connecticut State League

At the start of the Connecticut State League season, the Brooklyn club had made an agreement with the Holyoke (MA) Paperweights. They agreed that after watching the Paperweights play, the Superbas could choose one player off their roster. On a recent trip to Holyoke, Ned Hanlon watched a Paperweights game and the Brooklyn manager decided that 22-year-old second baseman John Hummel was that player.

A few days later President Charles Ebbets went to Holyoke to complete the transaction. Hummel, a right-handed batter who hit .330 in 110 games for Holyoke, joined the Brooklyn club in September.

Playing both infield and outfield, Hummel remained with the Superbas for the next ten seasons, playing more than 100 games in each year from 1907 through 1912. In 1915, the club released him after he batted .230 in 53 games. For his Brooklyn career, Hummel had a combined .253 batting average and 102 OPS+ in 1,139 games.

August 13, 1905: Signed Pitcher George Bell from the Amsterdam-Gloversville-Johnstown (NY) Jags of the New York State League

On the same trip that manager Ned Hanlon signed Holyoke second baseman John Hummel, he also signed right-handed pitcher George Bell from the Amsterdam-Gloversville-Johnstown (NY) Jags of the New York State League. Bell was assigned to the Altoona (PA) Mountaineers of the Tri-State League for 1906. He won 23 games for the Mountaineers, which earned him a promotion to Brooklyn in 1907.

A rookie at age 32, Bell pitched for the Superbas for five seasons, compiling a record of 43–79 (although his career earned run average was much better—2.85) for clubs that finished in the second division in each of those years. Bell had one winning season, 16–15 in 1909, but followed that with a league-leading 27 losses in 1910.

August 15, 1905: Signed Pitcher Jim Pastorius from the Albany Senators of the New York State League

Brooklyn drafted Jim Pastorius, a 5'9" left-hander, from the Albany Senators after the 1904 season, but lent him back to the Senators for 1905. The 24-year-old Pastorius struggled as a rookie in 1906, winning 10 and losing 14, with a 3.61 earned run average. He did much better in 1907, a 16–12 record and a 2.35 earned run average. Pastorius' ERA was a solid 2.44 in 1908, but he lost 20 of 24 decisions. He was 1–9 in 1909 when the club released him in August.

September 1, 1905: Purchased First Baseman Tim Jordan from the Baltimore Orioles of the Eastern League

The Superbas purchased 26-year-old Tim Jordan from Baltimore of the Eastern League after the 6'1" first baseman batted .312 for the 1905 Orioles. Jordan. A left-handed hitter. had played briefly in the American League—six games for Washington in 1901 and two for New York in 1903. In 1906, Jordan's first season with the Superbas, he led the National League with 12 home runs. He led again, with 12, in 1908, but in his other three seasons with the club he managed a total of only eight more home runs. Overall, Jordan played 532 games for Brooklyn with a combined OPS+ of 139.

September 1, 1905: Drafted Second Baseman Whitey Alpermann from the Davenport (IA) Riversides of the Three-I League

On September 1, 1905, the Superbas drafted second baseman Whitey Alpermann from Davenport of the Three-I League, where he had played this season as well as the previous three. The 26-year-old Alpermann played his entire four-season major league career with the Superbas, mostly at second base. He batted .237 in 450 games, with his career highlight coming in 1907, when he led the National League with 16 triples.

December 15, 1905: Traded Outfielder Jimmy Sheckard to the Chicago Cubs for Pitcher Button Briggs, Third Baseman Doc Casey, Outfielder Billy Maloney, Outfielder Jack McCarthy, and Cash

President Charles Ebbets and his new manager, Patsy Donovan, engineered the biggest trade (thus far) in Brooklyn baseball history. As a result of talks with new Chicago Cubs owner Charles Murphy, they sent their team captain, Jimmy Sheckard, to the Cubs for four players and a reported $2,000. Sheckard had played the last four seasons in his second stint with the Superbas, and in 1903 was considered among the game's greatest players. Sheckard batted .332 with a 158 OPS+ that year, while leading the league in home runs (9) and stolen bases (67). He tailed of sharply in 1904 but batted a solid .292 this past season.

Of the four players coming to Brooklyn, 27-year-old outfielder Billy Maloney was thought to be the best. Very popular with the Chicago fans and press, many considered him the equal of Sheckard, though nothing he had done in his three big league seasons gave any credence to that comparison. Nor would his three seasons as Brooklyn's center fielder, in which he batted a combined .217 in 408 games, with just 81 runs batted in.

The other outfielder coming from the Cubs, Jack McCarthy, had had a long and productive career but was now 36 years old. McCarthy would bat .304 in 91 games for Brooklyn in 1906 and be released after playing in 25 games in June 1907.

James "Doc" Casey had been Brooklyn's third baseman in 1899, although manager Ned Hanlon considered the 5'6", 156-pound Casey too light for the major leagues. He jumped to the American League's Detroit Tigers in 1901 and then back to the NL Cubs in 1903. The weak-hitting Casey would be the Superbas third baseman for the next two seasons, his final two as a major leaguer.

Button Briggs, a 30-year-old righthander had a 44–47 record in five seasons with the Cubs, but he would not pitch again in the major leagues.

The reaction to the deal in Chicago was that Charles Murphy, in his first transaction as the owner of the Cubs, had been swindled. Meanwhile, Sheckard, who had hoped to be traded to the New York Giants, vowed he would not go to Chicago. "But that deal is a dead one," he said. "I will not play with the Chicago team under any circumstances. My main reason is that I do not care for the West, and never could do, myself justice in a Western city, where the fans have peculiar ways or showing their feelings during contests."[1] Sheckard changed his mind and would play seven seasons for the Cubs.

Also in 1905:

Sold: Infielder Dutch Jordan to Atlanta Crackers of the Southern Association; Catcher Fred Jacklitsch to Providence Clamdiggers of the Eastern League

Chosen in Major League Draft: Catcher John Butler

Released: Pitcher Fred Mitchell; Shortstop Charlie Babb

1906

For the 1906 season, Patsy Donovan replaced Ned Hanlon as manager.

April 23, 1906: Traded First Baseman Doc Gessler to the Chicago Cubs for Pitcher Hub Knolls

The Chicago Cubs were one of several teams that tried to sign Doc Gessler in the summer of 1903, but Brooklyn outbid them all. In 1904 and 1905, Gessler, primarily an outfielder then, had back-to-back seasons in which he batted .290, with an accompanying OPS+ of 132 in 1904 and 127 in 1905. Overall, he batted .282 in 288 games for the Dodgers, with an OPS+ of 124. Manager Ned Hanlon had moved Gessler to first base in 1905, but new manager Patsy Donovan was impressed with his new first baseman, Tim Jordan, making Gessler expendable.

Hub Knolls was a 22-year-old right-hander with a reputation for a great fastball and eccentricities that rivaled those of Rube Waddell. Unfortunately, he could not pitch like Waddell. His entire Brooklyn (and major league) career consisted of the two games and 6 2/3 inning he threw in 1906.

September 1, 1906: Drafted Pitcher Nap Rucker from the Augusta (GA) Tourists of the South Atlantic League

Charles Ebbets selected three pitchers in the 1906 draft: right-handers Weldon Henley and Jesse Whiting, and left-hander Nap Rucker. Henley and Whiting combined for a 2–6 record in their brief careers with the Dodgers, while Rucker, who cost Ebbets $500, became the winningest left-hander in Brooklyn history.

Coming off a 27–9 season with Augusta in 1906, the 22-year-old Rucker picked right up as a rookie in 1907, with a 15–13 record and a 2.06 earned run average for a Brooklyn team that won only 65 games. His record in 1910 was a mediocre 17–18; nevertheless, he led the league in innings pitched (320 1/3), games started (39), complete games (27), and shutouts (6).

Rucker had his only 20-win season in 1911, finishing at 22–18. The next year he had a 20-loss season (18–21) despite an earned run average (2.21) that was more than a full run lower than the league average. A sore arm severely curtailed Rucker's appearances over his last three seasons (1914–1916). Overall, he won 134 games for Brooklyn and lost the same amount, but his 10-year career ERA was 2.42.

Also in 1906:
Purchased: Pitcher Chappie McFarland from Pittsburgh Pirates

1907

July 1, 1907: Purchased Outfielder Al Burch from the St. Louis Cardinals

Speedy outfielder Al Burch had a strong rookie season for the St. Louis Cardinals in 1906. He played so well Ned Hanlon, now the manager of the Cincinnati Reds, tried to trade for him, but Cardinals manager John McCloskey refused all offers. Burch had started slowly this season, as McCloskey had several new outfielders he was trying to assess. That greatly reduced Burch's playing time and his effectiveness.

Charles Ebbets' announcement that the Dodgers had purchased the 23-year-old Burch "will be good news for the fans," wrote the *Brooklyn Citizen*. "He is lightning fast, both on the bases and in the field, and is a fairly good batsman."[2]

Burch batted .292 in 40 games over the second half of the 1907 season, and he was a full-time outfielder from 1908 through 1910. He played in 54 games in 1911, the final one coming on July 30. His overall average with Brooklyn was .254 in 472 games. Burch's best season was in 1909, when he batted .271 with a team-high 38 stolen bases.

September 1, 1907: Drafted Pitcher Kaiser Wilhelm from the Birmingham Barons of the South Atlantic League

Unlike most players taken in major league drafts, 30-year-old right-hander Kaiser Wilhelm had previous big-league experience. He had pitched for Pittsburgh (5–3) in 1903 and for Boston in 1904 and

1905. Wilhelm was a 20-game loser in both seasons with the Beaneaters (14–20 and 3–23) with high earned run averages to match. He spent the 1906 and 1907 seasons with the Birmingham Barons of the South Atlantic League, where he had two 20-win seasons, including a league-high 23 in 1907. Two weeks after being drafted, he shut out Shreveport in both games of a doubleheader, raising his consecutive scoreless-innings streak to 59.[3]

For the 1908 Dodgers, Wilhelm had the fourth highest number of innings pitched in the National League (332), and the second most complete games (33). His record was 16–22, but his 1.87 earned run average and six shutouts were each the seventh best in the league. Wilhelm pitched half as many innings in 1909, and his record fell to 3–13. A case of typhoid fever in 1910 limited him to 68 1/3 innings and led to his sale to the Rochester Bronchos of the Eastern League.

September 1, 1907: Drafted Shortstop Tommy McMillan from the Jacksonville (FL) Jays of the South Atlantic League

The Dodgers played several spring training games against the minor league Jacksonville Jays in 1907 and came away impressed with Tommy McMillan, the Jays shortstop. When the end-of-season draft came around, they made McMillan one of their choices. He batted .214 over two and a half seasons, before the Cincinnati Reds claimed him on waivers on June 5, 1910.

December 14, 1907: Purchased Third Baseman Tommy Sheehan from the Pittsburgh Pirates

President Ebbets, in search of a third baseman to replace the weak-hitting 37-year-old Doc Casey, found him in Pittsburgh's Tommy Sheehan. Pirates president Barney Dreyfuss wanted pitcher Harry McIntire and offered to give Brooklyn Sheehan and one other player for McIntire. Ebbets did not want to part with McIntire and convinced Dreyfuss to take cash for Sheehan.

Ebbets said of the purchase: "I am pleased that we have landed Sheehan, especially as it did not necessitate giving up any player or players on our part.... While we wanted Sheehan, I could not see my way clear to giving up a seasoned pitcher."[4] Sheehan was not an improvement over Casey at third base, batting .214 in 146 games in 1908, his only season in Brooklyn.

Also in 1907:
Purchased: Infielder Simmy Murch from Brockton (MA) Tigers of the New England League
Chosen in Major League Draft: Pitcher Jim Holmes; Outfielder George Hunter
Released: Outfielder Jack McCarthy

1908

August 4, 1908: Purchased Third Baseman Pryor McElveen from the Nashville Volunteers of the Southern Association

Still searching for a third baseman, Charles Ebbets signed Pryor McElveen, the Nashville Volunteers third baseman, captain, and best player. McElveen, 26, who could also play shortstop and the outfield, would report to the Brooklyn club in 1909. Described as a fast runner, a good fielder, and a fair hitter, he was expected to be a strong competitor for the third base position. However, that competition was won by Ed Lennox, and for his three years in Brooklyn, McElveen was a backup. During that time, he played every position except pitcher, appearing in 171 games with a .209 batting average.

August 21, 1908: Purchased Third Baseman Ed Lennox from the Rochester Bronchos of the Eastern League

Although more than a month remained in the 1908 season, President Ebbets agreed to let newly purchased 23-year-old Ed Lennox finish the season in Rochester. He would report to the Dodgers in 1909, where he was expected to compete with Pryor McElveen for the third base job held in 1908 by Tommy Sheehan. Lennox's consistent hitting and superior defense earned him the job for the next two seasons, where he batted .261 in 236 games. Despite his solid performance, Lennox's inability to get along with new manager Bill Dahlen in 1910 led to his sale to the Louisville Colonels of the American Association for the 1911 season.

Also in 1908:
Purchased: Pitcher Pembroke Finlayson from Rochester (NY) Bronchos of the Eastern League

1909

For this season, Harry Lumley replaced Patsy Donovan as manager.

February 19, 1909: Purchased Catcher Doc Marshall from the Chicago Cubs

Charles Ebbets thought his club needed an experienced man for a backup catcher. He attempted to fill that need by purchasing 33-year-old Doc Marshall from the Chicago Cubs. Ebbets said it was up to his new manager, Harry Lumley, to decide whether he agreed with his choice. "I had a chance to buy Marshall, who is a seasoned backstop with plenty of ginger and a good hustler, so I took him," Ebbets said. "Had I waited to consult Lumley we would have lost him, so I took a chance."[5]

The well-traveled Marshall (Brooklyn would be his sixth National League team) had never played more than 84 games in a season; that was with St. Louis in 1907, when he shared the catching position with Pete Noonan. In 1908, Marshall appeared in only 18 games for the Cardinals and the Cubs. In his one season in Brooklyn, 1909, he batted .201 in 50 games as a backup to Bill Bergen.

June 7, 1909: Purchased Outfielder Wally Clement from the Philadelphia Phillies

Wally Clement was a speedy outfielder who spent seven seasons with the Jersey City Skeeters of the Eastern League. He made his major league debut with the Philadelphia Phillies in August 1908, batting .222 in 16 games. After three appearances as a pinch-hitter in 1909 (he struck out in two of them), Phillies manager Billy Murray wanted to send Clement back to Jersey City and asked for waivers on him. Brooklyn's Charles Ebbets and Boston's owner George Dovey claimed him and the two drew straws to decide his fate. Ebbets won the draw, and the 27-year-old Clement became the property of the Dodgers.

Sporting Life wrote, "To fill the vacancy caused by the poor work of [Jimmy] Sebring, Brooklyn claimed Clement, formerly of Jersey City. He is a fairly good player, but he hasn't any throwing arm."[6] Sebring was released two weeks later, and Clement was Brooklyn's left fielder for the rest of the 1909 season. He batted .259 in 92 games but was back in Jersey City in 1910, as rookie Zack Wheat became the team's regular left fielder.

July 15, 1909: Purchased Outfielder Zack Wheat from the Mobile Sea Gulls of the Southern Association

On July 15, 1909, Charles Ebbets made the most significant player purchase of his career. He acquired outfielder Zack Wheat from the Mobile (AL) Sea Gulls of the Southern Association for $1,200. Despite a .246 batting average for the Sea Gulls this year, the 21-year-old Wheat had impressed scout Larry Sutton who urged Ebbets to sign him. "What can I do with a fellow who hits only .245 [sic]?" Ebbets asked. "I don't care what he batted," Sutton replied. "This fellow is a ballplayer."[7]

"I had malaria all summer," Wheat replied when Dodgers manager Harry Lumley asked him about his poor 1909 season with the Sea Gulls. "But it didn't seem to bother me when I left Mobile. I think I'll hit all right up here."[8] The left-handed-hitting Wheat made his debut in September and batted .304 in 26 games. He would remain Brooklyn's left fielder through the 1926 season. "One of the grandest guys ever to wear a baseball uniform, one of the greatest batting teachers I have seen, one of the truest pals a man ever had and one of the kindliest men God ever created," said his Brooklyn teammate Casey Stengel.[9]

The Robins released Wheat after the 1926 season. He signed to play for the Philadelphia Athletics and batted .324 in 88 games. Wheat is the franchise's all-time leader in games (2,322), at-bats (8,859), hits (2,804), total bases (4,003), doubles (464), and triples (171). In 1959 the Veterans Committee voted him into the Hall of Fame.

July 31, 1909: Purchased Catcher Tex Erwin from the Rochester Bronchos of the Eastern League

Tex Erwin, a 23-year-old left-handed-hitting catcher, was batting .308 for Rochester when Charles Ebbets bought his contract on the last day of July. He would be allowed to stay with Rochester for the rest of the season, where he finished with a .275 mark. Erwin would spend four and a half seasons with Brooklyn, batting .232 in 260 games.

August 17, 1909: Purchased Pitcher Cy Barger from the Rochester Bronchos of the Eastern League

While accompanying his team from a series in St. Louis to one in Boston, Charles Ebbets made a side trip to Rochester where he purchased the contract of pitcher Cy Barger. The 24-year-old right-hander would finish the 1909 season with a 23–13 record for the Eastern League's pennant-winning Bronchos. Although Barger had appeared in three games for the Yankees in 1906 and 1907, he had spent almost all of the last four seasons in the minor leagues.

Barger had a good first season with Brooklyn, a 15–15 record and a 2.88 earned run average for a sixth-place team. The Dodgers dropped to seventh place in 1911, while Barger slipped to 11–15 with a 3.52 ERA. A 1–9 record and a 5.46 ERA in 1912 ended Barger's career in Brooklyn.

September 1, 1909: Drafted Catcher Otto Miller from the Duluth White Sox of the Minnesota-Wisconsin League

Otto Miller was 21 years old when he made his major league debut in 1910. The year before he had appeared in 107 games for the Class D Duluth White Sox, where he batted .193 but showed great skill as a receiver. That pattern would hold throughout Miller's thirteen-year major league career, all with Brooklyn. Although he was six-feet tall and close to 200 pounds, the right-handed-hitting Miller was not a power hitter. He hit only five home runs in 2,836 at-bats, with never more than one in a season. His career batting average was .245, and his on-base average was .275. Miller was a member of Brooklyn's first two National League pennant winners, batting a combined .136 in two games against the Red Sox in 1916 and six games against Cleveland in 1920.

Also in 1909:

Purchased: Outfielder Hi Myers from Connellsville (PA) Cokers of the Pennsylvania–West Virginia League; Pitcher Eddie Dent from Winston-Salem (NC) Twins of the Carolina Association; Shortstop

Chapter Four: 1905–1909

Lee Meyer from Anderson (SC) Electricians of the Carolina Association; Pitcher Pembroke Finlayson from Rochester (NY) Bronchos of the Eastern League; Pitcher Elmer Knetzer from Lawrence (MA) Colts of the New England League; Second baseman Harry Redmond from Winston-Salem (NC) Twins of the Carolina Association; Outfielder Red Downey from Oklahoma City Indians of the Texas League

Signed Free Agents: Shortstop Bill Dahlen

Chosen in Major League Draft: First Baseman Jake Daubert; Pitcher Rube Dessau

Released: Outfielder Jimmy Sebring.

Chapter Five

1910–1914

1910

For the 1910 season, Bill Dahlen replaced Harry Lumley as manager.

April 9, 1910: Traded Harry McIntire to the Chicago Cubs for Outfielder Bill Davidson, Outfielder Happy Smith, and Shortstop Tony Smith

Just before Opening Day, the Dodgers made a three-for-one trade, sending veteran right-hander Harry McIntire to the Chicago Cubs for rookie outfielders Bill Davidson and Happy Smith and shortstop Tony Smith.

McIntire, 31, had been a hard-luck pitcher for five mediocre-to-awful Brooklyn teams. He was a 20-game loser in three of those seasons, while compiling a record of 46–98 with an 82 ERA+. "I am glad to go with the Chicagos," McIntire said when learned of the trade. "In many ways I am sorry to leave Brooklyn, of course, where I have been well-treated in the past, but the Brooklyn club had so many pitchers and required strengthening in other departments."[1]

Cubs owner Charles Murphy had originally refused to part with Bill Davidson, but when pitcher Ed Reulbach came down with diphtheria, which seemed likely to keep him out of action for two months, manager Frank Chance persuaded Murphy to make the deal for McIntire.

Manager Bill Dahlen was pleased at the acquisition of Davidson, a 26-year-old center fielder who was considered the most promising of the three men coming to Brooklyn. Scouts who had seen him play in the minor leagues thought him to be one of the best rookies to come to the major leagues in recent years. Davidson was the Dodgers' center fielder for a season-and-a-half, batting .236 in 223 games.

Happy Smith batted .237 in 35 games in 1910, his one season in Brooklyn. He appeared in 16 games in the outfield and 19 as a pinch-hitter. Tony Smith was the Dodgers first-string shortstop in 1910 but batted just .181. The next season, his final one as a major leaguer, he played in 13 games and batted .150.

June 15, 1910: Traded Pitcher Frank Schneiberg and Cash to the Des Moines Boosters of the Western League for Outfielder Jack Dalton

Right-hander Frank Schneiberg's major league career consisted of one inning pitched. On June 8, 1910, against Cincinnati, he relieved Nap Rucker in the seventh inning. The 30-year-old Schneiberg allowed eight runs, five hits, four walks, and one hit batter. Seven of the runs were earned, resulting in a lifetime earned run average of 63.00. Four days later, he and $3,000 were sent to Des Moines in exchange for right-handed-hitting outfielder Jack Dalton. The arrival of Dalton led to the end of Happy Smith's tenure with the club.

Larry Sutton, Brooklyn's top scout who had recommended acquiring Jake Daubert and Zack Wheat, had high praise for Dalton. After watching him play in several games, he said: "Best ballplayer I have seen in many a day."[2] But Dalton was a disappointment, batting .227 in 77 games. He returned to the minor leagues for three years, batting better than .300 in two of them and .293 in the other. Back in Brooklyn in 1914, he became the player the team had expected when they traded for him. He batted .319, with an on-base average of .396 and an OPS+ of 132. But that would be the end of Dalton's time in Brooklyn. In 1915, he jumped to the Buffalo Blues of the Federal League.

September 1, 1910: Drafted Pitcher Raleigh Aitchison from the Wichita Jobbers of the Western League

Raleigh Aitchison was a 20-game winner for the Wichita Jobbers of the Western League in 1910, and the winner of 55 minor league games over the past three seasons. The 22-year-old left-hander appeared in only one game for Brooklyn in 1911, an April 19 loss, before spending the rest of the season with the Nashville Vols of the Southern Association.

He remained in the minors the next two seasons, winning 38 and losing 12, before returning to Brooklyn in 1914. Aitchison won 12 games that year (12–7), including five against the pennant-winning Boston Braves. He started poorly in 1915 and had an 0–4 record in June, when the club sent him back to the minor leagues, where he remained for the rest of his career.

A columnist for the *Brooklyn Eagle* wrote: "Aitchison is one of those peculiar ball players who lead good judges to think they are always on the verge of developing into stars, but never come through. The woods are full of such."[3]

September 1, 1910: Drafted Outfielder Bob Coulson from the Altoona Rams of the Tri-State League

Bob Coulson reached the major leagues in 1908, playing in eight games with the Cincinnati Reds. Brooklyn drafted him after he batted .302 for the 1909 Altoona (PA) Rams of the Tri-State League. He reported in September and appeared in 25 games, batting .247. Coulson played in 146 games in 1911, all but two in right field, but after batting .234 and leading the league with 78 strikeouts in 1912, he was sent back to the minors.

September 1910: Purchased Pitcher Pat Ragan from the Rochester Bronchos of the Eastern League

Pat Ragan's 29 wins for the 1908 Omaha Rourkes of the Western League earned him a brief stay in the major leagues the following season. He pitched two games for the Chicago Cubs and two for the Cincinnati Reds before he was returned to the minor leagues. His 16–11 record at Rochester led Charles Ebbets to outbid Connie Mack of the Philadelphia A's for Ragan's services in 1911. He was used mostly in relief that season, before being moved into the rotation in 1912.

Ragan a right-hander, had a 7–18 record in 1912. He lost 18 again in 1913 but led the team with 15 wins. By 1914, new manager Wilbert Robinson had added Jeff Pfeffer and Ed Reulbach to his pitching staff and had no room for the 31-year-old Ragan. He put him on waivers in late April 1915, where he was claimed by the Boston Braves. Ragan's composite record for his five years with Brooklyn was 37–54, with a 3.26 earned run average.

Also in 1910:
Purchased: Pitcher Jack Ryan from St. Paul Saints of the American Association
Sold: Shortstop Tommy McMillan to Cincinnati Reds; Pitcher George Crable to Rochester Bronchos of the Eastern League; Pitcher Fred Miller to Rochester Bronchos of the Eastern League
Chosen in Major League Draft: Pitcher Sandy Burk from Fort Worth Panthers of Texas League; Third baseman Eddie Zimmerman from Newark Indians of the Eastern League

1911

August 16, 1911: Purchased Outfielder Hub Northen from the Chattanooga Lookouts of the Southern Association

Outfielder Hub Northen, 24, played one game with Cincinnati this season before the Reds sent him to the Chattanooga Lookouts of the Southern Association. After Northen batted .312 in 135 games with Chattanooga, Charles Ebbets bought his contract. Northen joined the Dodgers after the sale and batted .316 in 76 at-bats.

In 1912, the left-handed-hitting Northen, played in 118 games, rotating between the three outfield positions. He batted .282 and had an OPS+ of 108. The following year, rookie Casey Stengel replaced him in the Brooklyn outfield, and Northen returned to the minor leagues.

September 1, 1911: Purchased Pitcher Frank Allen from the Mobile Sea Gulls of the Southern Association

Six major league teams were after Mobile pitcher Frank Allen, but Charles Ebbets secured him for $5,000 and a promise to send a pair of his surplus players to the Sea Gulls. Manager Bill Dahlen had hoped to have Allen with the club in September, but a case of malaria put off the 22-year-old left-hander's debut until 1912.

Allen had a disappointing rookie season, a 3–9 record and a 3.63 earned run average, albeit for a Dodgers' team that lost 95 games. It got even worse in 1913, when despite a 2.83 ERA his won-lost record was 4–18. Allen was struggling through 1914 with an 8–14 record, when late in the season he jumped to the Pittsburgh Rebels of the Federal League.

September 1, 1911: Drafted Outfielder Herbie Moran from the Rochester Bronchos of the Eastern League

Left-handed-hitting Herbie Moran batted .289 with nine home runs for Eastern League's Rochester Bronchos in 1911. A professional since 1904, the 26-year-old Moran had played for eight different minor league teams. He also had brief major league experience, with the Philadelphia Athletics (1908) and the Boston Doves (1908–1910).

Moran split his time between center field and right field with the 1912 Dodgers. He was the full-time right fielder in 1913, when rookie Casey Stengel took over in center. At 5'5" and 150 pounds, Moran was primarily a singles hitter, who also drew a lot of walks. His on-base average (OBA) in 1912 was .368. He played in 262 games in his two years in Brooklyn, batting .276 and .266 with a combined OBA of .351. The Cincinnati Reds claimed Moran on waivers in January 1914.

September 1, 1911: Drafted Outfielder Casey Stengel from the Aurora (IL) Blues of the Wisconsin-Illinois League

Casey Stengel, a 21-year-old outfielder drafted out of the Class C Wisconsin-Illinois League, would emerge as by far the best of Brooklyn's 1911 draft class. He led the Wisconsin-Illinois League in batting (.352) and hits (148) and had a .464 slugging percentage.

Stengel spent most of the 1912 season with the Montgomery Rebels of the Class A Southern Association. He handled the higher level of pitching well, batting .290. Called up in September, he made a spectacular debut On September 17 he had four hits in four at-bats, two runs batted in, and two stolen bases. Stengel would be the Dodgers' center fielder in 1913 and its right fielder from 1914 through 1917.

September 1, 1911: Drafted Pitcher Earl Yingling from the Toledo Mud Hens of the American Association

Earl Yingling, a 22-year-old left-hander, made his major league debut with the Cleveland Naps in April 1911. He pitched in four games, winning his only decision, before Naps manager George Stovall sent him back to the Toledo Mud Hens of the American Association. Yingling had an 18–11 record for the Mud Hens, following his 22–9 record with them in 1910.

Drafted at the suggestion of scout Larry Sutton, Yingling had a 14–19 record in his two seasons with Brooklyn (1912–1913). He also contributed offensively. A good-hitting pitcher, Yingling was sometimes used as a pinch-hitter by manager Bill Dahlen. In 71 plate appearances in 1913, he had a .383 batting average and a .464 on-base average. The Cincinnati Reds claimed Yingling on waivers in 1914.

December 14, 1911: Traded Pitcher Doc Scanlan to the Philadelphia Phillies for Pitcher Eddie Stack

William "Doc" Scanlan signed with the Dodgers as a free agent in August 1904. He split 12 decisions and threw three shutouts over the rest of that season. Scanlan pitched six more seasons for Brooklyn (1905–1907, 1909–1911); he sat out the 1908 season. During these years, he earned a degree in medicine and began practicing surgery in the offseason.

Overall, Scanlan had a 64–67 record with the Dodgers, including a 14-win season in 1905 and an 18-win season in 1906. After going 3–10 in 1911, he expressed his desire to be traded, claiming he was jinxed in Brooklyn. Scanlan said he preferred to be traded to the Philadelphia Phillies, but when he was, he refused to sign with them, ending his baseball career.

Eddie Stack was a 24-year-old right-hander who had won 11 games and lost 12 in his two seasons with the Phillies.

Also in 1911:

Purchased: Pitcher Elmer Steele from Pittsburgh Pirates

Sold: Pitcher Jack Ryan to Mobile Sea Gulls of the Southern Association; Third Baseman Ed Lennox to Louisville Colonels of the American Association

Chosen in Major League Draft: Second Baseman George Cutshaw from Oakland Oaks of the Pacific Coast League; Infielder Red Downs from Minneapolis Millers of the American Association; Catcher Bob Higgins from Chattanooga Lookouts of the Southern Association; Pitcher Maury Kent from Birmingham Barons of the Southern Association

1912

In January 1912, the McKeever Brothers, Steve and Ed, each bought 25 percent of the franchise from Charles Ebbets and Henry Medicus, who dropped out of ownership.

May 28, 1912: Traded Pitcher Bill Schardt and Shortstop Dolly Stark to the Newark Indians of the International League for Shortstop Bob Fisher and Outfielder Bill Kay

After four straight losses to the Giants, which dropped his team's record to 9–22, Charles Ebbets made a long-distance call to Newark Indians president George Solomon. (The Brooklyn club had a controlling interest in the Newark club.) The discussion ended in a two-for-two trade.

Newark was getting 6'4" righthander Bill Schardt, who as a 25-year-old rookie in 1911 had a 5–15 record. Schardt had appeared in seven games for the Dodgers this season, with a loss and a save. Also going to Newark was 27-year-old shortstop Dolly Stark, who at the time of the trade was out with an injury. Stark batted .295 in 70 games in 1911 but was a combined .245-hitter in his three years in Brooklyn.

The Dodgers were excited about getting Bob Fisher, a 25-year-old shortstop who was batting .267 for Newark. He would spend two years with Brooklyn, batting .252 in 214 games.

Outfielder Bill Kay had played 25 games for the 1907 Washington Senators. Kay was sent to the Albany Senators of the New York State League and never returned to the major leagues.

July 9, 1912: Purchased Pitcher Cliff Curtis from the Philadelphia Phillies

Cliff Curtis had a 2–5 record when the Philadelphia Phillies put him on waivers, with the intention of sending him to the minor leagues. But Dodgers manager Bill Dahlen claimed the 30-year-old right-hander, perhaps remembering the shutout he had pitched against his club the previous September. Curtis reached the major leagues with the Boston Doves in 1909. He had a three-year record of 11–37 with the Doves, including 24 losses (18 consecutive) in 1910. His 1911 record was 4–11, split among Boston, Chicago, and Philadelphia.

"Pitcher Cliff Curtis, just claimed from Philadelphia by Brooklyn, has been a baseball nomad," wrote *Sporting Life*. "He has never been anything more than a prospect."[4] Curtis won 12 and lost 16 in his two years with Brooklyn.

August 19, 1912: Traded Shortstop Bert Tooley to the Newark Indians of the International League for Infielder Enos Kirkpatrick

Because of his poor fielding, the trading of shortstop Bert Tooley surprised no one, including the *Brooklyn Eagle*. "His serious fielding errors, as well as his errors of judgment, were such a menace in close games that he was retired as soon as [Bob] Fisher, who also came from Newark, had recovered enough from his illness to play regularly."[5] Nor was Tooley much of a hitter—a .216 average in 196 games in his two seasons in Brooklyn.

Meanwhile, Enos Kirkpatrick was batting .305 in 119 games for Newark, while playing second base, third base, and shortstop, and excelling at all three positions. While the 27-year-old Kirkpatrick was an improvement over Tooley defensively, his offense was no better, a combined 1912–1913 average of .219 in 80 games. In 1914, he signed with the Baltimore Terrapins of the Federal League.

September 16, 1912: Drafted Catcher William Fischer from the Toronto Maple Leafs of the International League

Seeking to add a young catcher, manager Bill Dahlen drafted William Fischer, a left-handed batter from the International League's Toronto

Maple Leafs. The 22-year-old Fischer batted .267 in 62 games in 1913 and .257 in 43 games in 1914. The following year he signed with the Chicago Whales of the Federal League.

September 1912. Purchased Third Baseman Gus Getz from the Elmira Colonels of the New York State League

Brooklyn had Red Smith at third base in 1912 and no immediate need for 24-year-old, minor league third baseman Gus Getz. They sent him to the Newark Indians of the International League, where he had good seasons in 1913 and in 1914.

Getz was batting .289 in 107 games for Newark in 1914, when the Dodgers purchased him from the Indians to fill the roster spot of shortstop Ollie O'Mara, out with a broken leg. The right-handed-hitting Getz played three seasons at third base (full-time in 1915) batting .250 in 225 games. The Cincinnati Reds claimed him on waivers in April 1917.

Also in 1912:

Traded: Outfielder Hub Northen to Toronto Maple Leafs of the International League for Outfielder Benny Meyer

Purchased: Outfielder Leo Callahan from Elmira (NY) Colonels of the New York State League

Sold: Infielder Red Downs to Chicago Cubs; Pitcher Sandy Burk to St. Louis Cardinals

Chosen in Major League Draft: Pitcher Bull Wagner

1913

In 1913 the team moved from Washington Park to Ebbets Field.

July 26, 1913: Purchased Pitcher Jeff Pfeffer from the Grand Rapids Bill-eds of the Central League

Henry Medicus, the Brooklyn club's treasurer, had recently spent a month in Grand Rapids, Michigan, during which time he attended several games played by the local Central League club. Knowing the Dodgers were always in search of pitching help, Medicus paid particular attention to 25-year-old Jeff Pfeffer, a 6'3" right-hander. Suspecting he had uncovered a "find," Medicus telegraphed President Ebbets who sent scout Larry Sutton to Grand Rapids to look at Pfeffer. Sutton confirmed Medicus' opinion, and Ebbets made the purchase. The Grand Rapids team was leading the Central League and terms of the sale allowed Pfeffer to remain with them for the rest of the season. Grand Rapids would win the pennant by 15 games, aided by the pitching of Pfeffer, who led the league in wins (25) and strikeouts (232). After the Central League season ended, Pfeffer got into five late-season games for Brooklyn, losing his only decision.

August 5, 1913: Traded Pitcher Eddie Stack to the Chicago Cubs for Pitcher Ed Reulbach

For the past several weeks, manager Bill Dahlen had tried unsuccessfully to swing a deal for Cubs right-hander Ed Reulbach. Meanwhile, Reulbach had expressed dissatisfaction with Chicago and his desire to be traded. So, when Brooklyn was playing at Chicago, and Dahlen proposed the trade of Reulbach for pitcher Eddie Stack, new Cubs manager Johnny Evers was willing.

The 30-year-old Reulbach had been one of the National League's best pitchers in his nine years with the Cubs, with a 136–65 record and a 2.24 earned run average. But Evers had used him in only 10 games this season, with only three starts. Reulbach's record was 1–3 and his ERA was 4.42. Still, he was expected to strengthen Brooklyn's pitching staff, as a starter and as a reliever.

Reulbach did improve the staff; he made 15 appearances, 12 of which were starts, and he won seven of 13 decisions with a 2.05 ERA for a sixth-place team. In 1914, under new manager Wilbert Robinson, he was 11–18, with a 2.64 ERA. In 1915 Reulbach signed with the Newark Peppers of the Federal League.

Eddie Stack was originally the property of the Cubs but never pitched for them. The Dodgers acquired him from the Philadelphia Phillies in a December 1911 trade for Doc Scanlan. He had an 11–9 record and a 2.99 ERA in his two years in Brooklyn.

According to sportswriter Ring Lardner, the two managers and two pitchers were more than pleased with the trade. "Evers was wild to get Stack back, and Dahlen was wild to get Reulbach. Stack was wild to get back, and Reulbach was wild to get away."[6]

September 15, 1913: Drafted Shortstop Ollie O'Mara from the Fort Wayne Champs of the Central League

Ollie O'Mara was hitless in four at-bats for the Detroit Tigers as a 21-year-old in 1912. He would play with Brooklyn from 1914 to 1919, except for 1917, when he was sent to the minors after failing to agree with Charles Ebbets on his salary. O'Mara shared the shortstop position with Dick Egan as a rookie in 1914, was the full-time shortstop in 1915, and a backup to Ivy Olson in 1916. After a year in the minors, he was the Robins regular third baseman in 1918, but was returned to the minor league after two games in April 1919. O'Mara batted .231 in 411 games with Brooklyn.

December 13, 1913: Purchased Second Baseman Dick Egan from the Cincinnati Reds

Charles Ebbets had gone to Cincinnati ready to pay Reds president Garry Herrmann $15,000 for his shortstop, Joe Tinker. Ebbets had also agreed to pay Tinker a $10,000 bonus when he signed his contract. "Tinker is Now a Superba," read a headline in the *Brooklyn Citizen*, using a past name for the Brooklyn club. But Tinker, a hero in Chicago when he played for the Cubs, chose to return to that city and signed to play for the Whales, its team in the Federal League.

Ebbets did not get the man he was after, but he did get an option to buy second baseman Dick Egan, who had been with the Reds since 1908. The sale of Egan was completed on January 8. As a part of it, pitcher Earl Yingling and outfielder Herbie Moran were sold on waivers to the Reds. New manager Wilbert Robinson used Egan at shortstop in 1914 and sold him to the Boston Braves in April 1915.

Also in 1913:

Traded: Pitcher Cliff Curtis to Newark Indians of the International League for Outfielder Bill Collins

Purchased: Catcher Mike Hechinger from Chicago Cubs; Pitcher Elmer Brown from Montgomery (AL) Rebels of the Southern Association

Chosen in Major League Draft: Outfielder Joe Riggert

1914

Wilbert Robinson replaced Bill Dahlen as manager.

July 10, 1914: Sold Catcher Tex Erwin to the Cincinnati Reds

Tex Erwin's major league career seemed at an end when President Ebbets announced he was sending the 28-year-old catcher to the International League's Newark Indians. But that was before Tom Clarke, the Cincinnati's Reds first-string catcher, was injured in that afternoon's game. A foul tip from Brooklyn's Zack Wheat split Clarke's finger. Cincinnati president Garry Herrmann asked Ebbets to permit him to withdraw his waiver on Erwin. Ebbets consented, saying it had always been his policy to help ball players stay in the big leagues as long as possible. The next day, in his first game with the Reds, Erwin hit a two-run home run to beat his old team, 6–5. Erwin spent twelve days with Cincinnati. The Dodgers got him back on July 27. He played only one game for them before spending the rest of his career in the minor leagues.

August 8, 1914: Sold Third Baseman Red Smith to the Boston Braves

Third baseman Red Smith had been a star at Auburn University and one of the best players in the Southern Association when, at the urging of scout Larry Sutton, the Brooklyn club drafted him from the Nashville Vols in 1911. The 21-year-old Smith played in 28 games in September and October and was the team's regular third baseman in 1912 and 1913. He batted .286 and .296 in those two seasons, with OPS+ of 110 and 125. In 1913, the right-handed-hitting Smith led the National League with 40 doubles.

A popular player in his first two seasons, Smith lost that popularity after making threats to jump to St. Louis of the Federal League. Smith was also unhappy with new manager Wilbert Robinson, who considered him a troublemaker. Robinson asked waivers on Smith, but Braves manager George Stallings would not agree. Robinson wanted to trade Smith, but again Stallings did not want to give up any players. A straight sale was agreed to, which Robinson admitted was for a higher price than the proposed waiver sale. Weak-hitting Gus Getz replaced Smith at third base for the rest of the 1914 season. Smith played a significant role in helping the "Miracle Braves" win the 1914 pennant, batting .314 in 60 games.

September 15, 1914: Drafted Pitcher Wheezer Dell from the Seattle Giants of the Northwestern League

Wheezer Dell was a 28-year-old right-hander who pitched unimpressively in three games for the 1912 St. Louis Cardinals. But Dell won 20 games for the Class B Seattle Giants in 1913 and did even better with the 1914 Giants. He led the Northwestern League with 21 wins and a 2.50 earned run average.

Dell came highly recommended by scouts Amos Rusie, the great Giants' pitcher of the 1890s, and Tom Sheehan, who played for Brooklyn in 1908. In his three years with the Robins, Dell was 19–23 with a 2.50 earned run average. He was 8–9 with the 1916 pennant-winners and pitched one inning in the World Series.

September 15, 1914: Drafted Pitcher Leon Cadore from the Wilkes-Barre Barons of the New York State League

Wilbert Robinson liked big, hard-throwing pitchers, which halfway described 22-year-old right-hander Leon Cadore. He was big, 6'1", but was more a finesse pitcher than a hard thrower. One Brooklyn sportswriter later described Cadore as "a smart pitcher, with reasonable speed and a variegated delivery."[7]

Cadore got into just seven games with the Robins in 1915 and one in 1916. He spent those two seasons primarily with the International League's Montreal Royals, winning 10 games the first year and a league-leading 25 the second.

Beginning in 1917, Cadore was a double-digit winner for Brooklyn in four of the next five seasons. He missed only 1918, when he was drafted into the army and saw action in France. Cadore is best remembered for the May 1, 1920, game when he and Boston Braves pitcher Joe Oeschger each pitched all 26 innings of a 1–1 tie. Called on account of darkness, it remains the longest (by innings) major league game ever.

Cadore had a 4–1 record in 1923 and was dealing with a sore arm.

Ebbets asked for waivers on him and on July 6, the Chicago White Sox claimed him. His nine years in Brooklyn produced a 68–71 record and a 3.11 earned run average.

Also in 1914:

Purchased: Outfielder Joe Schultz from Rochester Hustlers of the International League; Pitcher Johnny Enzmann from Newark Indians of the International League; Pitcher Bill Steele from St. Louis Cardinals

Sold: Outfielder Joe Riggert to St. Louis Cardinals

Signed Free Agents: Shortstop Kid Elberfeld

Chosen in Major League Draft: Pitcher Sherry Smith

CHAPTER SIX

1915–1919

1915

January 17, 1915: Signed Pitcher Jack Coombs as a Free Agent

Jack Coombs was a star pitcher for Connie Mack's Philadelphia Athletics before an injury in 1913 limited him to two games that season and two in 1914. Mack released him following the 1914 season, and Wilbert Robinson, who was looking for a veteran pitcher, signed him.

Coombs, a six-foot righthander, had his greatest season in 1910. He led the American League with 31 wins, finished second in earned run average (1.30), and third in strikeouts (224). He led the AL in wins again in 1911, with 28, and added 21 more in 1912. Coombs had three complete game victories over the Chicago Cubs in the 1910 World Series and one against the New York Giants in the 1911 Series. "I am sure I will be in the finest condition possible when the season opens," he said, "and sincerely hope I may be as good as I was a couple of years ago. I have no doubt of this."[1]

While no one expected Coombs, now 32, to come near that level of success with Brooklyn, he proved to be an excellent addition. He won 15 games in 1915 and 13 for the pennant-winning Robins in 1916. Coombs was the starting and winning pitcher against the Boston Red Sox in Game Three the 1916 World Series, the first World Series game played at Ebbets Field. The win raised his World Series record to 5–0.

Coombs announced his retirement on August 30, 1918, after losing a 1–0 game to the Giants. With 7–11 and 8–14 records in 1917 and 1918, Coombs finished his Brooklyn career at 43–43. (He unretired in 1920, pitching in two games for the Detroit Tigers.)

April 23, 1915: Sold Infielder
Dick Egan to the Boston Braves

The injury to second baseman Johnny Evers led the defending world champion Braves to purchase Dick Egan as a backup at that position. Egan was also capable of playing shortstop and third base. Manager Wilbert Robinson had used him mostly at shortstop in 1914. He batted .226 with an on-base percentage of .273, and Robinson considered him expendable. A columnist who wrote under the name "RICE," thought Robinson had made a mistake.

"The departure of Egan will cause many regrets in Brooklyn," he wrote. "He is a ballplayer of the kind that helps the game on the field and off."[2] Egan did help the Braves, playing in 83 games and batting .259.

June 13, 1915: Purchased Pitcher
Phil Douglas from the Cincinnati Reds

On June 9, the Robins pounded Cincinnati pitcher Phil Douglas in a 5–1 victory. Four days later, Reds manager Buck Herzog persuaded a reluctant Wilbert Robinson to purchase the 25-year-old right hander for his club. Robinson's misgivings about the purchase were based on more than Douglas's 1–5 record and 5.40 earned run average this season. Douglas was an alcoholic, whose drinking had caused the Reds to suspend him in May.

Douglas was a talented pitcher—he would split 10 decisions for the Robins, with a 2.62 earned run average. But he broke the team's rules several times, leading a fed-up Robinson to put him on waivers. Boston and Chicago claimed Douglas, before National League president John Tener approved his sale to Chicago on September 9. The *Brooklyn Eagle* spoke for many when it wrote of Douglas's departure.

"The Superbas express little regret over the fact that Phil Douglas was shipped to the Cubs yesterday for the waiver price. Douglas had a reputation as a bad boy, and the Superbas did not like the constant newspaper reference to him as a member of their party. They thought the fans would gain a wrong impression of the whole outfit."[3]

July 16, 1915: Purchased Infielder
Ivy Olson from the Cincinnati Reds

The Robins 15–2–1 record in their last 18 games moved them to within two games of the first place Philadelphia Phillies. President Charles

Ebbets and manager Wilbert Robinson, seeing a chance for Brooklyn to win its first pennant since 1900, claimed infielder Ivy Olson from the Cincinnati Reds. Olson's ability to play many positions, they reasoned, would give the Robins a capable backup if any of their regulars got hurt.

Olson, 29, spent four seasons with the Cleveland Naps before his sale to the Reds in December 1914. In his first game with Brooklyn, he lined out as a pinch-hitter for Casey Stengel. But he was little-used and had only two hits in 25 at-bats the rest of the season.

Throughout his career, Olson was recognized as a good hitter but an erratic fielder.

Nevertheless, Robinson made him his full-time shortstop in 1916 and Olson helped the Robins win the pennant. He would retain that position through the 1921 season, then split his time between shortstop and second base in 1922. Olson's best season was 1919, when he led the National League with 164 hits. He played with Brooklyn for ten years, batting .261 with 1,100 hits. Olson was the Robins shortstop in the 1916 World Series against the Boston Red Sox and the 1920 Series against the Cleveland Indians, batting a combined .293. After getting his release in December 1924, he stayed on as a coach under Robinson.

August 29, 1915: Traded Third Baseman Joe Schultz and Cash to the Chicago Cubs for Pitcher Larry Cheney

Larry Cheney, a 6'1" right-hander, had been Chicago's winningest pitcher over the last three seasons. His 26 wins in 1912 were a National League high. He followed with 21 wins in 1913 and 20 in 1914. In addition, Cheney was a workhorse, leading the league in complete games in 1912 and total games in 1913 and 1914. After throwing more than 300 innings in each of the previous three seasons, a strained lower back had limited him to an 8–9 record and 131 1/3 innings with the 1915 Cubs. Cheney was unhappy at the way manager Roger Bresnahan was using him, and Bresnahan had become impatient with Cheney.

When Bresnahan offered to send the 29-year-old spitballer to Brooklyn for third baseman Joe Schultz and $3,000, Robinson agreed. The Robins manager had an excellent reputation as a judge of pitchers and believed Cheney's problems were only temporary. Brooklyn was fighting for a pennant and Robinson felt pitching help is what he most needed. "I need only one man to round out my staff," Robinson said, "and there is hardly one man I would rather have than Larry Cheney. Look out for Brooklyn now."[4]

Cheney lost his only two decisions in 1915, despite a 1.67 earned run average, but contributed 18 wins for the pennant-winning 1916 club. Cheney was 20–28 for the Robins over the next three seasons before he was claimed by the Boston Braves in June 1919.

Joe Schultz came to Brooklyn from the International League's Rochester Hustlers in May 1914. The 21-year-old right-handed hitter was batting .292 in 56 games and showing promise of becoming a fixture at third base for the Robins. But Schultz injured his shoulder in a May collision with the Cardinals' Cozy Dolan and his recovery had been slow. He had trouble making the throw across the diamond to first base, and Robinson was using him mostly as a pinch-hitter. Schultz would go on to play eight more years in the National League, as an outfielder and pinch-hitter.

August 31, 1915: Purchased Pitcher Rube Marquard from the New York Giants

A few days after Wilbert Robinson talked about Larry Cheney being the one pitcher he wanted for the stretch drive, he claimed left-hander Rube Marquard from the New York Giants. A once highly touted rookie, Marquard started slowly in 1909 and 1910, but blossomed as a 24-year-old in 1911, winning 24 games and leading the National League in winning percentage (.774) and strikeouts (237). In 1912, he won his first 19 decisions—a record-setting winning streak—and finished with a league-leading 26 wins. He won 23 in 1913 but slipped to 12–22 in 1914.

In his first 1915 start Marquard, now 28, pitched a no-hitter against Brooklyn, but he now had a mediocre 9–8 record for a Giants team that would finish in last place. After Marquard asked to be traded, Giants manager John McGraw put him on waivers. No one claimed him, but Robinson worked out a sale with McGraw, his former teammate and one-time close friend.

Brooklyn was hoping to reach the World Series and to have Marquard eligible, he would have to sign a contract by August 31. On that morning, Marquard, Robinson, and Charles Ebbets traveled to the Giants office in Manhattan to meet with McGraw and Giants owner Harry Hempstead, where the sale was formalized. The Brooklyn contingent then headed to Ebbets Field, where the Dodgers were playing a doubleheader against Pittsburgh that afternoon. Marquard signed his contract between games, and then won the second game in relief of—Larry Cheney.

Also in 1915:

Traded: Catcher Graeme Snow to Newark Indians of the International League for Catcher Mack Wheat; Outfielder Leo Callahan to

Newark Indians of the International League for Outfielder Bill Zimmerman; Pitcher Joe Chabek, Outfielder Bill Zimmerman, and Cash to Oakland Oaks of the Pacific Coast League for Outfielder Jimmy Johnston

Purchased: Outfielder Red Smyth from Fort Wayne (IN) Cubs of the Central League; Outfielder Al Nixon from Beaumont (TX) Oilers of the Texas League

Sold: Pitcher Johnny Enzmann to Newark Indians of the International League; Pitcher Pat Ragan to Boston Braves

Released: Pitcher Ed Reulbach

1916

February 10, 1916: Purchased Catcher Jack "Chief" Meyers from the New York Giants

Chief Meyers had been a mainstay for John McGraw's Giants since 1909. When the Giants won three consecutive pennants from 1911 to 1913, Meyers finished in the top ten in the voting for the Most Valuable Player Award each year. He was third in 1912, a year he batted .358 and led the league with a .441 on-base percentage.

When Meyers's batting average slipped to .232 in 1915, McGraw asked for waivers on his 35-year-old catcher. Robins manager Wilbert Robinson, a former catcher and a coach with the Giants during that three-year span, put in a claim. So did Percy Haughton, the new president of the Boston Braves. A coin toss was used as the method of deciding Meyers's fate, and Robinson won. No longer the player he had been, Meyers played two seasons in Brooklyn, batting .235. The Robins released him in August 1917, and the Braves finally got their man, signing him as a free agent.

February 20, 1916: Purchased Third Baseman Mike Mowrey from the Pittsburgh Rebels of the Federal League

Third Baseman Mike Mowrey spent 10 years in the National League, split between Cincinnati and St. Louis and one season, 1914, with Pittsburgh. Mowrey left the Pirates after that season to join the

Pittsburgh Rebels of the Federal League, which was now defunct. Wilbert Robinson signed the 32-year-old Mowrey, expecting him to be an improvement over incumbent third baseman Gus Getz. Although Mowrey was not a big improvement offensively, he was defensively. His .965 fielding percentage for the pennant-winning Robins in 1916 led all National League third basemen.

Sporting Life took note. "In Mike Mowrey, the Brooklyn team the past season had the best fielding third baseman in the National League.... And while he did not boast of any .300 batting average, he was a corking good timely hitter, especially in the early part of the season."[5] Mowrey held out in 1917, joining the team shortly before the opener. He never caught up and was batting just .214 when Robinson released him in August.

February 27, 1916: Purchased Outfielder Jim Hickman from the Baltimore Terrapins of the Federal League

Twenty-four-year-old Jim Hickman had batted well in the low minor leagues in 1914 and 1915. He also played in 20 games for the Baltimore Terrapins of the Federal League in 1915, batting a lowly .210. Nevertheless, Charles Ebbets thought Hickman had great promise. So too did his manager with the Terrapins, Otto Knabe, who called him the best young outfielder in the Federal League. "The big-league scouts must have been asleep last season, or they would have got [*sic*] wise to Hickman," he said.[6]

Despite Knabe's predictions of stardom, Hickman had a short and unexceptional career; he played 233 games for the Robins from 1916 through 1919, with a .218 batting average and an OPS+ of 76.

August 25, 1916: Traded Catcher Lew McCarty to the New York Giants for First Baseman Fred Merkle

Robins first baseman Jake Daubert was in his sixth consecutive .300 season, when he injured his hip in mid–August. The injury turned out to be more serious than originally thought, and Daubert was expected to be out for an extended period. With Brooklyn trying to protect its slim lead in the pennant race, Wilbert Robinson went shopping for a replacement. He found one on John McGraw's Giants, veteran

Fred Merkle. McGraw asked originally for three players in return, but his club was weak behind the plate, and he was glad to get 27-year-old catcher Lew McCarty.

Robinson was not happy about losing McCarty, who was having the best of his four seasons in Brooklyn, with a .313 batting average. But he had other catchers—Chief Meyers and Otto Miller—and desperately needed a first baseman.

"McCarty has been playing a grand game for Brooklyn," Robinson said. "But we are up against it so badly that I had to let Lew go.... He [Daubert] will not be able to get back in the game for at least 10 days anyway. And without a good first baseman during that time, we seriously would be affected."[7]

Merkle, who broke in with the Giants in 1907 and was in his tenth season, was still only 27 years old. He had been a consistently good hitter for New York but was batting just .237 at the time of the trade. Daubert returned on September 4, and the Robins did win the pennant Merkle contributed little; he batted .232 and drove in two runs in 23 games. After making only two appearances in 1917, Brooklyn sold him to the Chicago Cubs, where he again became a full-time player.

Also in 1916:

Purchased: Infielder John Kelleher from Denver Bears of the Western League

Chosen in Major League Draft: Catcher Jack Snyder

1917

August 6, 1917: Purchased Catcher Ernie Krueger from the New York Giants

Catcher Chief Meyers was 36 years old, and he was batting just .212. Manager Wilbert Robinson was making plans to release him and find someone else to replace Meyers as a backup to Otto Miller. He chose Ernie Kreuger of the New York Giants. The choice was risky, as the United States was now at war, and the 27-year-old Krueger was eligible for the military draft.

Kreuger escaped the draft and was able to finish the season with the Robins. After playing in 30 games in 1918, Krueger enlisted in the navy in June. He returned in 1919 and played through the 1921 season. Although he was primarily a backup, Kreuger played in 258 games for Brooklyn, with a .267 batting average.

October 16, 1917: Purchased Pitcher Clarence Mitchell from the Cincinnati Reds

Clarence Mitchell was a rarity among major leaguers, a left-handed pitcher who threw a spitball. In 1916, his first season with the Cincinnati Reds, the 25-year-old Mitchell won 11 and lost 10, a .524 winning percentage for a team that finished seventh with a 60–93 record.

Cincinnati moved up to fourth place in 1917, but Mitchell won only nine games with 15 losses. A good-hitting pitcher, he doubled as an outfielder-first baseman in those two seasons, batting .256 in 207 at-bats. Reds manager Christy Mathewson believed his pitching staff was strong enough to allow Mitchell to leave.

Also in 1917:

Purchased: Infielder Frank O'Rourke from Utica (NY) Utes of the New York State League; Pitcher Norman Plitt from Portland (ME) Duffs of the Eastern League

Sold: Third Baseman Gus Getz to Cincinnati Reds; Pitcher Duster Mails to Pittsburgh Pirates; First Baseman Fred Merkle to Chicago Cubs; Outfielder Red Smyth to St. Louis Cardinals; Catcher Jack Snyder to Toronto Maple Leafs of the International League

Chosen in Major League Draft: First Baseman Ray Schmandt

Released: Catcher Chief Meyers; Third Baseman Mike Mowrey

1918

January 9, 1918: Traded Outfielder Casey Stengel and Second Baseman George Cutshaw to the Pittsburgh Pirates for Pitcher Burleigh Grimes, Pitcher Al Mamaux, and Shortstop Chuck Ward

The Robins were the National League champions in 1916, yet many of their players had held out after receiving their contract offers for 1917.

Despite winning the pennant, owner Charles Ebbets was offering them either the same salary as 1916, or even a cut. Eventually, everyone signed except Casey Stengel. The Robins collapsed to a seventh-place finish in 1917 and some critic blamed Stengel. They pointed to his .257 batting average, ignoring that he led the team in runs batted in (73) and total bases (206).

Ebbets made no secret of his pleasure at getting rid of Stengel, who he felt never had shown proper deference to the owner. However, the 27-year-old outfielder was popular with the fans and had a .272 batting average and a 119 OPS+ in his six years with Brooklyn.

"Of the two Brooklyn has let get away, Stengel is the better and more valuable man in every way," wrote the *Brooklyn Times*.[8] Stengel was not happy about going to the last-place Pittsburgh club, even threatening to enlist rather than join the Pirates. He later changed his mind and signed but did enlist in the navy that season.

Negotiations for this trade had been ongoing for several weeks. The Pirates had hoped to get Zack Wheat, but the Robins were not letting their best player go. Meanwhile, Ebbets said he was pleased with the deal, which he predicted would help both clubs. "Now and then a player remains with a club so long that he considers himself indispensable, and then it's time to change," he said. "It was just as well that we should get rid of some of our veterans and take on some new blood to start the rebuilding which we plan in order to bring Brooklyn another pennant winner in a reasonable time."[9]

Thirty-one-year-old George Cutshaw joined the Brooklyn club in 1912 after being drafted from the Oakland Oaks of the Pacific Coast League in September 1911. Cutshaw had been the team's second baseman for the past six years, never failing to appear in more than 100 games. He led all National League second baseman in games played from 1914 through 1917, with Brooklyn, and again in 1918 and 1919 for the Pirates. In addition to being durable, he was a reliable hitter and a solid fielder, and like Stengel, popular with the fans. Playing in 845 games for Brooklyn, Cutshaw had 824 hits and a .260 batting average.

Just as Stengel was anxious to leave Brooklyn because of salary disputes with Ebbets, Al Mamaux was anxious to leave Pittsburgh because of salary disputes with Pirates owner Barney Dreyfuss. "Well, you can bet your Liberty Bonds I am glad" the 23-year-old right-hander replied when asked if he was glad to get away from the Pirates. "Why shouldn't I rejoice to break away from a lot of unpleasantness?"[10]

Mamaux won 21 games in both 1915 and 1916 for Pittsburgh, with earned run averages of 2.04 and 2.53. But he was coming off a season in which he had two wins and 11 losses with a 5.25 earned run average. Mamaux was also a discipline problem and been suspended for part of the 1917 season. Nevertheless, Ebbets thought Mamaux was Brooklyn's main acquisition from the trade, and manager Wilbert Robinson was convinced he could handle him. Mamaux missed all but two games in 1918, while doing defense work at the Fore River shipyard in Massachusetts, but he won 10 games in 1919, and 12 for the pennant-winning 1920 Robins. Mamaux pitched for Brooklyn into the 1923 season but won only four more games.

The Robins wanted right-hander Burleigh Grimes included in the trade because the military draft had claimed several of their top pitchers and they were desperate for help. Grimes, a 24-year-old spitballer, had a horrible 3–16 record as a rookie in 1917, but the *Brooklyn Eagle* agreed with several authorities who predicted a bright future for him.

"He has all the physical attributes of a successful pitcher and is said to have the mental capacity to learn," wrote Thomas S. Rice. "With a specialist like Robbie to coach him along, we should get excellent results from that big frame and powerful arm which are Grimes's distinguishing marks."[11]

The *Pittsburgh Post-Gazette* wrote, "Burleigh Grimes looks extremely promising," while noting some of his potential drawbacks. "But his career as a pitcher would be doubtful if the spitball is thrown into the discard. Although married, there is a chance that Grimes will be taken in the draft."[12]

Chuck Ward had the unenviable task in 1917 of replacing Honus Wagner as the Pirates' shortstop. (Wagner played mostly first base that year.) The 22-year-old rookie batted a most un–Wagner like .236. With Brooklyn, Ward spent all but two games of the 1918 season in the army. He returned in 1919 and spent the next four seasons as a backup at shortstop and third base, batting .217 in 111 games.

Also in 1918:

Purchased: Pitcher George Smith from New York Giants

Sold: Infielder Frank O'Rourke to New London (CT) Planters of the Eastern League; Pitcher George Smith to New York Giants; Catcher Jimmy Archer to Cincinnati Reds

Signed Free Agents: Shortstop Mickey Doolin; Catcher Jimmy Archer

1919

February 1, 1919: Traded First Baseman Jake Daubert to the Cincinnati Reds for Outfielder Tommy Griffith and Shortstop Larry Kopf

At the recommendation of scout Larry Sutton, Brooklyn drafted left-handed-hitting Jake Daubert from the Memphis Turtles of the Southern Association in September 1909. The following year Daubert replaced Tim Jordan as the Robins' first baseman and had occupied that position ever since. Daubert was highly thought of by teammates and opposing players and popular with the fans. But a money dispute relating to a suit he filed, related to Charles Ebbets withholding money from him, made his departure almost a certainty following the 1918 season.

Daubert was among the top players in the league, batting .305 over 1,213 games for the Robins. He was the National League's Most Valuable Player in 1913, a year his .350 batting average led the league. He led again in 1914, with a .329 mark, and was in the top 10 in hits for five consecutive seasons (1911–1915).

In return for Daubert, who would be 35, when the 1919 season began, Brooklyn was getting a speedy outfielder who was six years younger. One reporter called Tommy Griffith "One of the fastest players in the field and getting down to first base."[13] A left-handed batter, he played briefly with the Boston Braves in 1913 and 1914 and had been a regular with the Reds the past four seasons. His best season was 1915, when he batted .307 and had an OPS+ of 136, while playing a league-leading 160 games.

Larry Kopf refused to report to the Robins and just before the season began, Cincinnati sent second baseman Lee Magee to Brooklyn.

April 18, 1919: Acquired Second Baseman Lee Magee from the Cincinnati Reds

When Brooklyn traded Jake Daubert to Cincinnati in February, they were to get outfielder Tommy Griffith and shortstop Larry Kopf in return. But Kopf refused to report to the Robins and days before the season began, the Reds sent second baseman Lee Magee to the Robins in his place.

Magee, a 30-year-old switch-hitter, was in his ninth major league season. He was a man of questionable character who often clashed with management and teammates. Yet, Robins manager Wilber Robinson was more than pleased at getting him. "Lee will add hitting and fielding strength to my infield and also furnish some needed pep and aggressiveness," he said. "Lee is a fiery fellow and sometimes shows a tendency to tread on teammates corns, but all of the boys understand his temperament and there will not be any trouble."[14]

April 19, 1919: Purchased First Baseman Ed Konetchy from the Boston Braves

Left without a full-time first baseman following the trade of Jake Daubert, the Robins purchased veteran Ed Konetchy from the Boston Braves. The deal was contingent on the 33-year-old Konetchy, who had been a holdout with the Braves, agreeing to Brooklyn's salary offer. When the Robins agreed to meet his demands, he signed.

Konetchy, a right-handed batter, was a durable player who had twice led the National League in games played. An outstanding defender, his .992 fielding average led the league's first basemen in 1918; and he had been a consistent hitter, before slumping to .236 that year. His fall off in batting, his age, and his holdout contributed to Boston's seeking a replacement. In February they had traded for Cincinnati's 26-year-old first baseman Walter Holke. The Reds had acquired Holke in a trade with the Giants for Hal Chase earlier in the month. Three days later the Reds traded him to the Braves. Holke never played a game with Cincinnati.

Konetchy was a more than adequate replacement for Daubert. He batted .298 with an OPS+ of 118 in 1919 and had a .308 average with an OPS+ of 121 for the pennant-winning Robins of 1920. He played all seven games of the World Series, batting a lowly .174 with two runs batted in. Konetchy's Brooklyn career ended when he was sold to the Phillies on July 4, 1921. He had injured his wrist earlier, and his replacement, Ray Schmandt, stepped in and won the position.

June 22, 1919: Traded Second Baseman Lee Magee to the Chicago Cubs for Second Baseman Pete Kilduff

Wilbert Robinson expressed high expectations for Lee Magee when he acquired him in April, but two months later, he traded him to the Chicago Cubs for 26-year-old Pete Kilduff. Magee had appeared in

45 games and was batting .238. Kilduff had appeared in 31 games and was batting .273.

Kilduff was primarily a second baseman, but also had played shortstop and third base. His complaints to Cubs manager Fred Mitchell about his playing time, led to Mitchell making him available. Robinson used him at second and third for the remainder of the 1919 season and as his regular second baseman in 1920. Kilduff had an excellent .281 batting average for his two plus seasons with the Robins, but only two hits in 21 at-bats in the 1920 World Series against Cleveland. Unable to come to terms with the Brooklyn club on a 1922 salary, he left and joined the San Francisco Seals of the Pacific Coast League.

August 16, 1919: Purchased Outfielder Bernie Neis from the Saskatoon Quakers of the Western Canada League

After Robins outfielder Tommy Griffith made a midseason announcement that he would be retiring, the team went looking for outfielders. One they liked was 5'7" speedster Bernie Neis, who was batting .333 for the Saskatoon Quakers of the Class C Western Canada League.

Wilbert Robinson sent pitcher Jeff Pfeffer, who was out with an injury, to Canada to scout Neis and catcher Paul Beyers. Pfeffer came back with positive reports, and Brooklyn bought the pair for $2,000.

The 23-year-old Neis finished the season at Saskatoon, batting .297, fourth best in the league. Playing in only 101 games, he demonstrated his speed by leading the league in runs scored (86) and stolen bases (56). In 1920, Neis would begin an eight-year major league career, five with Brooklyn. Beyers would play one more season in the minors before his career ended.

August 29, 1919: Purchased Catcher Zack Taylor from the Charlotte Hornets of the South Atlantic League

Catcher Zack Taylor was yet another player the Robins drafted on the recommendation of their former star pitcher Nap Rucker. According to Warren Butts, Taylor's teammate at Charlotte, "Half a dozen major league scouts were looking Taylor over and bidding for him. Nap Rucker came along, boosted the price $500, and talked the Charlotte people into selling Taylor to Brooklyn before the other scouts knew what was happening."[15]

Chapter Six: 1915–1919

Ted Sullivan, a scout for the Chicago White Sox, said Taylor was the best-looking minor-league catcher he had seen in years. The report on him said he throws hard and accurately and gets the ball away very fast. Taylor would go on to have a 16-year major league career that began and ended with Brooklyn.

Also in 1919:

Purchased: Third Baseman Doug Baird from St. Louis Cardinals; Catcher Rowdy Elliott from Oakland Oaks of the Pacific Coast League

Sold: Outfielder Al Nixon to Beaumont (TX) Oilers of the Texas League; Pitcher Larry Cheney to Boston Braves

CHAPTER SEVEN

1920–1924

1920

January 12, 1920: Sold Catcher Mack Wheat to the Philadelphia Phillies

Mack Wheat was 22 in 1915 when he joined the Robins from the Newark Indians of the International League. The right-handed-hitting catcher became a teammate of his older brother Zack. Mack was the more energetic of the brothers, but nowhere near the player Zack was. He totaled 66 hits in 345 at-bats in his five years with the Robins, or about 35 percent of the elder Wheat's typical season. A month earlier Brooklyn had purchased catcher Rowdy Elliott from the Oakland Oaks of the Pacific Coast League. The addition of Elliott, who had major league experience with the 1916–1918 Chicago Cubs, made the weak-hitting Wheat expendable.

December 15, 1920: Traded Pitcher Rube Marquard to the Cincinnati Reds for Pitcher Dutch Ruether

While the Robins were in Cleveland, playing the Indians in the 1920 World Series, Rube Marquard was arrested on a charge of violating a city ordinance for alleged ticket speculating. Marquard paid a nominal fine and was released from custody. But the timing of the incident was unfortunate, coming shortly after the expose of "game-fixing" in the 1919 World Series between the Chicago White Sox and the Cincinnati Reds.

The Marquard incident paled in comparison to the Black Sox scandal, but Robins owner Charles Ebbets was furious. "I am through with him, absolutely," Ebbets said at the time. "He hasn't been released, however, and if anyone wants him, he can have him. But Marquard will never again put on a Brooklyn uniform."[1]

Ebbets remained true to his word. In an exchange of left-handers, he sent Marquard to Cincinnati for Dutch Reuther. Marquard spent six years with Brooklyn winning 56 and losing 48 with an earned run average of 2.58. His best season was 1917, when he was 19–12 with a 2.55 ERA. Marquard would win 17 for the Reds in 1921 and 11 for the Boston Braves in both 1922 and 1923.

On paper, it appeared to be a favorable trade for Brooklyn. Dutch Ruether had a 19–6 record, a league-leading .760 winning percentage, and an ERA+ of 154 for the 1919 world champion Reds. His 1920 record was 16–12, with a 123 ERA+. And, at 27, he was seven years younger than Marquard. But Reuther had some controversy surrounding him, as well. Reds manager Pat Moran had named him as the originator of the dissension that prevented his club from repeating as pennant winners in 1920. Moran called Wilbert Robinson to suggest the trade and Robinson agreed. Marquard had expressed a desire to return to the Giants but made no fuss about going to the Reds.

Also in 1920:

Purchased: Infielder-Outfielder Bill McCabe from Chicago Cubs; Outfielder Bill Lamar from Louisville Colonels of the American Association

Sold: Outfielder Wally Hood to Pittsburgh Pirates; Third Baseman Doug Baird to New York Giants

1921

January 11, 1921: Traded Minor League Outfielder Horace Allen and Cash to the Birmingham Barons of the Southern Association for Minor League Outfielder Bert Griffith

In the middle of the 1920 season, scout Nap Rucker had recommended that Brooklyn acquire Southern Association outfielder Bert Griffith. The Robins did not, but made their move after the season, one in which the speedy 24-year-old Griffith batted .304 for the Birmingham Barons. After some holdup about what the Barons would receive in return, the deal was made, with Brooklyn sending outfielder Horace Allen to Birmingham. Allen's first professional experience came in 1919 when he played in four games for the Robins. He would spend the rest of his career in the minor leagues.

Griffith expected to be in Brooklyn in 1921, but the Robins sent him back to the Southern Association, to the New Orleans Pelicans. A disappointed Griffith strengthened his case for big league status with a .355 batting average and a league-leading 224 hits.

Griffith had a successful two seasons in Brooklyn. He played mostly right field in 1922 and left field in 1923, while batting a combined .302 in 185 games. After holding out all spring in 1924, the Robins put him on waivers. When no National or American League team claimed Griffith, he was sent to the minor leagues.

June 18, 1921: Traded Pitcher Jeff Pfeffer to the St. Louis Cardinals for Pitcher Ferdie Schupp and Infielder Hal Janvrin

Jeff Pfeffer had been an outstanding pitcher for the Robins since 1914, amassing 113 wins, including twice winning more than twenty. Pfeffer was the pitching ace of Brooklyn's 1916 pennant winners, with 25 wins, and he added 16 more for the 1920 pennant winners. World War I interrupted Pfeffer's career, and he had started slowly this year. He was only 1–5 in June, leading the Robins to trade him. But the 33-year-old right-hander was far from through. Pfeffer won nine and lost three after going to St. Louis and then won 19 more for the Cardinals in 1922.

In return, the Dodgers got virtually nothing out of 30-year-old pitcher Ferdie Schupp and 28-year-old infielder Hal Janvrin. Schupp, a left-hander, won 21 games for the 1917 Giants and came back after the war to win 16 for the Cardinals in 1920. He was 2–0 for St. Louis this season but won only three games with four losses for Brooklyn. After the season the Robins sold Schupp to the Chicago White Sox.

Hal Janvrin played for seven years in the American League (six with Boston and one with Washington) primarily as a utility infielder. Janvrin batted .224 over 573 games as an American Leaguer. Since September 1919 he had been a utility infielder with St. Louis. He filled that same role for Brooklyn for a year and a half, after which his big-league career ended. Janvrin batted .235 with a 51 OPS+ over 74 games with the Robins.

July 1, 1921: Purchased Third Baseman Andy High from the Memphis Chicks of the Southern Association

Andy High was another Southern Association player scouted and recommended by Nap Rucker. The 23-year-old left-handed-hitting High was the league's best all-around third basemen in 1921, finishing the season with 191 hits and a .321 batting average. The Robins considered bringing him up after the end of the Southern Association season, but High would not make his Brooklyn debut until 1922.

July 23, 1921: Purchased Catcher Hank DeBerry from the New Orleans Pelicans of the Southern Association

Needing a catcher to replace the aging Otto Miller, Brooklyn purchased 26-year-old Hank DeBerry from the New Orleans Pelicans on the recommendation of scouts Nap Rucker and Larry Sutton. Aside from the 1918 season, which he spent in the navy, DeBerry had been playing professional baseball since 1914. Most of his career had been in the minor leagues, but he did have brief stints with the Cleveland Indians in 1916 and 1917.

July 23, 1921: Purchased Pitcher Dazzy Vance from the New Orleans Pelicans of the Southern Association

When the Robins purchased Hank DeBerry from the New Orleans Pelicans, DeBerry said he would not sign unless they also purchased his batterymate. The pitcher DeBerry wanted was Dazzy Vance, a 6'2", 200-pound right-hander with a history of arm trouble. The 31-year-old Vance had spent ten seasons in the minor leagues, compiling 117 wins, with brief unsuccessful trials with the Pittsburgh Pirates and New York Yankees.

Despite his 21-win season with the Pelicans, Charles Ebbets was reluctant to add a pitcher with a history of arm trouble. "I could have drafted him long ago if I wanted him," Ebbets told Sutton on the telephone. "You go back and tell them if we have to take Vance the deal is off." Soon Sutton called his boss back. "They say, no Vance, no DeBerry."

"In that case," Ebbets replied, "tell them they can...." Sutton interrupted: "Wait a minute, Mr. Ebbets. I just talked to DeBerry. He wants to go to Brooklyn, naturally, but he says he don't want to go without Vance. He says to tell you that if he looks good down here, it's because Vance makes him look good. And, really, Daz is hot. He's knocked around a long time and he's learned how to pitch. And he has a fastball. A real good fastball. He's the best pitcher in the league."[2]

Wilbert Robinson, who liked matching pitchers and catchers, and was impressed by Vance's size and his fastball, convinced Ebbets to make the deal. And in this serendipitous way, the team acquired the greatest pitcher in their history in Brooklyn.

Also in 1921:

Purchased: Pitcher Sweetbread Bailey from Chicago Cubs; Pitcher Eddie Eayrs from Boston Braves; Catcher Bernie Hungling from Memphis Chicks of the Southern Association

Sold: First Baseman Ed Konetchy to Philadelphia Phillies; Pitcher Ferdie Schupp to Chicago White Sox; Catcher Rowdy Elliott to Sacramento Senators of the Pacific Coast League; Outfielder Bill Lamar to the Toledo Mud Hens of the American Association

1922

September 18, 1922: Sold Pitcher Sherry Smith to the Cleveland Indians

On September 17, left-hander Sherry Smith made his twenty-eighth appearance of the 1922 season and the 229th of his seven-year career in Brooklyn. After the game Charles Ebbets announced he had asked waivers on the 31-year-old Smith, and the Cleveland Indians had claimed him.

Smith began his Robins career in 1915, after he was drafted from the Newark Indians of the International League. He had four double-digit win seasons, including two in which he won 14. His loss the previous afternoon to the Chicago Cubs dropped his record with the Robins to 69–70, but with an excellent earned run average of 2.91.

Smith is best-remembered for his 14-inning 2–1 loss to Babe Ruth and the Boston Red Sox in the 1916 World Series. He also pitched well in the 1920 Series against Cleveland, pitching two complete games with an 0.53 earned run average. That performance likely influenced Tris Speaker, the Indians manager, then and still, to make the claim.

Speaking to the press, Ebbets praised "Smith's conscientious and loyal service to the Brooklyn club and to Brooklyn fans. From the day he joined the team at the training camp in 1915 he has been a man who played to win."[3]

Ben Rosenberg, writing in the *Brooklyn Times Union*, called Smith "a picturesque ball player, with a winning and pleasing personality." He added that his release came as a surprise, "and undoubtedly is the first step on the part of the club to build for next year."[4]

October 15, 1922: Drafted Catcher Charlie Hargreaves from the Pittsfield (MA) Hillies of the Eastern League

Charles Ebbets came away from the draft meeting in Chicago with the addition of Charlie Hargreaves, a 26-year-old catcher. Hargreaves, a six-foot right-handed-hitter, started his professional career in 1921 with the Class AA Rochester Colts of the International League. He played in only 11 games with the Colts when manager George Stallings decided he had too many catchers and sent Hargreaves to Class A Pittsfield. Hargreaves batted .277 for the Hillies over the remainder of the 1921 season and upped his average to .302 in 1922.

Also in 1922:

Purchased: Shortstop Sam Crane from Cincinnati Reds; Outfielder Possum Whitted from Pittsburgh Pirates; Pitcher Leo Dickerman from Memphis Chicks of the Southern Association; Infielder Billy Mullen from Mobile Bears of the Southern Association; Pitcher Paul Schreiber from Saginaw (MI) Aces of the Michigan-Ontario League

Sold: Outfielder Possum Whitted to Toledo Mud Hens of the American Association; Pitcher Lew Malone to Rochester Tribe of the International League; Pitcher Johnny Miljus to Rochester Tribe of the International League

Signed Free Agents: Pitcher Art Decatur

Chosen in Major League Draft: Outfielder Gene Bailey; Second Baseman Stuffy Stewart

1923

February 15, 1923: Traded Pitcher Clarence Mitchell to the Philadelphia Phillies for Pitcher George Smith

Several of the contracts President Ebbets sent to his players for the 1923 season called for reductions in salary. One was to left-hander Clarence Mitchell, which called for a $2,000 cut from his 1922 salary. "We reduced Mitchell's figure because it was felt he would be useful in only a utility capacity," Ebbets said.[5] An unhappy Mitchell, who was a successful automobile salesman in the offseason, claimed he could make more money selling cars full time than playing for a reduced salary. Ebbets gave his response at the winter meetings; he traded Mitchell to the Philadelphia Phillies.

Mitchell had been with the Robins for five seasons, compiling a 23–20 record. His best season was 1921, when he won 11 games and led the league with three shutouts. His record in 1922 was 0–3 and he pitched in only five games. But Mitchell based his argument against the salary cut on his work as a first baseman. A left-handed-hitter, he played 42 games at first base and batted .290. The 32-year-old Mitchell would play another 10 seasons in the National League, mostly as a pitcher.

Manager Wilbert Robinson thought George Smith had the makings of a good pitcher if properly handled. Smith was 6'2" right-hander out of Columbia University. He had pitched previously for the Giants, the Reds, the Phillies, and in 1918 with Brooklyn, where he had a 4–1 record. Overall, he was 36–75, including a 27–63 mark in his four years with Philadelphia. Smith won three games and lost six with a 3.66 earned run average for the 1923 Robins and was released the following winter.

February 15, 1923: Traded Outfielder Hi Myers and First Baseman Ray Schmandt to the St. Louis Cardinals for First Baseman Jack Fournier

"Brooklyn Outfielder Given for an Erratic Infielder," was the *Brooklyn Eagle's* subheading announcing this trade. President Ebbets said he made it on the advice of his manager, who believed the Robins were long on outfielders but short on first basemen. Jack Fournier was expendable for the Cardinals who had rookie Jim Bottomley waiting to take his place.

Hi Myers had been with Brooklyn for eleven seasons and was its full-time center fielder since 1915. A right-hand hitter, he twice led the National League in triples, including 1919, when he also led in slugging average, runs batted in, and total bases. Myers played in 1,166 games for Brooklyn; he had 1,253 hits and a .282 batting average. In 1922, at age 33, he played 153 games and batted .317.

While Myers was still considered a star, the *Eagle*'s headline seemed unfair to Jack Fournier. The left-handed-hitting first baseman was three years younger than Myers and had been a leading batsman in both leagues. His batting average was .282 for his six years with the Chicago White Sox, and .317 in three years with the Cardinals. Fournier was coming off a season in which he batted .295 with 61 runs batted in. On the downside, he had a career-long reputation as a liability in the field.

Complications arose when Fournier said he would not play for any team but St. Louis. "I have gone into the insurance business here as a profession, which I intend to follow," Fournier said. "I am making more money selling insurance during the winter than I can possibly make playing baseball during the summer."[6]

Fortunately for Fournier, and for Brooklyn, he did join the Robins in 1923. In his first three seasons with them, he batted .351, .334, and .350, with corresponding home run totals of 22, a league-leading 27, and 22, and runs batted in totals of 102, 116, and 130. An average of .284 in 1926, still left him with a .337 average, 82 home runs, and 396 RBIs for his four seasons, with the club. The Robins released him at his request after the 1926 season.

Brooklyn drafted Ray Schmandt, the third man in the trade, from the Lincoln (NE) Links of the Western League in September 1917. Schmandt, 27, played five years with the Robins, mostly as a first baseman. His best season was 1921, when he batted .306 in 95 games after replacing the injured Ed Konetchy. Overall, Schmandt batted .270 in 314 games with Brooklyn.

Also in 1923:

Traded: Outfielder Bert Griffith to Washington Senators for Pitcher Bonnie Hollingsworth; First Baseman Dutch Schliebner to St. Louis Browns for Pitcher Dutch Henry and Cash

Purchased: Shortstop Johnny Mitchell from Boston Red Sox; Outfielder Turner Barber from Chicago Cubs

Sold: Pitcher Leon Cadore to Chicago White Sox; Catcher Bernie Hungling to Des Moines Boosters of the Western League
Signed Amateur Free Agents: Moe Berg
Signed Free Agents: Shortstop Ray French; Catcher Eddie Ainsmith

1924

April 25, 1924: Traded Catcher Mike González to the St. Louis Cardinals for Third Baseman Milt Stock

Thirty-three-year-old catcher Mike González was a veteran of nine seasons in the National League. But for the past two seasons, he had been a member of the St. Paul Saints of the American Association. The Cincinnati Reds purchased him from the Saints on February 26, 1924, and sold him to Brooklyn that same day. González never played a league game for the Robins. On April 25, they traded him to the Cardinals for third baseman Milt Stock, who had held out all spring and had not appeared in a game for St. Louis.

The 30-year-old Stock had been a third baseman in the National League since 1913. Manager Robinson continued to play him at third base in 1924 but moved him to second base in 1925. Stock seemed to profit from the change of position. He raised his batting average from .242 in 1924 to .328 in 1925. That season he set a still untied major league record with four consecutive four-hit games. Stock was again a holdout in 1926 and then played poorly in his first three games, going hitless in eight at-bats. Brooklyn released him on May 3.

May 16, 1924: Purchased Pitcher Tiny Osborne from the Chicago Cubs

Baseball players have a penchant for giving other players nicknames in direct contrast to their appearance or habits. Thus, 6'4", 215-pound Earnest Osborne was given the name "Tiny." Osborne, a right-hander, reached the major leagues with the Chicago Cubs in 1922. The 29-old-rookie appeared in 41 games, mostly in relief, with a 9–5 record and a 4.50 earned run average. His ERA was about the same in 1923 (4.56), but his record fell to 8–15.

When the sale was made, Osborne had appeared in two games, with no decisions. He won six and lost five for Brooklyn in 1924, and in 1925 matched the 8–15 mark he had with the 1923 Cubs. The Robins released him after the season.

May 21, 1924: Traded Pitcher Rube Yarrison to the Portland Beavers of the Pacific Coast League for Outfielder Dick Cox

In September 1923, the Brooklyn club purchased pitcher Rube Yarrison from the Portland Beavers of the Pacific Coast League for $25,000. Yarrison had appeared in three games for the Robins this season, two of which were starts and in both of which he was the losing pitcher. In May the Robins traded him back to Portland for outfielder Dick Cox, or so they thought. But the Portland club owners repudiated the transaction, saying the club official who made the deal did not have the authority to do so. At the urging of Charles Ebbets, the dispute was referred to baseball commissioner Kenesaw Landis. On June 16, Landis decided in favor of Brooklyn.

Yarrison reported to Portland and Cox remained with the Beavers for the entirety of the 1924 season. It was his sixth consecutive season with Portland, all of which had been successful, but 1924 was his best. He batted .356 and had 248 hits in 185 games of the long PCL season. His slugging percentage was .565 and he had 393 total bases.

Cox, who was 29 in 1925, was Brooklyn's primary right fielder that season and the next. A 5'7" right-handed hitter, he batted .329 in 1925 and .296 in 1926, with excellent on-base averages of .382 and .375. However, Cox's several injuries and inability to get along with Wilbert Robinson resulted in his returning to the Pacific Coast League in 1927.

June 4, 1924: Traded Shortstop Binky Jones and Outfielder Gene Bailey to the Indianapolis Indians of the American Association for Outfielder Eddie Brown

The hitting of Indianapolis outfielder Eddie Brown made an impression on Wilbert Robinson during two spring training games Brooklyn played against the Indians. The Robins recent lack of success against left-handed pitching made the right-handed Brown a desirable addition. Now 32, Brown had been playing professionally since 1913. In his one full big-league season, he batted .281 in 70 games for the 1921 pennant-winning New York Giants. But he was back in the minor leagues with Indianapolis in 1922. He batted .338 that year and .361 in 1923. Brown had hit well wherever he played, but he was held back by a weak throwing arm that earned him the nickname "Glass Arm Eddie."

Going to Indianapolis, with whom Brooklyn had a working agreement, were right-handed hitting outfielder Gene Bailey and shortstop Binky Jones. "Neither Bailey nor Jones will be missed here, while they may help the American Association club," wrote Charlie Segar of the *Brooklyn Citizen*.[7]

The Robins drafted Bailey in 1922 from the Houston Buffaloes of the Texas League. He batted .265 in 1923 but Robinson expected he would get more production from Brown. Jones had a .108 batting average in 10 games this season, his only season in the major leagues.

June 14, 1924: Traded Pitcher Leo Dickerman to the St. Louis Cardinals for Pitcher Bill Doak

Brooklyn had high hopes for right-hander Leo Dickerman when they purchased him from the Memphis Chicks of the Southern Association in 1922. He won 20 games (20–7) with a 2.14 earned run average for the Chicks that season. The 6'4" rookie had an 8–12 record in 1923, but he had been ineffective this season. Dickerman pitched 19 2/3 innings over seven games with a 5.49 ERA. He would do much better in St. Louis, a 7–4 record and a 2.41 earned run average. Dickerman's major league career ended after his 4–11 record and 5.58 ERA for the 1925 Cardinals.

In return for Dickerman, the Robins were getting a pitcher they hoped would solidify their staff as they pursued the 1924 pennant. Bill Doak was a 13-year veteran, all but one game with the Cardinals. He had 144 big-league wins and had twice led the league in earned run average. The 33-year-old right-hander, known as "Spittin' Bill," was one of the seventeen major league pitchers allowed to continue using the spitball after the pitch was banned following the 1920 season.

Doak's 11 wins (11–5) did help the Robins in their run for the pennant, which fell one-and-a-half games short of the Giants. In one July–September stretch he had a 10-game winning streak. Doak retired after the 1924 season and spent 1925 and 1926 as a real estate salesman in

Florida. He returned to the Robins in 1927 and 1928 with a combined 14–16 record. In 1929, Doak returned to the Cardinals for his final season.

December 17, 1924: Sold Pitcher Dutch Ruether to the Washington Senators

Left-hander Dutch Ruether came to Brooklyn from Cincinnati in a December 1920 trade for Rube Marquard. After winning 19 and 16 games for the Reds in 1919 and 1920, Ruether won only 10 for the 1921 Robins. He rebounded with a career-high 21 wins and a 116 ERA+ in 1922. He won 15 in 1923 but was 8–13 in 1924 and of little help down the stretch when the Robins were trying to overtake the Giants. Nevertheless, it came as a surprise when all National League clubs waived on Ruether, allowing the Robins to sell him to the world champion Washington Senators.

"The departure of Walter Ruether is not calculated to call for the half-masting of any Brooklyn flags," wrote the *Brooklyn Standard Union*. "Walter has been more or less persona non grata here for some time."[8]

Ruether, who was 31 at the time of the trade, won 18 games for Washington's repeat American League pennant winners in 1925, and another 27 for the Senators and New York Yankees over his final two seasons.

Also in 1924:

Traded: Pitcher Nelson Greene and Cash to Little Rock Travelers of the Southern Association for Pitcher Jim Roberts; Infielder Billy Mullen and Cash to Fort Worth Panthers of the Texas League for Pitcher Guy Cantrell

Purchased: Pitcher Bonnie Hollingsworth from New Orleans Pelicans of the Southern Association; Pitcher Tex Wilson from Des Moines Boosters of the Western League

Sold: Shortstop Ray French to Chicago White Sox

Chosen in Major League Draft: Pitcher Andy Rush; Jerry Standaert

Released: Pitcher George Smith; Shortstop Ivy Olson

CHAPTER EIGHT

1925–1929

1925

Charles Ebbets and Ed McKeever died.

February 4, 1925: Traded Outfielder Bernie Neis to the Boston Braves for Second Baseman Cotton Tierney

This trade, involving two men who had injury problems in 1924, seemed to favor the Braves. In 29-year-old Bernie Neis, Boston was getting a player who appeared in only 80 games in 1924 but had a .303 batting average and an OPS+ of 120. Brooklyn bought him from the Saskatoon club of the Western Canada League in the summer of 1919 after outfielder Tommy Griffith announced his retirement. When Griffith changed his mind, Neis became a fill-in for most of his five years with the team, years in which he was often injured and in contract disputes. He played in 464 games for the Robins with a batting average of .269.

Cotton Tierney, six days shy of his thirty-first birthday, made his major league debut with the Pittsburgh Pirates in 1920. In 280 games with Pittsburgh, he had a .315 batting average. His .345 mark in 1922 was the fifth highest in the National League, and his 36 doubles the next year was second in the league. With the Phillies in 1923, he batted .317, but was traded to the Braves after the season. He did not hit nearly as well in his one season with Boston—a .259 mark in 136 games.

Manager Wilbert Robinson assumed the presidency of the club after Charles Ebbets' death on April 18, 1925.

Chapter Eight: 1925–1929

April 25, 1925: Traded Pitcher Art Decatur to the Philadelphia Phillies for Pitcher Bill Hubbell

The death of club president Charles Ebbets made this trade the first by manager Wilbert Robinson in which he did not have to get Ebbets' approval; Robinson now was also the team's president. The deal was a minor one, involving two mediocre right-handed pitchers, but it indicated the change in the Brooklyn club's managerial policy.

"That the McKeevers lay no restraining hand on Robby in his barterings is significant" wrote Thomas Meany. "Ed and Steve realize that no advice that they could give would aid Robby and knowing that the leader of the Flatbush crew is one of the most sagacious pilots in the pastime, are quite willing to let him do with the Robins as he will, while they devote themselves to the business angle."[1]

Art Decatur joined the Robins in 1922 as a free agent. Now 31, he had a 16–16 record and a 3.31 earned run average in his three seasons with Brooklyn. Decatur would win four and lose thirteen for the Phillies this season.

Twenty-eight-year-old Bill Hubbell was in his seventh big league season. He had a record of 1–2 with the 1919–1920 New York Giants and a 36–55 mark with the hapless Phillies after they acquired him in 1920. Hubbell won three and lost six for Brooklyn in this, his final year as a major leaguer.

May 9, 1925: Traded Outfielder Tommy Griffith to the Chicago Cubs for a Player to be Named

Tommy Griffith had been Brooklyn's right fielder since coming from Cincinnati in a February 1919 trade for Jake Daubert. Since then, the left-handed-hitting Griffith played in 724 games for the Robins with a .285 batting average. But he was now 35, and Dick Cox had taken his place in right field.

"The passing of Tommy Griffith from the Dodger line-up is to be regretted," noted the *Brooklyn Times Union*. "There are few ball players in the big show as likeable as the sweet-swinging sunfielder. Brooklyn's loss is Chicago's gain."[2]

The Robins and Cubs had agreed that the player to be named would be an infielder and would be sent to Brooklyn when Cubs shortstop Rabbit Maranville returned from his leg injury. On May 23 the Cubs sent 26-year-old Bob Barrett to the Robins. Barrett batted .241 as a rookie in 1924, but he was off to a good start this season, with 10 hits in 32 at-bats. Having an excess of infielders, the Robins sent Barrett to the Memphis Chicks, where he batted .306 in 82 games.

July 25, 1925: Sold Infielder Andy High to the Boston Braves

In July 1921, when the Robins purchased Andy High from Memphis of the Southern Association, it was as a third baseman. Manager Wilbert Robinson used him there in 1922 and 1923, although he often used High at shortstop, as well. In 1924, the versatile High was almost exclusively a second baseman and his limited appearances this season were at all three positions.

High hit well in his first two years with Brooklyn, .283 and .270, and exceptionally well in 1924 when he batted .328. His 191 hits were fourth best in the league, and his 98 runs scored were sixth best. A broken ankle suffered in spring training limited him to just 44 games this season, 20 as a pinch-hitter. His batting average was .200, and with Milt Stock having taken his place at second base, High was put on waivers. The Braves claimed him and paid the $4,000 waiver price. It turned out to be a bargain for Boston. High regained his batting prowess for the Braves in the second half of the season and for the 1926 and 1927 seasons.

There was another part of this deal worked out in secret between Robinson and Boston owner Judge Emil Fuchs. The Robins would pay the Braves an undisclosed amount of money in exchange for Boston pitcher Jesse Barnes. Unlike High, who became Braves property this day, Barnes was allowed to remain with Boston for the remainder of the season and report to Brooklyn in 1926.

July 25, 1925: Purchased Pitcher Jumbo Elliott from the Terre Haute (IN) Tots of the Three-I League

James "Jumbo" Elliott began his career with the Class B Terre Haute Tots of the Three-I league as a 20-year-old, in 1921. Elliott, a left-hander, stood 6'3" and weighed more than 230 pounds, hence the nickname Jumbo. He was with the Tots for three seasons, compiling a record of 48 wins and 29 losses. The St. Louis Browns gave Elliott a one-game (one inning) look in April 1923. He allowed three runs in that inning, and it was back to Terre Haute, where he remained in 1924 and 1925, including a brief stay in 1924 with the Class A San Antonio Bears of the Texas League. Scout Spencer Abbott recommended Elliott, whose record at the time of the purchase was 18–3. He would go on to lead the Three-I League in wins (25) and earned run average (3.04).

August 14, 1925: Purchased First Baseman Del Bissonnette from the York (PA) White Roses of the New York–Pennsylvania League

The Robins purchased Del Bissonnette, a 25-year-old left-handed hitter, during his sensational 1925 season in the Class B New York–Pennsylvania League. Playing first for the Binghamton Triplets and then for the York White Roses, he batted .381, with 18 home runs and 46 doubles.

Bissonnette had an excellent spring training with the Robins in 1926 but was slowed by a bad case of influenza and sent back to the minors. He played in the International League for the Jersey City Skeeters and the Rochester Tribe that year, and for the Buffalo Bisons in 1927. Bissonnette was the most dominant hitter in the league with Buffalo, batting .365 and leading in home runs (31), runs batted in (167), runs (168), and hits (229). His outstanding season earned him a return trip to spring training with the 1928 Robins.

September 13, 1925: Purchased First Baseman Babe Herman from the Seattle Indians of the Pacific Coast League

Floyd "Babe" Herman was only 22 years old, but he had already played for eight minor league teams and been on the rosters of the Detroit Tigers and the Boston Red Sox. Herman, a 6'4" left-handed hitter, began his professional career in 1921 by batting .330 for the Class B Edmonton Eskimos of the Western Canada League. Edmonton sold him to Detroit in the middle of the season. He went to the Tigers training camp in 1922 before being sent to the Omaha Buffaloes of the Class A Western League. A .416 batting average after 92 games resulted in Herman getting a brief eight-game stay with the Reading Aces of the Class AA International League.

At the end of the 1922 season, the Tigers sent Herman to the Red Sox as part of a multiplayer trade. In 1923 he played for Atlanta and Memphis in the Class A Southern League, batting a combined .339. Boston kept him for a while in 1924, before sending him to the San Antonio Bears of the Texas League, and then to the Little Rock Travelers of the Southern Association. He had a combined .326 average for the two teams.

At Little Rock, Herman was spiked so badly by Al DeVormer, he went on the voluntarily retired list. Near the end of the 1924 season, Seattle Indians manager Wade Killefer heard Herman had healed and acquired him for 1925. Herman batted .316 with 206 hits for the Indians. Previously considered a defensive liability, his skills around first base showed great improvement under Killefer's tutelage. Brooklyn scout Spencer Abbott, who recommended Herman to the Robins, added he was fast enough to play the outfield.

Herman's path to a big-league job had been hindered by his eccentricities, occasional bad temperament, and sporadic lack of concentration. But Babe Herman could hit, and he had proved it everywhere he played.

October 6, 1925: Traded Third Baseman Jimmy Johnston, Catcher Zack Taylor, and Outfielder Eddie Brown to the Boston Braves for Catcher Mickey O'Neil and Outfielder Gus Felix

This trade began as a trade of outfielders—Eddie Brown for Gus Felix—and grew as the negotiations continued. It resulted in three players leaving the Robins who had been popular with the fans, none more so than versatile Jimmy Johnston. Primarily a third baseman, Johnston had played the three other infield positions as well as right field. In short, he played whenever and wherever Wilbert Robinson needed him. Johnston had been a minor leaguer from 1908 to 1915, except for playing one game with the 1911 Chicago White Sox and 50 for the 1914 Chicago Cubs. He was back in the minors with the Pacific Coast League's Oakland Oaks in 1915, where he batted .348 with a league-leading 274 hits in 206 games.

Johnston signed to play for the Federal League's Newark Peppers in January 1916, but following the demise of the league the Peppers sold him to Brooklyn. He played 10 seasons with Brooklyn—including the 1916 and 1920 pennant winners—and had a .297 batting average and a 102 OPS+ in 1,266 games.

Now 35, Johnston was also one of the cleverest players in the league, especially adept at spotting weaknesses in opposing batters and pitchers. That knowledge was expected to be a big help to Dave Bancroft, the Braves third-year manager who had been after Johnston for a long time.

Center fielder Eddie Brown played in all of Brooklyn's games in 1925, a league-high 153. He batted .306 following his .308 average in 1924, his first year with the Robins. Aside from a weak throwing arm, Brown was an excellent outfielder, one of the best he ever saw said manager Robinson. In 1926, the 34-year-old Brown batted .328 for Boston and led the National League with 201 hits.

Zack Taylor, 27, had been a member of the Robins since 1920. He shared the catching duties with Hank DeBerry the past three seasons, with Taylor playing the majority of games in each one. During that time, he batted .288, .290, and .310. And he was the catcher of choice for Burleigh Grimes, the Robins' best pitcher.

Despite all Taylor had done, getting catcher Mickey O'Neil was the Robins primary target in making this deal. O'Neil was the same age as Taylor, but a lesser hitter. He batted .283 in 1920, his first full season with Boston, but had not approached that level since. What appealed to Robinson, a catcher in his playing days, was O'Neil's "sprightliness" behind the plate and that he was a better thrower, all-around defender, and handler of pitchers than Taylor.

Gus Felix, a speedy 30-year-old right-handed-hitter, had a fine rookie season with the Braves in 1923, batting .273 in 139 games. He slipped the next year but rebounded with a .307 average and 66 runs batted in this past season. Felix had a much stronger throwing arm than Eddie Brown ("Glass Arm Eddie"), but the accuracy of his throws had been a problem in Boston.

While pitcher Jesse Barnes is often listed as part of this trade, his sale to Brooklyn had been arranged in July of this year as part of the negotiation in which the Braves acquired Andy High for the waiver price. Barnes was allowed to finish the season with Boston and would join the Robins in 1926. His 11–16 record with the 1925 Braves brought his career totals to 140 wins and 129 losses in twelve seasons, split evenly between Boston and the New York Giants. His greatest success had come with New York, where he had two 20-win seasons, including a league-leading 25 in 1919. By contrast, his two seasons leading the league in losses had come with Boston, 21 in 1917 and 20 in 1924.

Barnes pitched his final two major league seasons with the Robins, winning 10 with 11 losses in 1926, and winning two with 10 losses in 1927. His combined earned run average for the two seasons was 5.40.

Also in 1925:
Traded: Pitcher Nelson Greene, Pitcher Tex Wilson, and Cash to Minneapolis Millers of the American Association for Pitcher Bob McGraw

Purchased: Pitcher Joe Oeschger from Philadelphia Phillies: Infielder Horace Ford from Philadelphia Phillies; Shortstop Rabbit Maranville from Chicago Cubs; Third Baseman William Marriott from Boston Braves; Pitcher Jesse Petty from the Indianapolis Indians of the American Association; Pitcher Hank Thormahlen from Dallas Steers of the Texas League; Outfielder Roy Hutson from Topeka (KS) Senators of the Southwestern League; Pitcher Ray Moss from Memphis Chicks of the Southern Association

Sold: Pitcher Hank Thormahlen to Rochester Tribe of the International League; Pitcher Andy Rush to Waterbury (CT) Brasscos of the Eastern League; Catcher Moe Berg to Chicago White Sox

Signed Amateur Free Agents: Jay Partridge

Signed Free Agents: Outfielder Whitey Witt

Released: Pitcher Tiny Osborne; Pitcher Joe Oeschger

1926

February 1, 1926: Traded Third Baseman Cotton Tierney, Infielder Horace Ford, Pitcher Bonnie Hollingsworth, Pitcher Bill Hubbell, and Outfielder Dick Loftus to the Minneapolis Millers of the American Association for Shortstop Johnny Butler

Despite Johnny Butler's age, 32, the Robins traded five players for him. Rated among the best infielders in the minor leagues, Butler was coming off a 1925 season in which he batted .339 with 204 hits in 147 games for the American Association's Minneapolis Millers.

Originally the deal called for outfielder Dick Loftus and pitcher Bill Hubbell to go to Minneapolis for Butler, but Millers manager Mike Kelley insisted that Brooklyn send more players. Brooklyn wanted to stick to the original terms but finally agreed to Kelley's demand.

Butler spent the 1926 and 1927 seasons with the Robins, playing shortstop and third base, and batting .253 in 296 games. Wilbert Robinson was not satisfied. In December 1927 he traded Butler to the Chicago Cubs for infielder Eddie Pick and then sent Pick and cash to the Milwaukee Brewers of the American Association to complete a September deal with the Brewers in which they acquired infielder Harry Riconda.

Cotton Tierney spent just one season in Brooklyn, batting .257 in 93 games, well below his production in earlier years. He would not return to the major leagues. Thomas Meany of the *Brooklyn Eagle* paid a fond farewell to the popular third baseman. "There were better fielders and harder hitters than Tierney," he wrote, "but there were few ball players who enjoyed the friendship of fans, owners, and fellow players to the degree that Cotton did."[3]

It was also the last major league season for pitcher Bill Hubbell, acquired from the Phillies in a May 1925 trade. Hubbell appeared in 33 games for the Robins with a 3–6 record.

The Robins had purchased 28-year-old infielder Horace Ford on waivers from the Philadelphia Phillies the previous May. Ford batted .273 in 66 games in 1925, his only season in Brooklyn.

Pitcher Bonnie Hollingsworth, 30, was purchased from New Orleans of the Southern Association in July 1924. His career with the Robins consisted of three games with one win later that season.

Outfielder Dick Loftus came to Brooklyn from the Bridgeport Americans of the Eastern League in 1924. His hitting over two seasons was not what the Robins expected, a .250 average with no home runs in 97 games.

August 4, 1926: Purchased Pitcher Watty Clark from the Terre Haute (IN) Tots of the Three-I League

While scouting the Three-I League for the Brooklyn club, former pitcher Joe McGinnity was impressed with the pitching of Terre Haute's Watson "Watty" Clark. McGinnity even helped arrange the Robins purchase of the 24-year-old left-hander. Clark, who had a brief stay with the 1924 Cleveland Indians, was 9–7 for the Tots at the time of the signing but was on his way to a 19–9 record.

"One thing I like about him is his willingness to listen to advice and his eagerness to absorb information," McGinnity said. "Clark has speed but no curve whatever. But you can teach a fastball pitcher how to throw a curve and nothing whatever can give a pitcher speed if nature hasn't taken care of him in that respect. In my opinion he's just about a year away from the big leagues and may be ready to stick with the club next summer."[4]

August 17, 1926: Purchased Outfielder Max Carey from the Pittsburgh Pirates

National League president John Heydler announced that Brooklyn had obtained long-time star outfielder Max Carey from Pittsburgh for the waiver price of $4,000. The announcement came in what the *Brooklyn Eagle* called "the climax of one of the most sudden and surprising upheavals in organized baseball."[5] Earlier in the month Pirates owner Barney Dreyfuss had suspended Carey and released unconditionally two other longtime Pirates—pitcher Babe Adams and outfielder Carson Bigbee.

The veteran trio had protested the presence of former manager Fred Clarke sitting on the bench alongside current manager Bill McKechnie and frequently questioning McKechnie's decisions. Following a doubleheader loss in Boston on August 7, team captain Carey held a meeting that called for a resolution banning Clarke from the bench.

"As the team's captain, Carey felt that he should represent the players in their dispute, and his stand resulted in his becoming the fall guy for the whole ugly affair," wrote Carey biographer John Bennett.[6] Dreyfuss suspended and then asked for waivers on him. Carey appealed to Commissioner Kenesaw Landis, who referred the case to Heydler.

In Carey the Robins were getting a switch-hitting speedster and outstanding defender who had been with the Pirates since 1910, first as a left fielder and since 1916 as a center fielder. In his 17 seasons he had 2,416 hits and an OPS+ of 111. His 10 times leading the National League in stolen bases remains a league record. Carey had six seasons of 50 or more stolen bases, and his 738 stolen bases is the major leagues' ninth highest total ever.

Carey was 36 when he came to Brooklyn and never regained the form that made him a star in Pittsburgh. He batted .260 in 298 games, though he did steal 32 bases in 1927 and 18 in 1928. The Robins released him on October 7, 1929, but Carey would return to Brooklyn in 1932, when he replaced Wilbert Robinson as manager.

Also in 1926:

Traded: Pitcher Ray Moss, a Player to be Named, and Cash to New Orleans Pelicans of the Southern Association for Outfielder–First Baseman Harvey Hendrick

Purchased: Infielder-Outfielder Chick Fewster from Cleveland Indians; Infielder Sam Bohne from Cincinnati Reds; Outfielder Merwin Jacobson from Jersey City Skeeters of the International League
Signed Amateur Free Agents: Paul Richards
Chosen in Major League Draft: Pitcher Oscar Roettger
Released: First Baseman Jack Fournier; Second Baseman Milt Stock; Shortstop Rabbit Maranville

1927

January 9, 1927: Traded Pitcher Burleigh Grimes to the New York Giants in a Three-Way-Deal that brought them Catcher Butch Henline from the Philadelphia Phillies

Originally reported as a trade that sent pitcher Burleigh Grimes to the Giants for catcher Butch Henline, it soon became a three-team, five-player transaction. Brooklyn sent Grimes to the Giants; the Giants sent pitcher Jack Scott and second baseman Fresco Thompson to the Philadelphia Phillies; and the Phillies sent outfielder George Harper to the Giants and Henline to Brooklyn. For the Robins it was simply exchanging Burleigh Grimes for Butch Henline, which made it one of the worst trades in franchise history.

Grimes, 33, won 158 games in his nine years with the Robins, trailing only Dazzy Vance and Bill Kennedy among Brooklyn pitchers. He had four 20-win seasons, led the league in complete games three times and innings pitched twice. But because of his losing record the past two seasons, the trade did not seem so one-sided at the time. In addition, Grimes was unable to get along with Wilbert Robinson, openly criticizing the manager's judgement this past season. His departure left the team with no one who had played on the Robins pennant-winning 1920 club.

Henline, 32, was a right-handed-hitter who batted .304 in 576 games for the Phillies since joining them in 1921. He had held out in the spring of 1926, which cost him his team captaincy and some playing time, as Phillies manager Art Fletcher made more use of 25-year-old Jimmie Wilson.

Brooklyn had never had a top-flight catcher, which may account for sportswriter Dan Daniel's praise of the acquisition. "Henline embodies what many critics regard as the ideal factors of catching, effectiveness as a backstop, effectiveness as a hitter, and the ability to hold up a pitcher."[7]

Henline told the *Brooklyn Times Union*, "You can't imagine what playing in Brooklyn means to me. I have been dissatisfied with the conditions in Philadelphia for the last five years. I hope I catch every game for Robby."[8]

But Henline ended up splitting the 1927 catching duties with Hank DeBerry and Charlie Hargreaves. He started only 50 games and hit a career low .266. Things got worse for him over the next two seasons. He hit .212 while starting 35 games in 1928, and .242 in 15 starts in 1929. Moreover, Henline had "sciatica" in his throwing arm and had difficulty throwing to bases. He passed through waivers in December 1929 and was sent to the Toledo Mud Hens of the American Association. Henline later became a National League umpire.

Meanwhile, Grimes won 19 for the Giants in 1927 and a league-leading 25 for the Pirates in 1928. He continued to pitch until age 40, in 1934. He finished with 270 wins and is now in the Hall of Fame.

March 28, 1927: Sold Catcher Mickey O'Neil to the Washington Senators

With Opening Day less than two weeks away, Brooklyn still had four veteran catchers on its roster—Hank DeBerry, Charlie Hargreaves, Mickey O'Neil, and newly acquired Butch Henline. One had to go, and O'Neil was manager Wilbert Robinson's choice. The Robins asked for waivers on O'Neil, and when no National League club claimed him, he was sold to the Washington Senators. Robinson was surprised that neither the Giants nor the Cardinals had claimed O'Neil, as both needed a catcher. He had hoped to work out a trade for an infielder with one of those teams.

Much had been expected of O'Neil when he came to the Robins in the October 1925 multi-player trade with the Boston Braves. But his 1926 performance was disappointing, a .209 batting average in 75 games. He batted a combined .114 in 1927, playing for the Senators and the Giants in what was his final major league season.

April 28, 1927: Traded Pitcher Bob McGraw to the St. Louis Cardinals for Infielder Jake Flowers

Bob McGraw pitched briefly for the New York Yankees from 1917 through 1920 but had spent the past four seasons with the Minneapolis Millers of the American Association. McGraw's work for the Millers in 1925 caught Wilbert Robinson's attention. The Brooklyn manager sent former Robins pitchers Nelson Greene and Tex Wilson, now in the minor leagues, and $25,000 to obtain the 30-year-old right-hander.

McGraw finished the 1925 season with a 22–13 record for Minneapolis. He joined the Robins late in the 1925 season and lost his only two decisions. He had nine wins and 13 losses for Brooklyn in 1926 and had lost his only decision this season.

Jake Flowers, 27, played 13 games for the Cardinals in 1923 and 40 in 1926, with a combined batting average of .217. He had yet to see action this season. The Robins planned to play Flowers at shortstop and move Johnny Butler to third base, the position he preferred. "You perspire like a gentleman at third base and sweat like a ditch digger at short" was the way Butler described the two positions.[9]

August 26, 1927: Purchased Catcher Al Lopez from the Jacksonville (FL) Tars of the Southeastern League

Because Brooklyn already had three catchers on their roster, some in the press considered the addition of 19-year-old Al Lopez an indication that one of them, likely Charlie Hargreaves, would be traded to Pittsburgh for outfielder Kiki Cuyler. If not, they said, adding Lopez was like "carrying coals to Newcastle."

The Robins brain trust thought differently. Wilbert Robinson, scout Nap Rucker, and veteran pitcher Bill Doak believed the Robins had picked up the brightest catching prospect in the minor leagues. Robinson remembered a spring game against Jacksonville in which Lopez doubled and tripled against Dazzy Vance and displayed aggressiveness and an accurate throwing arm behind the plate.

Doak, who lived in Bradenton, Florida, had seen Lopez in action when the young catcher played for the Tampa Smokers in the Florida State League in 1925 and 1926, when he was age sixteen and seventeen. "Certainly, he was a better catcher than several I have thrown to in my fifteen years on the big time," Doak said. "The manner in which he handled those wild Class D League pitchers convinced me that he knows what it is all about."[10] Doak told Robinson about him, and Robinson had Rucker scout him this season at Jacksonville. Lopez batted .276 and impressed with his style and actions as a catcher. The Robins purchased him for $10,000, a then record price for a Class B Player.

September 10, 1927: Traded Two Players to be Named to the Buffalo Bisons of the International League for Outfielder Ty Tyson

On December 15, Wilbert Robinson announced that third baseman Bob Barrett and outfielder Gus Felix would be the two players sent to the Buffalo Bisons of the International league to complete the September 10 trade for outfielder Ty Tyson.

Barrett came to Brooklyn in the same manner. He was the player to be named in the May 1925 trade of Tommy Griffith to the Chicago Cubs. Barrett played in one game for the Robins that season and was sent to Memphis. He batted .306 for the Southern Association Chicks in 1925 and .321 in 1926. But he could not match that success with Brooklyn in 1927, where his batting average was .259 and his on-base average was .289.

Felix, now 32, was part of the three-for-three trade with the Boston Braves that also brought catcher Mickey O'Neil and pitcher Jesse Barnes to Brooklyn. He was an outfield regular in his two seasons with the Robins, batting .273 in 264 games.

"Felix and Barrett are better ball players than ever they showed," wrote Tom Meany. "Their main trouble is mental and temperamental rather than physical. In a pinch, neither is able to loosen up and play naturally."[11]

Before they sent him to Buffalo in July 1927, Ty Tyson had been a member of the New York Giants for the first half of that season and all of 1926. A .293 hitter in 1926, he was batting .264 at the time of his departure. In 1928, his final major league season, he batted .271 in 59 games for the Robins.

October 14, 1927: Signed Free Agent Shortstop Dave Bancroft

Wilbert Robinson was gambling that 36-year-old shortstop Dave Bancroft had one or two good seasons left. In his prime, the future Hall of Famer had been the best all-around shortstop in the National League. He played the most games at the position five times, led in putouts four times and assists three times. Offensively he had five .300 seasons and one where he fell just short, at .299.

Bancroft reached the big leagues with the pennant-winning 1915 Philadelphia Phillies but reached stardom after his June 1920 trade to the New York Giants. Beginning in 1921 the Giants won four consecutive pennants. Bancroft captained the first three pennant winners, the first two of which also won the World Series. He batted above .300 in each of those three seasons.

Bancroft had spent the last four seasons as a player/manager for the Boston Braves. He hit well his first three seasons in Boston, but his legs were hurting, and he had tailed off significantly in the last two. Bancroft played 10 games for the 1930 Giants before his aching legs forced him to retire as a player.

As the manager, his team's finished eighth, fifth, seventh, and seventh in his four seasons. Moreover, attendance was poor and to no one's surprise, owner Emil Fuchs jettisoned Bancroft and replaced him with Jack Slattery for the 1928 season.

Bancroft filled the shortstop position for Brooklyn in 1928 and 1929, batting .259 in 253 games. Released in October 1929, he signed a month later with John McGraw's Giants, the team where he had his greatest glory.

Also in 1927:

Sold: Pitcher Guy Cantrell to Baltimore Orioles of the International League; Pitcher Norman Plitt to New York Giants
Signed Amateur Free Agents: Hal Lee
Signed Free Agents: Outfielder Irish Meusel
Chosen in Major League Draft: Infielder Howard Freigau; Pitcher Lou Koupal
Released: Outfielder Zack Wheat

1928

March 13, 1928: Purchased Outfielder Rube Bressler from the Cincinnati Reds

In 1914, at age nineteen, left-hander Rube Bressler had a 10–4 record and a 1.77 earned run average for Connie Mack's pennant-winning Philadelphia Athletics. Bressler did not pitch in the World Series, won in an upset by the Boston Braves. Mack, faced with salary challenges from the Federal League, sold off or traded several of his key players, and the A's sank to last place in 1915. Bressler's record sank as well—four wins and 17 losses. Arm problems curtailed his pitching career. After joining the Cincinnati Reds in 1917, Bressler gradually transitioned from a left-handed pitcher to right-handed-hitting position player, eventually becoming a full-time outfielder His career record on the mound was 26–32 with a 3.40 earned run average.

Bressler was a much better hitter, with a .311 batting average and an OPS+ of 115 in 745 games with Cincinnati. In the three seasons from 1924 through 1926, he batted .347, .348, and .357, playing in more than half the Reds' games. Bressler's OPS+ those years was 133, 131, and 148. Playing a full season in 1927, he batted .291 and drove in 77 runs.

"I'm sure to hit more than .300 for the Robins this year, and if anybody you know doesn't think so, you can just bet me," Bressler said a few days after Brooklyn acquired him.[12] He would have lost that bet, but not by much. Bressler batted .295, and his career average for his four years in Brooklyn was .302, with a 109 OPS+. In 1931, at age 36, he played in only 67 games and was released in January 1932.

June 8, 1928: Traded Catcher Charlie Hargreaves to the Pittsburgh Pirates for Catcher Johnny Gooch and First Baseman Joe Harris

Charlie Hargreaves had been with the Robins since 1923, but only in 1926 had he played in more than half the team's games. He left with a .267 batting average in 231 games. A broken finger limited him to just 20 games so far this season, with a .197 average.

"I used him often earlier in the season," said manager Wilbert Robinson, "but he failed to prove that he was O.K. I was then thoroughly convinced that he would be of no further value to the club and looked around to see if I could do business with some club. I think the team is greatly strengthened by the deal."[13]

Johnny Gooch, 30, had been a consistent hitter in his eight seasons with the Pirates—a .286 batting average in 551 games. "It seems a bit strange after all those years at Pittsburgh to find myself with another club," Gooch said, adding that he was pleased with the trade. "And it's a relief to be with a club that has some other good catchers in condition who can share the grind of a season."[14] Gooch expected to share the catching duties with Butch Henline.

Robinson said he was anxious to add a right-handed pinch-hitter like Joe Harris to his roster, something the team badly needed. The 37-year-old Harris was a combination first baseman and outfielder. Before going to Pittsburgh, he played eight years in the American

League—with New York, Cleveland, Boston, and Washington—and never batted below .300. In his final big-league season, Harris did not live up to his manager's expectations. He played in 55 games for the Robins, 41 as a pinch-hitter, and he broke his streak of .300 seasons by batting .236.

September 8, 1928: Purchased Pitcher Clise Dudley from the Atlanta Crackers of the Southern Association

Twenty-five-year-old Clise Dudley played his first four professional season with two South Carolina teams in the Class B South Atlantic League—Greenville and Spartanburg. In 1928, the 6'1" right-hander moved up to the Class A Atlanta Crackers of the Southern Association, where he won 11 and lost 15. Dudley had captured Wilbert Robinson's attention in a spring training game the Robins played at Atlanta.

In a ghost-written column for the *Brooklyn Standard Union*, Robinson wrote: "I was impressed then with his size and actions and instructed [scout Nap] Rucker to keep close tabs on him. Evidently Nap was impressed, too, as he had recommended his purchase more than two months ago. I like those big fellows with a fastball. The rest can be taught or acquired. With speed and a measure of control to start with, any pitcher has a chance."[15]

September 9, 1928: Purchased Outfielder Johnny Frederick from the Memphis Chicks of the Southern Association

Scout Nap Rucker had recommended several players from the Southern Association who found success with Brooklyn. Outfielder Johnny Frederick of the Memphis Chicks would be one more. Rucker had followed Frederick all season, as the 26-year-old outfielder led the league with 221 hits in 150 games and had a .359 batting average and a .510 slugging percentage. Brooklyn's West Coast scout Larry Sutton seconded Rucker's recommendation. The left-handed swinger had spent the previous five seasons, in the Pacific Coast League, batting better than .300 in four of them.

December 11, 1928: Traded Pitcher Jesse Petty and Infielder Harry Riconda to the Pittsburgh Pirates for Shortstop Glenn Wright

Jesse Petty of the Indianapolis Indians was the American Association's best pitcher in 1924. He led the league with 29 wins (29–8) and a 2.83 earned run average. The Robins purchased the 30-year-old lefthander in late March 1925. After a 9–9 rookie season, Petty had a spectacular start in 1926. Replacing an injured Dazzy Vance as Brooklyn's opening day starter, he pitched a 3–0, one-hit shutout against the Giants at the Polo Grounds. Frankie Frisch's sixth-inning double was New York's lone hit.

Petty won his next four decisions but finished the season at 17–17. The 17 wins were the team's most, and the 17 losses were the league's most. His ERA+ was an excellent 133, as it was again in 1927, when he was 13–18. Petty had a 15–15 record in 1928, but it had become obvious it would be his last year in Brooklyn after Robinson suspended him without pay during the season. Harry Riconda played one season for the Robins, 1928. He appeared in 92 games and batted .224.

Meanwhile, Glenn Wright was having salary difficulties with the Pirates and was glad to leave. He had played only 108 games in 1928, batting .310, but still was recognized as among the game's best shortstops. Wright had a .298 average and 793 hits to show for his five years in Pittsburgh. After the trade was announced, he made it clear the Robins were his preferred destination. "I would as soon, if not rather, play for Brooklyn than for any club the Pirates could have sent me to," Wright said. "I feel sure that the change will benefit my playing immensely."[16]

The Robins were expecting the 28-year-old Wright to replace Dave Bancroft at shortstop. But Wright had injured his shoulder playing handball during the offseason, which allowed Bancroft to put in a final season with the Robins. Wright's 1929 season consisted of only 25 at-bats, mostly as pinch-hitter. The arm healed in time for the 1930 season, and he captained a team that won 86 games and finished in fourth place. Wright batted .321 that season, with 126 runs batted in. He battled injuries in each of the next three seasons and finished his five-year stay in Brooklyn with a .289 average and 423 hits. The Robins released him in February 1934.

Also in 1928:
Purchased: Pitcher Cy Moore from Macon (GA) Peaches of the South Atlantic League
Sold: Infielder Howard Freigau to Boston Braves
Chosen in Major League Draft: Pitcher Win Ballou

1929

April 18, 1929: Traded Pitcher Rube Ehrhardt and Catcher Johnny Gooch to the Cincinnati Reds for Catcher Val Picinich

Rube Ehrhardt, a 6'2" right-hander, had pitched three seasons in various semipro leagues when the Robins signed him in July 1924. The 29-year-old Ehrhardt won five of eight decisions in the second half of that season. He made 25 starts and had a 10–14 record for the Robins in 1925, before spending the next three seasons as a relief pitcher. During that stretch, Ehrhardt appeared in 118 games, all but six in relief, and twice led the league in games finished.

Johnny Gooch's stay in Brooklyn was brief. He came in a trade for one catcher, Charlie Hargreaves, and was leaving in a trade for another catcher, Val Picinich. Gooch arrived from Pittsburgh in June 1928, batted .317 in 42 games, and had only one appearance this season, as a pinch-hitter.

Val Picinich was nineteen years old when he made his major league debut with the 1916 Philadelphia Athletics. After two seasons with the A's, Picinich played five seasons for the Washington Senators, three for the Boston Red Sox, and the last three for Cincinnati. The 1928 season with the Reds was his career best in games (96) and batting average (.302).

And Picinich came highly recommended. When Brooklyn's new catcher was with Washington, Walter Johnson called him the best batterymate he ever had. "Picinich is the peppery catcher I've been looking for," said Wilbert Robinson.[17] Picinich was the first-string catcher in his first season with the Robins but a little-used backup in the next three. Dodgers manager Max Carey released him in May 1933.

May 13, 1929: Purchased Second Baseman Eddie Moore from the Toledo Mud Hens

To add to the woes of the last place Robins, second baseman Jake Flowers was stricken with an attack of appendicitis. Flowers was scheduled to undergo an operation for the removal of his appendix and would likely be out of action until late in the summer. Manager Robinson, feeling he had no capable reserve to take Flowers' place, purchased infielder Eddie Moore from the Toledo Mud Hens of the American Association.

Moore came up with Pittsburgh late in the 1923 seasons. He batted .301 in 263 games for the Pirates, before being sold to the Boston Braves in July 1926. The right-handed-hitting Moore had his best season in 1927 when he batted .302 in 112 games. He slumped in 1928 and was sent to Toledo.

June 26, 1929: Purchased Pitcher Johnny Morrison from the Kansas City Blues of the American Association

With the Robins badly in need of pitching help, Wilbert Robinson turned to Glenn Wright, his injured shortstop. Robinson asked Wright, who was recovering at his Kansas home, to travel to Kansas City to evaluate Johnny Morrison, his former Pittsburgh Pirates teammate. Known for throwing an outstanding curve ball, Morrison had been a star pitcher for the Pirates. In the five years from 1921 to 1925, he won 79 games, led the league in games started and shutouts twice and saves once. Upset with the way the Pirates handled his assignments in the 1925 World Series against the Washington Senators, along with arm problems, heavy drinking, and insubordination ended his stay in Pittsburgh.

Morrison returned to the minor leagues, going 1–6 for the Kansas City Blues of the American Association in 1928 and had a 3–2 record with the Blues this season. Robinson, who had dealt with alcoholic players before, with mixed success, signed the 33-year-old right-hander to a 30-day contract. Morrison would pitch batting practice and work in relief. But Morrison pitched well enough in relief for Robinson to also use him as a starter. Working in both roles, Morrison won 13 games, lost seven, and led the National League with eight saves. He had a 1–2 record in 1930, when he left the club on June 19 and did not return. It was one too many drinking sprees and the Robins released him.

July 1929: Purchased Pitcher Ray Phelps from the Jacksonville (FL) Tars of the Southeastern League

The Robins had high hopes for Ray Phelps, the 6'2" right-hander they signed from the Jacksonville (FL) Tars of the Class B Southeastern League. He came with recommendations from scout Nap Rucker and from former Brooklyn pitcher Rube Marquard, Phelps's manager at Jacksonville. Pitching for the Tars for the full season in 1929, Phelps, 25, had a 23–11 record, a 2.58 earned run average, and a league leading 136 strikeouts.

Phelps exceeded expectations as a rookie in 1930, with a 14–7 record and an ERA+ of 120. But like many rookie stars, he slumped badly in his second season, with a 7–9 record and an ERA+ of 77. He was 4–5 with an ERA+ of 65 on August 18, 1932, when new manager Max Carey sent him to the minor leagues. Carey did so to make room for pitcher Fay Thomas, purchased from the Oakland Oaks of the Pacific Coast League. He said he expected Phelps would return to Brooklyn, but he never did. Thomas's career in Brooklyn consisted of one loss in 1932.

October 7, 1929: Drafted Pitcher Sloppy Thurston from the San Francisco Seals of the Pacific Coast League

"Thurston seems to be a pretty good pitcher and also a pretty good hitter," said Wilbert Robinson after he drafted the 30-year-old right-hander from the Pacific Coast League's San Francisco Seals. Thurston won 22 games for the Seals in 1929 in a league one step below the majors. He had also been a good enough hitter in his years in the American League to be used as a pinch-hitter. "I'm not sure what we'll do with him," Robinson said. "But with his varied talents he ought to help us."[18]

Thurston began his major league career with the 1923 St. Louis Browns, but feeling he was overworked by manager Lee Fohl, he refused to pitch batting practice. The Browns asked waivers on him, and Thurston was claimed by the Chicago White Sox. In 1924, his first full season in Chicago, he won 20 games, including five against the Browns. Thurston, who led the league in games finished in 1923 (30), led in complete games in 1924 (28). After two lesser seasons with the White Sox and one with Washington, he returned to the minors in 1928, with the Seals.

Also in 1929:

Traded: Pitcher Lou Koupal to Philadelphia Phillies for Pitcher Luther Roy

Purchased: Pitcher Alex Ferguson from Philadelphia Phillies; Pitcher Kent Greenfield from Boston Braves; Third Baseman Jack Warner from Toledo Mud Hens of American Association

Chosen in Major League Draft: Pitcher Jim Faulkner

Released: Max Carey; Dave Bancroft

Chapter Nine

1930–1934

1930

For the 1930 season, the National League names Frank York to replace Wilbert Robinson as president and to arbitrate between the Ebbets and McKeever factions, who held equal numbers of shares and were constantly fighting.

February 5, 1930: Traded Pitcher Doug McWeeny to the Cincinnati Reds for Pitcher Dolf Luque

Disagreements among members of Brooklyn's management regarding Wilbert Robinson's resignation as club president resulted in a settlement imposed by the National League. Robinson remained the manager, with Frank York, a lawyer for owner Steve McKeever, replacing him as president. The first deal of the new regime was a trade of veteran right-handers. The Robins sent Doug McWeeny, who would be 34 in the upcoming season, for Dolf Luque, who would be 40.

The Robins drafted the 6'2", 190-pound McWeeny after he went 20–5 for the 1925 San Francisco Seals of the Pacific Coast League. McWeeny had decent years with the Robins in 1926 and 1928 but won only four games and lost ten in 1929. His four-year totals for Brooklyn were 33 wins, 45 losses, and a 3.77 earned run average. The Reds released him in June 1931. He had appeared in eight games and lost his only two decisions. McWeeny never again pitched at the professional level.

Luque, a native of Cuba, had been with the Reds for twelve years. Foremost among them was his spectacular 1923 season, when he led the National League in wins (27), earned run average (1.93), and shutouts (6). His ERA that year was half the league average. In 1925, despite a 16–18 record, he again led the league in earned run average and shutouts. Luque's overall record with the Reds was 154–152, with a 3.09 ERA.

Although he was just 5'7", Luque had a powerful physique and was a fiery competitor. And despite his advanced age, manager Robinson had hopes that Luque had two or three more winning seasons in him. He did in 1930, his first season with the Robins. His 14 wins (14–8) and 115 ERA+ helped the team to a fourth-place finish, following five consecutive sixth-place finishes. Luque was 7–6 in 1931 and was released in January 1932.

February 11, 1930: Traded a Player to be Named and Cash to the Mission (CA) Reds of the Pacific Coast League for Shortstop Gordon Slade and Second Baseman Mickey Finn

Three days before this trade, new president Frank York had told the press about the Robins troubling double-play combination. Shortstop Glenn Wright played only three games in the field in 1929, and second baseman Jake Flowers played only 39. "We don't dare to trust on Glenn Wright's ability to throw or to the chance of Jake Flowers regaining his health. We need additional infield strength. I think we ought to get it now."[1]

They found the potential replacements for Wright and Flowers in the Pacific Coast League, with 25-year-old shortstop Gordon Slade and 26-year-old second baseman Neal "Mickey" Finn. Slade and Finn had performed as a double-play combination beginning in 1925 with the Vernon Tigers of the PCL, and for the past four seasons with the Mission club after the franchise was moved to San Francisco.

"I don't know why Slade and myself worked so well on the Coast," Finn told sportswriter Thomas Holmes, "unless it is the fact that we're roommates, and we talked baseball about all the time we were awake."[2]

Both were highly thought of as hitters and fielders, and each was coming off a strong 1929 season for the pennant-winning Reds. Finn batted .347 with 244 hits in the extended PCL season, and Slade had a .303 mark with 222 hits in 197 games. A cash sum of $50,000 or more reportedly accompanied the player to be named to California.

June 30, 1930: Purchased Outfielder Ike Boone from the Mission (CA) Reds of the Pacific Coast League

Ike Boone had played at the major league level in five seasons, but only in two was he a regular. In those two, with the 1924 and 1925

Boston Red Sox, Boone was one of the best hitters in the American League. In 1924, he batted .337, had 98 runs batted in, and an OPS of .901. His numbers in 1925 were a .330 batting average, 68 RBIs, and an OPS of .885. Boone's OPS+ for the two seasons were 132 and 125, and he gathered Most Valuable Player votes in both. The last-place Red Sox rewarded him by sending him back to the minor leagues because Boone's defense was a substantial liability.

In 1929, playing for the Mission Reds of the Pacific Coast League, Boone had one of the greatest offensive seasons ever. He batted .407 with 323 hits in 794 at bats, hit 55 home runs and drove in 218 runs in 198 games. This season the 33-year-old left-handed slugger was batting .448 with 98 RBIs at the time of his purchase by the Robins.

Yet Boone had not been Brooklyn's first choice for a hard-hitting outfielder. They had been turned down in attempts to trade for Cincinnati's Harry Heilmann and the Phillies' Lefty O'Doul. Scout Larry Sutton completed the deal for Boone under instructions from President Frank York. Wilbert Robinson had not been consulted on the purchase.

"They tell me that Boone is a great hitter," the manager said, "and there's always room on our team for a hitter. Larry Sutton insists that Boone will help our club and his judgment is good enough for me until I can see for myself."[3]

Boone did help the club in 1930, playing in 40 games, he had a .297 batting average and 13 runs batted in. He spent the next two season in the International League, with the Newark Bears in 1931 and the Jersey City Skeeters in 1932, while playing a combined 19 games for Brooklyn. On January 7, 1933, the Dodgers sent Boone back to the International League by selling him to the Toronto Maple Leafs, a Detroit Tigers affiliate.

September 7, 1930: Purchased Pitcher Van Mungo from the Winston-Salem (NC) Twins of the Piedmont League

Pitching for the Winston-Salem (NC) Twins of the Class C Piedmont League in 1930, 19-year-old Van Lingle Mungo had an 11–11 record and an unimpressive 5.26 earned run average. But scout Nap Rucker saw something in the 6'2" hard-throwing right-hander and recommended the Robins sign him. In December, Mungo broke his arm playing football near his South Carolina home. Fortunately, it was his left arm, and it was expected to be fully healed by the start of spring training.

Mungo joined the Robins late in the 1931 season, after going 15–5 for the Hartford Senators of the Eastern League. "He is another [Dazzy] Vance, another Dazzy, I'm telling you," said Wilbert Robinson. "Hasn't the best disposition in the world. You know some of those Carolina fellows get funny ideas sometimes, but he certainly can buzz that ball over. Best young pitcher I've seen since Rube Marquard. Only he is faster than Rube was. Say, maybe he is another Walter Johnson. I'll bet he will be winning 20 to 25 games a year for this club for a long time."[4]

October 13, 1930: Traded Pitcher Clise Dudley, Pitcher Jumbo Elliott, Outfielder Hal Lee, and Cash to the Philadelphia Phillies for Outfielder Lefty O'Doul and Second Baseman Fresco Thompson

During the 1930 season, the Robins had been turned down by the Philadelphia Phillies in their attempt to trade for outfielder Lefty O'Doul. After the season ended, they tried again. Following their denial a few days earlier that they were seeking a trade for O'Doul and second baseman Fresco Thompson, the deal was consummated on October 13. Robins president Frank York and Phillies owner William Baker made the announcement following their meeting in Manhattan. The reaction in the press was that Brooklyn had gotten much the better of the deal. The players they had surrendered were of lesser quality than those the Phillies had asked for during the negotiations. The difference, the newspapermen speculated, would be made up by the amount of money going to the cash-strapped Phillies—$50,000 or more was the guess.

Phillies manager Burt Shotton viewed the deal differently. "If you have stars and they cannot win for you, get rid of them and try someone else," he said. "I thought I had a winner last spring and when the team failed, I was one of the most disappointed men in baseball."[5] The Phillies had finished in fifth place in 1929, their highest finish since 1917, but dropped to eighth place in 1930.

Clise Dudley won six and lost 14 with a 5.69 earned run average as a 25-year-old Robins' rookie in 1929. Manager Robinson used him less frequently in 1930. His appearances dropped from 35 to 21, his starts from 20 to seven, and his innings pitched from 156 2/3 to 66 2/3. Shotton made him a part of the Phillies rotation in 1931, and Dudley made 24 starts and had a 121 ERA+ despite an 8–14 record.

Jumbo Elliott had been in poor physical condition for several years and had missed most of the 1929 season. He pitched brilliantly in several early starts in 1930, but his strength seemed to leave him in the summer heat. Nevertheless, it had been Elliott's best season, a 10–7 record and an ERA+ of 125. Overall, Elliott had a 26–38 record and an earned run average of 3.89 in his five years with Brooklyn. He did even better in his first year in Philadelphia, winning a league-leading 19 games for a sixth-place team. (It was the first time in National League history that no pitcher won at least twenty games.)

The Robins signed Hal Lee in 1927 as an amateur free agent. As a 25-year-old rookie in 1930, he batted .162 in 22 games. Wilbert Robinson had always thought highly of Lee's future and wanted to keep him, but the Robins' manager had played little part in Brooklyn's transactions since Frank York replaced him as president. Two years later, Lee batted .303 with an OPS of .841 in 149 games for the Phillies.

Robinson was glad to have a hitter like Lefty O'Doul, but worried about having two defensive liabilities in his outfield—O'Doul in left and Babe Herman in right. That left a lot of room for center fielder Johnny Frederick to patrol.

Fresco Thompson, 28, had spent four seasons as the Phillies second baseman, amassing 700 hits and compiling an even .300 batting average. Joe McCarthy, recently named to replace Bob Shawkey as manager of the Yankees, thought Thompson would give the Robins their best infield the former Cubs manager had seen. "A smooth, hustling ball player, that kid," he said, "and I think he'll play a lot better for a winning club than he did for the Phillies last year."[6] McCarthy was wrong. Thompson batted .265 in 74 games for Brooklyn in 1931. In May 1932, he appeared in only three games for the Dodgers and spent the rest of the season with the Jersey City Skeeters of the International League.

The major addition for Brooklyn was 33-year-old Lefty O'Doul. Early in his career (1919–1923) O'Doul was a mostly fringe pitcher with the Yankees and the Red Sox. He spent the next four years playing the outfield for the Salt Lake City Bees, the Hollywood Stars, and the San Francisco Seals in the Pacific Coast League. O'Doul totaled 973 hits in those four seasons, leading the league in 1925 and 1927, and had batting averages of .392, .375, .338, and .378.

John McGraw brought O'Doul to the New York Giants in 1928. He missed six weeks with a broken ankle but batted .319 in 114 games. In October the Giants traded him to the Phillies. This was a hitter's era; nevertheless, O'Doul's 1929 season with Philadelphia stands out. He led the league in batting (.398), hits (254), and on-base percentage (.465), and had an OPS of 1.087. His performance earned him a close second-place finish to Rogers Hornsby of the Cubs in voting for the Most Valuable Player Award. His 1930 numbers were not quite as high, but still striking, a .383 batting average, 202 hits, and a 1.057 OPS.

Adding O'Doul and Thompson to a lineup that included Babe Herman, Glenn Wright, Del Bissonette, Johnny Frederick, Wally Gilbert and Al Lopez was expected to make facing the 1931 Robins a formidable task for pitchers.

"I see that Brooklyn has made a good deal," McCarthy said. "A swell deal, in fact. It makes my regret at leaving the pleasant association of the National League behind a bit easier to bear. I'd hate to sit on the bench doping out ways and means of foiling O'Doul along with those other murderous Brooklyn hitters. That job will give many a manager gray hair."[7]

Also in 1930:
Traded: Pitcher Jim Richardson and Cash to the Toledo Mud Hens of the American Association for Pitcher Fred Heimach
Purchased: Outfielder Alta Cohen from Macon (GA) Peaches of the South Atlantic League; Pitcher Phil Gallivan from Macon (GA) Peaches of the South Atlantic League
Sold: Infielder Billy Rhiel to Boston Braves; Pitcher Luther Roy to Chattanooga Lookouts of the Southern Association
Chosen in Major League Draft: Pitcher Pea Ridge Day
Released: Pitcher Johnny Morrison

1931

January 19, 1931: Traded Catcher Hank DeBerry, Infielder-Outfielder Eddie Moore, and Cash to the Oakland Oaks of the Pacific Coast League for Catcher Ernie Lombardi

Hank DeBerry spent nine years with the Robins, batting .267 in 608 games. During that time, he shared the catching position with Zack Taylor and others. Only twice, in 1922 and 1928, did he catch more than half the team's games. DeBerry's skills and intelligence behind the plate had been a big reason for the development of many young Brooklyn pitchers, most noticeably Dazzy Vance. He was Vance's preferred catcher and had been since 1922, when he and the team's best pitcher joined the club.

Columnist Murray Robinson summed up DeBerry's stay in Brooklyn. "In losing DeBerry, the National League loses one of the finest characters it has ever housed—a gentleman and a scholar, and a great catcher when he was at his best. It was always easy to underestimate his ability because he was not showy."[8] At age 36, DeBerry played one final season in the minor leagues.

Versatile Eddie Moore played mostly at second base, but also at shortstop and the outfield in his two seasons with Brooklyn. He batted a combined .291 with a .365 on-base percentage in 187 games.

Hank DeBerry and Eddie Moore were not enough to get Oakland to surrender Ernie Lombardi, the best young catcher in the minor leagues. It was reported that $50,000 dollars was sent to the Oaks. Lombardi, 22, was 6'3" and well over 200 pounds. He was slow afoot and clumsy behind the plate, but he had a strong throwing arm and was a prolific hitter. In the past three seasons with the Oaks, the right-handed-hitting Lombardi batted .377, .366, and .370, with slugging percentages of .557, .587, and .594. He was expected to challenge the Robins other young catcher, Al Lopez, for playing time in 1931.

February 9, 1931: Signed Free Agent Pitcher Jack Quinn

No one was sure where Jack Quinn was born or how old he was. It was generally accepted that he was born in the coal mining region of western Pennsylvania in 1885. Later research revealed Quinn was born in the Slovakian region of the Austro-Hungarian Empire on July 1, 1883. He began pitching in the major leagues for the 1909 New York Yankees and had been a major league pitcher, for several teams, for twenty years. Quinn had a 9–7 record with the 1930 world champion Philadelphia Athletics, but manager Connie Mack let him go after the season to make room for younger pitchers.

Quinn attributed his longevity to a strict regimen of physical training and his ability to throw the spitball, a pitch that was easier on the arm. The 46-year-old right-hander attended the winter meetings in New York and made a case with several clubs to continue his career. He finally convinced Brooklyn's president, Frank York, to sign him. "There's many a good game left in this arm," Quinn told the press. "I've taken care of it, and if I get the chance, I'll show it."[9]

Manager Wilbert Robinson gave him the chance, and Quinn showed he was still a valuable pitcher. He appeared in 81 games in his two seasons with Brooklyn, all but one in relief. His combined record for his age 47 and 48 seasons, was only 8–11, but in both those seasons he led the National League in games finished and saves. After he was released, he signed for one final season with the Cincinnati Reds.

May 7, 1931: Sold Outfielder–First Baseman Harvey Hendrick to the Cincinnati Reds

Harvey Hendrick had hit well wherever he played, including the minor leagues and two partial seasons with the New York Yankees and one with the Cleveland Indians. Playing for the New Orleans Pelicans of the Southern Association in 1926, the left-handed-hitting Hendrick batted .370 with a .564 slugging percentage. Scout Nap Rucker alerted manager Wilbert Robinson, and the Robins purchased him for the 1927 season.

Hendrick continued to hit well with Brooklyn. In his first three seasons, he batted .310, .318, and .354 with OPS+ of 106, 129, and 138. But he played in just 68 games in 1930, and his average fell to .257. The sale to Cincinnati came after Hendrick had appeared in only one game this season, but he regained his form with the Reds, batting .315 with an OPS+ of 120.

June 14, 1931: Sold Second Baseman Jake Flowers to the St. Louis Cardinals

David Driscoll, the Robins business manager, announced the club had sold second baseman Jake Flowers to the St. Louis Cardinals for slightly over the $7,500 waiver price. Flowers had played in only 22 games this season and was batting .226. Cardinals manager Gabby Street needed a reserve infielder, and he got one in Flowers, who could play second, short, and third. The Robins had traded pitcher Bob McGraw to get him in April 1927. Flowers played five seasons for the Robins, but in only one, 1928, did he play more than 100 games (103). His best season was 1930, when he batted .320 in 89 games.

Also in 1931:

Traded: A Player to be Named and Cash to Baltimore Orioles of the International League for Outfielder Denny Sothern
Sold: Pitcher Bobo Newsom to Little Rock Travelers of the Southern Association; Pitcher Ray Moss to Boston Braves
Signed Free Agents: Pitcher Joe Shaute

1932

For the 1932 season, Max Carey replaced Wilbert Robinson as manager. With Robinson's departure, a new nickname had to be found to replace Robins. The club's executives asked the local sportswriters to choose one. At their January 22, 1932, meeting they overwhelmingly chose Dodgers. Kings was the only other name that received serious consideration. (The borough of Brooklyn is coextensive with Kings County.)[10]

January 23, 1932: Traded Minor League Outfielder–First Baseman Bob Parham and Cash to the St. Louis Cardinals for Outfielder Hack Wilson

Hack Wilson began his major league career playing in three games for the 1923 New York Giants. But his fame rests with the six seasons he spent with the Chicago Cubs. For the years 1926 through 1931, the 5'6", 190-pound Wilson *had* 190 home runs, 769 runs batted in, and a 1.002 OPS. He led the league in home runs four times and runs batted in twice, topped off by a record-breaking 1930 season. That year, the right-handed slugger set a National League record with 56 home runs and a still-standing major league record 191 runs batted in.

Through it all, Wilson had a downside. He was an alcoholic and a brawler, on and off the field. The fans loved him, and the front office tolerated him, but in 1931 the Cubs replaced manager Joe McCarthy with Rogers Hornsby. Unlike McCarthy, Hornsby had no tolerance for the fun-loving Wilson and limited his playing time. In December, Chicago traded him to the St. Louis Cardinals for pitcher Burleigh Grimes.

The Cardinals had no place for Wilson, but knew Brooklyn needed a right-handed hitter. Owner Sam Breadon and president Branch Rickey asked for Dazzy Vance or Johnny Frederick in return, but Dodgers president Frank York said no. Instead, the Cardinals accepted $50,000 and Bob Parham, a minor league outfielder who would never play in the major leagues. It was the first major deal made under newly named manager Max Carey.

"I'm gratified with the result of the deal," York said after getting off the phone with Rickey. "If Wilson can come back for us, we ought to be right in the middle of next year's pennant race."[11]

In response to a telegram from the *Brooklyn Eagle*, Wilson, replying from his Martinsburg, West Virginia, home, wrote. "I expect to have the greatest year I ever had. The deal suits me fine."[12]

Wilson had an excellent but not his "greatest year" with the Dodgers in 1932: a .297 average, 123 RBIs, and an OPS+ of 141. He never reached those numbers again, and Carey released him in early August 1934. The Phillies signed Wilson a few days later, and he lasted a month before they released him, ending his major league career.

March 14, 1932: Traded Outfielder Babe Herman, Third Baseman Wally Gilbert, and Catcher Ernie Lombardi to the Cincinnati Reds for Second Baseman Tony Cuccinello, Third Baseman Joe Stripp, and Catcher Clyde Sukeforth

This deal, which had been pending for four days, was the most satisfactory of several propositions made by the Reds, claimed Jack Ryder of the *Cincinnati Enquirer*. Reds owner Sidney Weil set a deadline at one o'clock this afternoon and informed the Brooklyn people that his offer would be withdrawn if not accepted by that time. Promptly at one, Weil was summoned from the dining room to the telephone. President Frank York had called to notify Mr. Weil that the deal was acceptable.[13]

"A baseball trade is made, I imagine, for the purpose of strengthening a ball club," wrote Brooklyn columnist Murray Robinson in assessing the three-for-three trade. "Another important factor to be taken into consideration should be the public's reaction to the deal. Judged by both of the foregoing standards, the Brooklyn-Cincinnati swap is a knockout victory for the Reds—and a flop for the Dodgers."[14] Robinson was right—this would turn out to be a most questionable trade for the Dodgers.

In losing Babe Herman, they lost the man who had been their best hitter for six years, averaging .340, with 1,084 hits, 111 home runs, and 585 runs batted in. From 1928 to 1930, he batted .340, .381, and .393. This was an era of hitter dominance, so Herman never won a batting title, finishing fifth, second, and second in those three seasons. In five of his six seasons with Brooklyn, he finished in the top 10 in OPS+. His 1931 season did not match his previous two. When the Dodgers tried to reduce his salary for 1932, Herman held out, so they traded him. (Stripp and Cuccinello were also holdouts.) Only 29, Herman had five more good seasons left.

Another factor that made this such a bad trade for the Dodgers was trading catcher Ernie Lombardi after just one season. Lombardi had an excellent rookie year in 1931, batting .297 as the backup to Al Lopez. But having Lopez made Lombardi expendable, and he went on to be a star for the next 16 seasons. He won an MVP Award, a couple of batting titles, was an eight-time All-Star, and was voted into the Hall of Fame. It is interesting to contemplate what Lombardi might have accomplished as a Dodger.

Also leaving was Wally Gilbert, who had been Brooklyn's third baseman for the past three years. In his three plus seasons with the club, he batted .281 in 477 games. But Gilbert would play only one season with the Reds, batting .214, before returning to the minor leagues for another 10 seasons.

Twenty-nine-year-old Joe Stripp would take Gilbert's place at third base. Stripp was coming off two seasons in which he batted .306 and .324 for the Reds. While Gilbert played only one more season in the major leagues, Stripp would be Brooklyn's third baseman for the next six. That part of the trade was a strong positive for the Dodgers.

So too was getting 24-year-old Tony Cuccinello, who in his two seasons with the Reds batted .312 and .315, with runs batted in totals of 78 and 93. He would be Brooklyn's second baseman for the next four seasons.

The third man the Dodgers received was catcher Clyde Sukeforth, who played five seasons with the Reds, but only in 1931 had he been the first-string catcher. Sukeforth was a risky acquisition having suffered a serious eye injury during the offseason. He would recover, but in his three years with Brooklyn, he would be strictly a reserve behind Al Lopez.

Manager Max Carey, who engineered the trade on behalf of the Dodgers, explained his thinking. "We unloaded two players who were not to figure in my plans this year. I had no intention of using either Wally Gilbert or Ernie Lombardi. Herman is a fine player, but not effective enough for me to figure in championship plans. I'm not claiming any pennants, but with the addition of Stripp, Cuccinello, and Sukeforth, I think I recommended a trade to Mr. York that will more than offset the loss of the departed players."[15]

April 7, 1932: Traded Pitcher Pea Ridge Day and Cash to the Minneapolis Millers of the American Association for First Baseman George Kelly

The spring training injury to first baseman Del Bissonette's leg now seemed likely to keep him out for the entire year. With the season-opener only five days away, the Dodgers needed someone to fill that position. When attempts to get Sam Leslie or Joe Judge fell through, manager Max Carey found his man in George Kelly, a 36-year-old veteran of 15 National League seasons, most notably with John McGraw's New York Giants. In return, the Dodgers sent pitcher Pea Ridge Day and a reported $15,000 to the Millers. Day's 2–2 season for Brooklyn in 1931 was his last in the major leagues

Kelly, a 6'4" right-handed hitter and future Hall of Famer, was a consistent hitter and an excellent defensive player. He led the NL in home runs in 1921 (23) and in RBIs in 1920 (94) and 1924 (136). Kelly was coming off an excellent 1931 season for the Minneapolis Millers of the American Association. He batted .320 with 194 hits and 20 home runs.

Kelly was Brooklyn's first baseman until he injured his hand in late July. The Dodgers sent him to the International League's Jersey City Skeeters, ending his major league career. In 64 games, Kelly batted .243 with an OPS+ of 82. Carey used Bud Clancy, purchased from Jersey City, at first base for the rest of the season.

May 7, 1932: Purchased Outfielder Danny Taylor from the Chicago Cubs

The Dodgers left Chicago with one player more than when they arrived after manager Max Carey purchased outfielder Danny Taylor. Cubs manager Rogers Hornsby happily let Taylor go. In the sixth innings of a May 3 game at Pittsburgh, Taylor, playing right field, let three successive base hits get by him, resulting in two triples and a double. An unhappy Hornsby sent Marv Gudat to right field to replace him.

Taylor, 31, had a reputation as a good right-handed hitter and a fair fielder, so the May 3 game was not a typical occurrence for him. He batted .300 and .319 the past two seasons but had played in only six of Chicago's 20 games in 1932. Taylor proved to be a good addition for Brooklyn, batting .324 for the remainder of the 1932 season. He was around .300 throughout his five years with the Dodgers, finishing with a batting average of exactly .300. Taylor's OPS+ for those years was always above 100, ranging from 103 to 143, and was a cumulative 129. On July 11, 1936, the Dodgers sold him to the Indianapolis Indians of the American Association, ending Taylor's career as a major leaguer.

December 14, 1932: Traded Pitcher Earl Mattingly and Cash to the Nashville Vols of the Southern Association for Shortstop Lonny Frey

Earl Mattingly was a 28-year-old right-hander who appeared in eight games for Brooklyn in 1931, losing his only decision. He spent the 1932 season with the Jersey City Skeeters of the International League, where he had a 5–6 record and a 5.16 earned run average. On December 14 the Dodgers traded Mattingly and cash to the Nashville Vols of the Southern Association. In return, they received Lonny Frey, a 22-year-old shortstop. Playing for the York (PA) White Roses this past season, Frey batted .290 and was rated the best all-around shortstop in the New York–Pennsylvania League.

According to Nashville owner Jimmy Hamilton, five major league clubs were after the young shortstop, but the Dodgers won the bidding war. Brooklyn agreed to allow Nashville to keep Frey in 1933 and delay his reporting to the Dodgers until the spring of 1934. Nevertheless, the Dodgers brought the switch-hitting Frey to Brooklyn in late August 1933.

December 15, 1932: Traded Second Baseman Mickey Finn, Pitcher Cy Moore, and Infielder Jack Warner to the Philadelphia Phillies for Pitcher Ray Benge and Cash

A Dodgers-Phillies deal had been in the works since the end of the 1931 season. Phillies manager Burt Shotton was after Mickey Finn to replace weak hitting Les Mallon at second base, while Dodgers manager Max Carey was looking for a pitcher like Ray Benge to strengthen his staff. The holdup had always been what players, in addition to Finn, would go to Philadelphia.

"Shotton insisted on Carey handing over [outfielder] Johnny Frederick as well as Finn for Benge, but Carey wouldn't regard this exchange at all," said Dodgers business manager Dave Driscoll. "Max stood firm, and after hours of debating he convinced Shotton and [Phillies owner Gerald] Nugent that Finn, pitcher Cy Moore, infielder Jack Warner, plus $15,000 was a fair return. Our rivals are pleased with the transfer and I might add that President [Steve] McKeever and Carey are elated."[16]

Finn came to Brooklyn in a February 1930 trade with the Mission

(CA) Reds of the Pacific Coast League. He batted .278 as a rookie and .274 in 1931, while earning a 19th place finish in the voting for the Most Valuable Player. In 1932 he appeared in only 65 games with a .238 batting average. Finn was batting .237 for the 1933 Phillies when he played his last game on June 17. Three weeks later, he died after undergoing an operation to deal with stomach pains caused by a duodenal ulcer. He was 29 years old.

Cy Moore was a 27-year-old right-hander whom Brooklyn purchased from the Macon Peaches of the Class B South Atlantic League in September 1928. The high hopes they had for him never materialized. Moore spent the past four seasons with both Brooklyn and the Jersey City Skeeters of the International League. He appeared in 76 games for the Dodgers, all but six in relief, with a 4–8 record, two saves, and an ERA+ of 88.

Jack Warner had previous major league experience—four seasons with the Detroit Tigers—before Brooklyn purchased him from the Toledo Mud Hens of the American Association in August 1929. He batted .297 for the Dodgers from 1929 through 1931 but appeared in only 47 games. Warner, who spent the 1932 season with Jersey City, played second and third base for the Phillies in 1933, his final big-league season.

Ray Benge, a 5'9", 160-pound right-hander who would turn 31 in April, had spent the past five seasons with the mostly second division Phillies. Benge's first season, 1928, when he had an 8–18 record was his worst and the last two, 1931 and 1932, were his best. Fourteen wins and an ERA+ of 134 in 1931, and 13 wins and an ERA+ of 109 in 1932.

"I think he's a mighty good pitcher and that he's proved it for the last three or four years in Philadelphia," Carey replied when asked about Benge. "He has speed strength and control. No club in the league finds him easy. If he isn't hurt and things go well, I think he can win 15 maybe 20 games for us."[17]

Also in 1932:

Purchased: Pitcher Boom-Boom Beck from Memphis Chicks of the Southern Association; First Baseman Dick Siebert from New York Yankees

Sold: Outfielder Denny Sothern to Hartford Senators of the Eastern League; Catcher Paul Richards to Minneapolis Millers of the American Association; Pitcher Fay Thomas to Chicago Cubs; Fresco Thompson to Jersey City Skeeters of the International League

Signed Free Agents: Pitcher Waite Hoyt

Released: Pitcher Dolf Luque; Outfielder Rube Bressler; Pitcher Waite Hoyt

1933

February 8, 1933: Traded Pitcher Dazzy Vance and Shortstop Gordon Slade to the St. Louis Cardinals for Second Baseman Jake Flowers and Pitcher Ownie Carroll

Dazzy Vance is the winningest pitcher in Brooklyn history. (He had 187 wins at the time of the trade and would add three more in 1935.) The Dodgers purchased him from the New Orleans Pelicans in 1921 over the objections of Charles Ebbets, who did not want a sore-armed, 31-year-old pitcher. Vance led the National League in strikeouts in each of his first seven seasons with Brooklyn. He also led twice in wins and complete games, three times in earned run average, and four times in shutouts. His greatest season was 1924, when he won the pitchers Triple Crown by leading in wins (28), earned run average (2.16), and strikeouts (262). Although the Robins fell just short of winning the pennant that year, Vance was the voted the league's Most Valuable Player. But he was now one month short of his forty-second birthday and had not been as effective the past two seasons. That, along with the economic hard times in baseball as well as elsewhere, led the team's ownership to propose a healthy cut in Vance's salary.

In a letter to a friend two weeks earlier, Vance had written how rudely shocked and surprised he was when he saw his 1933 contract. "I realized how tough conditions were, but I never figured the Brooklyn club would reduce my salary over 50 percent. I don't mind a reduction in pay, but I certainly won't stand for so big a cut," he continued. "Brooklyn offered me $7,500 for the coming season. I won't sign for that figure. It's the lowest I have been offered since I became a regular member of the Brooklyn club. Last year I drew down $16,500."[18]

The Dodgers had offered $10,000 (not $7,500) which they said was non-negotiable and was a good salary for a pitcher who they claimed was almost useless when he was needed most. A trade, which now seemed inevitable, was announced on February 8. It was a two-for-two deal said business manager Dave Driscoll, who negotiated the transaction with Cardinals president Branch Rickey.

The *Brooklyn Eagle*'s Thomas Holmes summed up one aspect of Vance's years in Brooklyn. "He never was as popular here as he might have been. On more than one occasion he received the regal raspberry of the mob. One of the contributing factors to the crowd's reaction to Vance was his propensity for becoming inflicted with some obscure ailment at a time when the club needed him most. As last season when the Dodgers in early August were within striking distance of the lead, he developed neuritis in his pitching shoulder. Vance did not win a game last season after August 1."[19] (Vance did not win a start, but he did have a win in relief on August 10.)

Shortstop Gordon Slade accompanied Vance to St. Louis. Slade was an excellent fielder, but he batted a lowly .238 in 189 games in three seasons with Brooklyn. After a poor season with the Cardinals, he would do much better offensively in his next two seasons with Cincinnati.

While Slade was primarily a shortstop, Jake Flowers, who was returning to Brooklyn, could play equally well at second, short, and third. Flowers spent five seasons with the Robins before being sold to St. Louis in June 1931. He played in 78 games for the 1933 Dodgers, giving him a career total of 405 games played for Brooklyn, with a .260 batting average.

Right-hander Ownie Carroll had been a member of the Cardinals for a little over a month. The 30-year-old Carroll was sent to St. Louis by Cincinnati to complete a December 1932 deal between the two teams. Carroll had engendered high praise after starring for the College of the Holy Cross in Worcester, Massachusetts, where he won 50 of 52 decisions. However, he had not lived up to expectations after breaking into the big leagues with the Detroit Tigers in 1925.

Carroll had spent the last three seasons with Cincinnati. His 19 losses for the last-place Reds in 1932 was the league high, although many of the Dodgers considered him that team's best pitcher. Bothered from time to time by arm problems, he seemed to have recovered, as his 15 complete games in 1932 would indicate. Carroll had a 13–15 record for the 1933 Dodgers and a 1–3 record in 26 games for the team in 1934, his final major league season.

After two seasons with St. Louis and Cincinnati, 44-year-old Dazzy Vance returned to Brooklyn in 1935, as a free agent. In his final major league season, he had a 3–2 record in 20 games, all in relief, for manager Casey Stengel.

June 7, 1933: Traded First Baseman Del Bissonette and Cash to the Baltimore Orioles of the International League for Outfielder Buzz Boyle

To strengthen their outfield, the sixth-place Dodgers traded veteran first baseman Del Bissonette and a reported $7,500 to the Baltimore

Orioles of the International League for outfielder Buzz Boyle. After a brief trial with the Boston Braves, the 25-year-old left-handed-hitting Boyle was in his third and best season with the Orioles. Following the 1931 and 1932 seasons, in which he batted .312 and .314, he was batting a lofty .364 in 51 games at the time of the trade. Boyle was expected to report immediately, and manager Max Carey planned to use him immediately. He would replace Hack Wilson in center field, playing between Lefty O'Doul in left and Johnny Frederick in right.

Del Bissonette had been a popular player with Brooklyn fans ever since his spectacular rookie season of 1928. In addition to a .320 batting average that year, his 25 home runs were the fourth most in the league, and he had 106 runs batted in, 319 total bases, and an OPS+ of 145. He played in only 116 games the following year, after being beaned by Philadelphia's Les Sweetland in the first week of the season but batted .281 with a 105 OPS+. He followed with an OPS+ of 120 in 1930 and 110 in 1931.

Bissonette missed the entire 1932 season following several operations on his left leg, which he injured in spring training. He was attempting to resume his career this year, but the Dodgers were unsure he would be able to do so and purchased 39-year-old first baseman Joe Judge from the Washington Senators. Bissonette appeared in 35 games in 1933, bringing his total games in a Dodgers uniform to 604, with a .305 batting average, a .371 on-base average and a 119 OPS+.

June 15, 1933: Traded Outfielder Lefty O'Doul and Pitcher Watty Clark to the New York Giants for First Baseman Sam Leslie

A week after trading away popular Del Bissonette, the Dodgers parted with two more fan favorites, outfielder Lefty O'Doul, 36, and pitcher Watty Clark, 31. Crossing the East River in return was 27-year-old Giants first baseman Sam Leslie.

Dissatisfied with the two first baseman he had, manager Max Carey had traded Del Bissonette and soon would release Joe Judge. Leslie, a left-handed-hitter, had been a backup to Bill Terry in New York the past two seasons. Used mostly as a pinch-hitter, he batted .302 and .293. "We are building for the future," Carey said. "With the acquisition of Leslie, I now feel that we are well fortified at a position that has been a perennial sore spot since I took charge of the team."[20]

Brooklyn expected offensive firepower when they acquired O'Doul from Philadelphia in 1930, and he had delivered: a .336 batting average with a 135 OPS+ in 1931, and a league-leading .368 average with a 163 OPS+ and a third-place finish in the MVP race in 1932. But O'Doul was batting just .252 this season, and Carey thought the pitchers had discovered how to pitch to him. "It is skillful pitching, on low curve balls, which has slowed Frank [O'Doul] up from his league-leading pace this season as much as the deadened ball," Carey said.[21]

Watty Clark had been a reliable member of Brooklyn's pitching staff since joining the club in 1927. Clark won 84 and lost 69 and had better earned run averages than the league's ERA each year. He twice led the National League in games started and once in innings pitched.

When Terry, the Giants player-manager, was asked about the deal he replied: "I wouldn't have made the trade, unless I thought that the acquiring of Clark and O'Doul would strengthen the Giants. We can use a left-hand pitcher and despite the fact that Clark's work this spring has not been entirely satisfactory, I believe that he will do a lot better with us when the warmer weather sets in. Clark will take his regular turn on the mound." Terry concluded by saying, "Brooklyn must certainly have needed Leslie in a bad way to be willing to make a sacrifice of two players and no cash."[22]

August 22, 1933: Purchased Pitcher Dutch Leonard from the York (PA) White Roses of the New York–Pennsylvania League

The Dodgers paid the York (PA) White Roses of the New York–Pennsylvania League $800 to bring right-handed pitcher Emil "Dutch" Leonard to Brooklyn for a 10-day trial. Leonard was 24 years old and had pitched in the minor leagues since 1930, for seven different teams. His 12–15 record this season, for last-place York, was the best he had done.

Leonard began his trial at Ebbets Field on August 31, in the first game of a doubleheader against the St. Louis Cardinals. He relieved Van Mungo in the second inning and allowed three earned runs in seven 1/3 innings.

"The kid has something," manager Max Carey said after the game. "He displayed exceptionally fine control, a good curve ball, and a floater which teased the Cardinals. We shall see more of him later." Catcher Al Lopez also praised the newcomer. "He has plenty of speed, and his control is perfect," Lopez said. "He was able to put the ball just where I wanted it. I think he has the goods."[23]

October 11, 1933: Traded Pitcher Sloppy Thurston, Pitcher Ray Phelps, Outfielder Joe Hutcheson, and Cash to the St. Paul Saints of the American Association for Pitcher Les Munns

New business manager Bob Quinn continued the process of getting rid of holdovers from the Wilbert Robinson regime. He traded right-handed pitchers Sloppy Thurston and Ray Phelps to the St. Paul Saints of the American Association for right-handed pitcher Les Munns. Also going to the Saints was rookie Joe Hutcheson, a slow-footed outfielder who batted .234 in 55 games in 1933, in what would be his only major league season.

Thurston was well-liked by teammates and fans during his four years in Brooklyn. Pitching for poor teams, he won more games (33) than he lost (29), something few Dodgers pitchers had accomplished in recent years. Thurston was at his best when he had a week's rest between starts, but he was now 34, and manager Carey was seeking younger arms who would be able to pitch more frequently.

Phelps, like Thurston, came to Brooklyn in 1930. He had an excellent rookie season, with a 14–7 record and an ERA+ of 120. He slipped to 7–9 with an ERA+ of 77 in 1931. Phelps was 4–5 with an ERA+ of 65 in 1932 when Carey sent him to the Jersey City Skeeters of the International League.

Dodgers scout Bob Connery recommended Les Munns, as did scouts from the Indians, Reds, Phillies, and Athletics to their bosses. Rated a "sure fire" prospect, Munns, who would be 25 in December, was a 6'5" right-hander who was coming off a 19–16 season with St. Paul. He appeared in 54 games for the Dodgers over the 1934 and 1935 seasons, winning four and losing 10, with a 5.02 earned run average. Munns finished his career with an 0–3 record in seven games for the 1936 St. Louis Cardinals.

December 4, 1933: Purchased Pitcher Art Herring from the Detroit Tigers

For the last five seasons, 26-year-old Art Herring had bounced between the Detroit Tigers and the minor leagues. He had little success with the Tigers, a 14–21 record with a 4.55 earned run average. He was 1–2 in 24 games this past season. Herring's time in Detroit ended after he issued a bases-loaded walk to pitcher Herb Pennock in a game against the Yankees. Tigers manager Bucky Harris was so upset with Herring, he demoted him to Beaumont of the Texas league.

But Brooklyn's business manager, Bob Quinn, saw something he liked in the 5'7" right-hander. "Herring is a good pitcher. You can take my word for it," Quinn said. "He had trouble with the Detroit Club, that's why he couldn't make a go of it. But I feel certain that he will win for Brooklyn."[24]

Herring had a 2–4 record for the 1934 Dodgers. He spent the next ten years in the minor leagues, except for seven games for the 1939 Chicago White Sox. On August 12, 1944, the Dodgers, on their way to a seventh-place finish, brought Herring back to Brooklyn when they purchased him from the St. Paul Saints.

"Herring is an important addition to our staff," said Branch Rickey. "He can thread the eye of a needle and is as fast as Curt Davis."[25] Herring, now 38, won three and lost four over the last six weeks of the 1944 season and followed with 7–4 and 7–2 records in 1945 and 1946. In October 1946, the Dodgers sold him to the Pittsburgh Pirates.

Also in 1933:

Sold: Second Baseman Fresco Thompson to the Buffalo Bisons of International League; Pitcher Joe Shaute to Cincinnati Reds; Outfielder Max Rosenfeld to Washington Senators; First Baseman Bud Clancy to Jersey City Skeeters of the International League

Chosen in Major League Draft: Catcher Ray Berres; Infielder Jim Bucher: Outfielder Glenn Chapman

Released: Pitcher Jack Quinn; Catcher Val Picinich; First Baseman Joe Judge; Pitcher Fred Heimach; Outfielder Alta Cohen

1934

For the 1934 season, Casey Stengel replaced Max Carey as manager.

June 12, 1934: Traded Pitcher Ray Lucas and Cash to the Mission (CA) Reds of the Pacific Coast League for Pitcher Johnny Babich

After 20-year-old Johnny Babich won 20 games for the second division Mission Reds of the Pacific Coast League in 1933, the Chicago

Cubs and New York Yankees made efforts to acquire him. The Missions retained him for 1934 but finding themselves short of money put the 6'1" right-hander on the market in June. Babich's 10–3 record and 2.03 earned run average made even more clubs anxious to get him. New Dodgers manager Casey Stengel and coach Chick Fraser had seen Babich pitch the previous winter in California. They convinced business manager Bob Quinn Babich was worth whatever the Missions wanted. Quinn, in turn, convinced owner Steve McKeever, who sent pitcher Ray Lucas and a reported $33,000 to California. Lucas, 25, had a 1–1 record in 10 games for Brooklyn this season and would never return to the major leagues. A week later, Babich made his major league debut, a start, and a loss at Cincinnati.

June 29, 1934: Purchased Pitcher Watty Clark from the New York Giants

One year after manager Max Carey traded left-hander Watty Clark to the New York Giants, manager Casey Stengel brought him back. The trade had not worked out well for Clark. A sore arm limited his appearances for the second half of 1933 and the first half of 1934. Clark's combined record for 21 games in the two half-seasons was a 4–6 record and a 5.31 earned run average. He had pitched in five games this season, most recently on June 22, and was generally ineffective. The Giants had obtained waivers on him and were set to return him to the minor leagues, but Brooklyn stepped in and bought Clark for what they said was slightly under the $7,500 waiver price.

"It's this way," said Giants manager Bill Terry. "I'd like to hang on to Clark a little longer and see if he can't come back. But I can't.... I know what my other pitchers can do, and I don't know how far Watty can come back."

Stengel's response was like those he would make thirty years later as the manager of the New York Mets. "I don't know how far Clark can come back either," he said, "but that doesn't matter so much to me because he can't do much worse than some of my present pitchers."

Clark would outlast Stengel. He went 2–0 for Brooklyn in the second half of 1934 and won 13 (13–8) in 1935. Following a 7–11 season in 1936, new Dodgers manager Burleigh Grimes released him in May 1937. Clark's won-lost record for his 11 seasons in Brooklyn was 106–88, with a 3.55 earned run average.

December 26, 1934: Traded Outfielder Johnny Frederick, Pitcher Art Herring, and Cash to the Sacramento Senators of the Pacific Coast League for Outfielder Frenchy Bordagaray

The Dodgers and the Sacramento Senators of the Pacific Coast League had recently signed a working agreement. Outfielder Stan "Frenchy" Bordagaray was Sacramento's best player and expectations that he was heading to Brooklyn had begun during baseball's winter meetings two weeks earlier. Bordagaray, a 25-year-old right-handed batter, had been a star with Sacramento for the past three seasons, hitting over .300 in each one. In a brief trial with the Chicago White Sox this past season, he batted .322 in 29 games.

"He's not a big fellow [he was 5'7"] but he has a lot of flash and color and plenty of the old confidence," said Jimmy Dykes, his manager with the White Sox. "He knows he can play ball. And the one thing I'll guarantee is that he can hit. Unlike most men who aren't near giants, he isn't a place-hitter. He tees off on everything and wallops bullets over the infield. His weakness is in the field. It isn't that he isn't fast. In fact, he's real fast. He can catch a ball too and has a good arm. He'll make a lot of great catches, but he'll also give you a heart attack now and then."[26]

"If Bordagary is only one-half as good as all the scouts say he is, then I think our left field problem will be solved," said business manager Bob Quinn. "We tried to get Pepper Martin, but the Cardinals refused to give him up. We made overtures for Wally Berger, too, and the Braves laughed at us. In taking Bordagaray, we considered his youth and speed. We could have had several National League outfielders, but they are ten-year men. Stengel wanted a youngster and we acted accordingly."[27]

When Johnny Frederick was a rookie in 1929, Wilbert Robinson put him in the leadoff spot, and Frederick was an immediate success. He batted .328, with a .372 on-base percentage, a .545 slugging average, 24 home runs, and among his 206 hits was a league-leading 52 doubles. (Frederick's 52 doubles are still the major league record for most ever by a rookie. It was also the Brooklyn/Los Angeles franchise record until broken by Freddie Freeman in 2023.) Frederick matched the 206 hits in his sophomore season, along with a .334 batting average, a .383 on-base percentage, and a .524 slugging average. He scored 120 runs, seven short of his rookie total.

No Brooklyn player had ever had such a successful first two seasons, but Frederick suffered a broken ankle late in the 1930 season, and it impeded the rest of his career. While he never matched his early totals over the next four seasons, he remained a major contributor to Brooklyn's offense. And to their defense, where he was the center fielder his first three seasons, before splitting his appearances between center and right in his last three.

Frederick's departure left only two Dodgers who had played under manager Robinson: pitcher Van Mungo and catcher Al Lopez. Frederick had a short but notable career with the Dodgers. He played 805 games in his six years with the club, batting .308 with 85 home runs and a 117 OPS+. He had six more successful seasons in the PCL, one with Sacramento and five with the Portland Beavers.

Pitcher Art Herring, 2–4 with a 6.20 ERA in his one season in Brooklyn, was sent to Sacramento as a part of the trade. The money going to the Senators was said to be $10,000.

Also in 1934:

Traded: Pitcher Howard Craghead to Seattle Indians of the Pacific Coast League for Pitcher Phil Page

Purchased: Pitcher Harry Smythe from New York Yankees

Sold: Pitcher Phil Page to Kansas City Blues of the American Association; Pitcher Charlie Perkins to Buffalo Bisons of the International League; Pitcher Harry Smythe to Montreal Royals of the International League; Pitcher Boom-Boom Beck to Mission (CA) Reds of the Pacific Coast League

Signed Free Agents: Pitcher Tom Zachary; First Baseman Johnny McCarthy

Released: Shortstop Glenn Wright; Outfielder Hack Wilson; Second Baseman Jake Flowers

CHAPTER TEN

1935–1939

1935

January 2, 1935: Purchased Catcher Babe Phelps from the Chicago Cubs on Waivers

Business manager Bob Quinn and manager Casey Stengel had pursued 27-year-old catcher Babe Phelps at the Louisville and New York winter meetings. The Cubs were unwilling to let him go, but Quinn and Stengel continued to ask and finally persuaded Cubs manager Charlie Grimm to make the deal. The acquisition of Phelps filled two needs with one player—a good backup catcher to Al Lopez and a reliable pinch-hitter.

Rookie Ray Berres, drafted from the Southern Association's Birmingham Barons in October 1933, had served as the backup to Lopez in 1934. Berres was adequate defensively, but a poor hitter. Appearing in 39 games, 37 as a catcher, he batted .215 with a minuscule OPS+ of 34. The previous month's trade of Johnny Frederick left Stengel without a powerful left-handed batter to come off the bench. Phelps, who stood 6'2" and weighed well over 200 pounds, was expected to fill both those roles. Stengel said he planned for Phelps to catch twice a week so as not to overwork Lopez.

Stengel remembered the left-handed-hitting Phelps's two-run pinch-hit home run in the top of the ninth inning of a 10–9 loss to the Cubs. That May 21 blast traveled more than 400 feet and was the longest home run hit at Ebbets Field in 1934. For the season, Phelps batted .286 with an OPS+ of 111 in 44 games as the backup to Gabby Hartnett.

May 15, 1935: Purchased Pitcher George Earnshaw from the Chicago White Sox

Bob Quinn, whose title was now general manager, announced that the Dodgers had paid the $7,500 waiver price to secure veteran pitcher George Earnshaw from the Chicago White Sox. The 6'4" righthander had a 1–2 record this season after winning 14 games for the last-place White Sox in 1934. Before that he spent six seasons with the Philadelphia Athletics and had a 67–28 record for the pennant-winning A's of 1929, 1930, and 1931. Earnshaw's overall record in Philadelphia was 98–58, with an ERA+ of 106. When economic hard times forced Connie Mack to break up the A's, Earnshaw was one of the first to go.

Despite the 35-year-old Earnshaw's a reputation for being a heavy eater and a heavy drinker, Quinn had hopes for his new acquisition. "If Earnshaw is in good physical condition, and I'm told he is, I look for him to be of help to the Brooklyn club," Quinn said.[1]

September 7, 1935: Traded Outfielder Glenn Chapman, and Cash to the Baltimore Orioles of the International League for Pitcher Max Butcher

The Dodgers were in Pittsburgh when they announced the acquisition of Max Butcher, a 6'2" right-hander, from the Baltimore Orioles of the International League. The 25-year-old Butcher had a 24–11 record and a 2.23 earned run average for the Galveston Buccaneers of the Texas League this season. (Baltimore had sent him to Galveston under an optional agreement.) Butcher was ordered to report to manager Casey Stengel next Spring.

In addition to cash, Brooklyn gave Baltimore outfielder Glenn Chapman, who batted .280 in 67 games for the Dodgers in 1934. Chapman split this past season between the Montreal Royals of the International League and the Sacramento Senators of the Pacific Coast League. He would continue to play in the minor leagues through 1946.

December 12, 1935: Traded Catcher Al Lopez, Second Baseman Tony Cuccinello, Pitcher Ray Benge, and Pitcher-Outfielder Bobby Reis to the Boston Bees for Pitcher Ed Brandt and Outfielder Randy Moore

There was no unanimity among Dodgers fans regarding this deal, which they viewed as a trade of catcher Al Lopez for pitcher Ed Brandt.

Chapter Ten: 1935–1939

Some thought Brooklyn came out on top; some thought it was Boston; and some thought it was an even swap. As it turned out, those who thought Boston got the better of it were correct.

Al Lopez had been Brooklyn's first-string catcher for the past six seasons. Lopez was an excellent defensive backstop and a solid hitter, batting .279 with 274 runs batted in as a Dodger. He finished in the top five in putouts among National League catchers five times, and in assists six times. He led the league assists in 1932 and 1933 and gathered Most Valuable Player votes in 1933 and 1934. Lopez would go on to play another 12 big league seasons before becoming a Hall of Fame manager.

But, according to Bill McCullough of the *Brooklyn Times Union*, there was an underlying reason for Brooklyn to trade Lopez. While the fans loved him, McCullough wrote, most of the players on the club disliked him. For one, they did not think he rated a $14,000 salary. For another, he had the club in disfavor with the umpires because of his baiting of them. Most importantly, the pitchers challenged his handling of them. Three of them asked manager Casey Stengel to use Babe Phelps, in his first season with the team, or old-timer Zack Taylor when they were the starting pitcher. One claimed he lost seven games in 1934 because Lopez overruled him and demanded another kind of pitch. McCullough concluded by saying "ball players are the most clannish individuals in the world. Seldom do they knock one of their own, even if he's on a rival club, without reason."[2]

Tony Cuccinello had been Brooklyn's starting second baseman since coming from Cincinnati four years earlier. He had a composite batting average of .271 and an above average OPS+ in three of the four seasons. (His OPS+ in 1934 was 100.) Cuccinello earned MVP votes in 1932 and was an All-Star in 1933. Stengel felt Cuccinello was expendable after the team acquired 25-year-old Vince Sherlock from the Indianapolis Indians of the American Association in September 1935. Sherlock had impressed Stengel by batting .462 in the nine games he played after arriving. But they would be the only nine major league game Sherlock would play. Before the start of the 1936 season, the Dodgers returned him to Indianapolis. Meanwhile, Cuccinello played another nine seasons in the big leagues. World War II kept his career alive, and in 1945, with the Chicago White Sox, he just missed winning the American League batting championship.

Two of the players going to Boston were no loss for Brooklyn. Ray Benge was a pitcher who had been around for ten seasons, the last three as a Dodgers' starter after arriving in a December 1932 trade with the Phillies. He had a 33–38 record with a 4.00 earned run average for Brooklyn, but his career was basically over. Bobby Reis was a part-time pitcher and part-time outfielder. He had not been good in either role for Brooklyn, or he would be for Boston.

Stengel made this trade to get Ed Brandt, a quality left-handed pitcher. In the four years from 1931 to 1934, Brandt won 68 games for not very good Boston teams. But in 1935, the Braves collapsed, losing 115 games, and Brandt won only 5 while losing 19.

The Dodgers thought getting Randy Moore was a bonus. In his six years with Boston, Moore had a .286 batting average with 287 runs batted in. His best season was 1933, when he batted .302 with 70 RBIs and an OPS+ of 120.

Overall, this was not a good deal for the Dodgers. While Cuccinello and Lopez went on to play for many more years, Brandt spent only one season with Brooklyn, and Randy Moore played only 55 games for the Dodgers.

Also in 1935:

Traded: First Baseman Dick Siebert, a Player to be Named, and Cash to Indianapolis Indians of the American Association for Pitcher Johnny Cooney and Second baseman Vince Sherlock

Purchased: Outfielder Buster Mills from St. Louis Cardinals; Outfielder Gene Moore from St. Louis Cardinals; Outfielder Ox Eckhardt from Mission (CA) Reds of Pacific Coast League

Signed Amateur Free Agent: Shortstop Rod Dedeaux

Signed Free Agents: Pitcher Dazzy Vance

1936

February 6, 1936: Traded Pitcher Johnny Babich and Outfielder Gene Moore to the Boston Bees for Pitcher Fred Frankhouse

Johnny Babich, for whom the Dodgers sent $33,000 and pitcher Ray Lucas to the Mission (CA) Reds of the Pacific Coast League in July 1934, never lived up to the promise he had shown in the PCL. Babich won seven games in each of his two seasons as a Dodger, with 11 losses in 1934 and 14 in 1935. His earned run averages for the two seasons were 4.20 and 6.66. "[Bees] manager Bill McKechnie thinks maybe he can do something with Babich and good luck to him. Most of the boys locally are tired of watching him get his ears knocked off by line drives" wrote Tommy Holmes of the *Brooklyn Eagle*.[3]

"I strung along with Babich, whom the club bought for $30,000 [sic] three years ago, for two seasons and Johnny showed no signs of improving," said manager Casey Stengel. "Of course, he's only a young man and he may show me up this summer. But Babich pitched only 12 complete games in two years and the fact that I could never really count on him prompted me to part with him when I saw the chance to get Frankhouse."[4]

Bob Quinn was Brooklyn's GM when the club purchased minor-league outfielder Gene Moore from the St. Louis Cardinals in September 1935. Moore never played a game for the Dodgers, but Quinn, now the president of the Bees, insisted that before he would let Fred Frankhouse go Moore had to be part of the deal.

Frankhouse, a 32-year-old right-hander, had one of the best curve balls in the game. He was 17–8 in four years with the Cardinals before being traded to Boston for Burleigh Grimes in June 1930. Moved from the bullpen to a starting role in 1933, Frankhouse was a 16-game winner that year and a 17-game winner with a 118 ERA+ in 1934. Stengel believed the addition of Frankhouse gave him a pitching staff equal to any in the National League.

February 20, 1936: Sold First Baseman Sam Leslie to the New York Giants

In conjunction with adding minor league first baseman Buddy Hassett from the Yankees, the Dodgers were disposing of first baseman Sam Leslie. They had acquired Leslie from the New York Giants in June 1933, in a trade that sent outfielder Lefty O'Doul and pitcher Watty Clark to New York. The Giants sold Clark back to Brooklyn a year later, and now the Dodgers were selling Leslie back to New York

In 1934, Leslie's first full season with Brooklyn, he batted .322 with 102 runs batted in and an OPS+ of 136. He had another good season in 1935, batting .308 with 93 runs batted in and an OPS+ of 117. But Casey Stengel was dissatisfied with Leslie's defense at first base and thought newly acquired Buddy Hassett would be a big improvement. The reported price of the sale was $25,000.

February 20, 1936: Traded First Baseman Johnny McCarthy, Outfielder Buzz Boyle, and Cash to the New York Yankees for First Baseman Buddy Hassett

The Dodgers used the reported $25,000 they got from the sale of Sam Leslie, added another reported $15,000 and packaged it with two players to add first baseman Buddy Hassett to their roster. Hassett was one of the two standout left-handed-hitting first basemen in the minor leagues in 1935; the other was the more publicized Johnny Mize. Casey Stengel may have been more interested in Mize, but the St. Louis Cardinals would not let Mize go and would bring him to St. Louis this season.

Hassett, 24, was a native New Yorker who had played successfully for three years in the Yankees farm system. But with Lou Gehrig playing first base for the parent club, Hassett realized he had no future with the Yankees and asked to be traded. Stengel was pleased with getting him, predicting he would be a valuable man for many years to come, and Hassett was excited about getting a chance in the big leagues.

The two players leaving Brooklyn, Buzz Boyle and Johnny McCarthy, did not fit into Stengel's plans for the 1936 season. "Boyle is a good, aggressive outfielder, but is not a strong enough hitter," wrote columnist Lou Niss, "while McCarthy is a fancy Dan around first base, but his stick work failed to improve enough to make him a major leaguer."[5]

July 15, 1936: Traded Pitcher George Earnshaw to the St. Louis Cardinals for Outfielder Eddie Morgan

This deal was made possible by the St. Louis Cardinals need for a healthy pitcher and the decision by all the clubs in the National League to allow George Earnshaw to pass through waivers. With Dizzy Dean, Paul Dean, and Roy Parmelee nursing injuries, the Cardinals were fortunate to get a battle-tested veteran like Earnshaw, as they battled the Giants and Pirates for first place.

Earnshaw had an 8–12 record for the 1935 Dodgers after coming over from the White Sox in May. He was 4–9 this season but would likely do better with the pennant-contending Cardinals. At age 36, he did not figure prominently in Brooklyn's future. His departure would allow manager Stengel to give more work to three of his younger pitchers: Tom Baker, Max Butcher, and George Jeffcoat.

Coming to Brooklyn in the trade was Eddie Morgan, a 21-year-old left-handed-hitting outfielder—but not until 1937. Morgan, who played eight games for St. Louis early in the 1936 season, would spend the rest of the season with the Columbus (OH) Red Birds of the American Association.

August 1, 1936: Purchased Outfielder Tom Winsett from the St. Louis Cardinals

Tom Winsett was a 6'2" left-handed-hitting outfielder with a terrific batting record in the minor leagues but had failed in brief stays with the Boston Red Sox. The St. Louis Cardinals picked him up in 1934, and Winsett batted .356 with 21 home runs for their International League team, the Rochester Red Wings. Winsett began the 1935 season with the Cardinals, but they were loaded with good outfielders and after 15 games they sent him to their Columbus (OH) Red Birds team in the American Association, where he batted .348 with 20 home runs. Winsett was back with Columbus in 1936, where he led the league in batting (.355), home runs (50), runs batted in (154), and runs scored (144). The Dodgers paid a reported $25,000 for Winsett, who would report to them after the American Association season ended. Scout Chick Fraser had followed Winsett and predicted success in Brooklyn for the 26-year-old slugger.

"Winsett hits the ball a mile," Fraser said. "I have seen him drive as far as Babe Ruth ever did. I am not hailing him as another Ruth, but I will say that no man in baseball today, not even Lou Gehrig, can hit a ball as far as Winsett. He is a pull hitter and that right-field fence at Ebbets Field and around the National League in general, will be a set up for his style."

Fraser also addressed Winsett's reputation for lack of ambition and indifference to his craft. "Don't think for a minute Winsett is a clown in the field. Winsett is taking baseball seriously, now. I had a long talk with him the day Brooklyn bought him, and he said, among other things, that when he goes into the big league this time he is going to stay."[6]

But Winsett proved again to be one of those players who could do well against minor league pitchers but not against major league pitchers. He was the team's primary left fielder in 1937, but batted .237, with five home runs and 42 runs batted in. On May 2, 1938, the Dodgers sold him to the New York Giants, who sent him to their Jersey City farm team, ending Winsett's big league career.

The Dodgers acquisition of Winsett, originally announced as a straight cash purchase, was completed on December 3 with the transfer of three Brooklyn players to the Cardinals. The press had suspected all along that the Cardinals would receive players after the season. On December 3, business manager John Gorman made public the names of the three players: outfielder Frenchy Bordagaray, pitcher Dutch Leonard, and infielder Jimmy Jordan.

Several National League clubs were interested in Bordagaray, who batted .282 and .315 in his two seasons with the Dodgers and was thought to be the best of the three. He would return to the Dodgers during World War II.

Leonard came to Brooklyn in 1933. He won 14 games in 1934, and though he had a 2–9 record in 1935, his eight saves that season led the National League. He would spend 1937 in the minor leagues, but was back in the major leagues in 1938, where he would remain until 1953.

For Jordan, who batted .257 in his four seasons in Brooklyn, 1936 was his final one in the big leagues.

September 29, 1936: Drafted Pitcher Luke Hamlin from the Detroit Tigers

At the annual draft of minor league players, the Dodgers selected 32-year-old Luke Hamlin, a 6'2" right-handed pitcher. Hamlin spent six seasons in the minor leagues before pitching briefly for the Detroit Tigers in 1933 and 1934, splitting six decisions. For the past two seasons he had been with the Milwaukee Brewers of the American Association, where he was a 19-game winner in 1936.

December 4, 1936: Traded Pitcher Ed Brandt to the Pittsburgh Pirates for Second Baseman Harry Lavagetto and Pitcher Ralph Birkofer

One year earlier, the Dodgers had given up Al Lopez and Tony Cuccinello to get left-hander Ed Brandt from the Boston Bees. Manager Casey Stengel thought Brandt would be a significant addition to his pitching staff, but Brandt spent only one season with Brooklyn, in which he won 11 games. Newly named Dodgers manager Burleigh Grimes was reluctant to part with Brandt, but Pirates manager Pie Traynor insisted there would be no deal without Brandt.

Left-hander Ralph Birkofer won 31 and lost 26 with a league average ERA in his four years in Pittsburgh. "This fellow Birkofer is a better pitcher than he has shown," said Grimes. "The fellow needs to be put in shape and given lots of work."[7]

But Birkofer was not a better pitcher than he had shown. He was 0–2 for the 1937 Dodgers when they traded him to the Detroit Tigers for shortstop Lindsay Brown in July. It was the end of Birkofer's major league career. Brown batted .270 in 48 games for Brooklyn in the second half of the season, the only 48 games of his big-league career.

Harry "Cookie" Lavagetto, began his career in 1933 as a 20-year-old second baseman for the Oakland Oaks of the Pacific Coast League. He batted .312 and was signed by the Pittsburgh Pirates, for whom he had been a part-time second baseman for the past three seasons. His combined .249 batting average and 75 OPS+ disappointed the Pirates, and they had made him available. Grimes expected he would do better with the Dodgers. "Lavagetto is a player of much promise," he said. "And in Brooklyn, where he'll be a regular, I think he'll find himself."[8]

Unlike his prediction about Birkofer, Grimes was correct about Lavagetto. After playing mostly at second base in 1937, he moved to third base in 1938, where he remained for the rest of his career. He was selected to the National League's All-Star team from 1938 through 1941 and appeared in the voting for the league's Most Valuable Player Award in 1939 and 1941.

When the war broke out, Lavagetto enlisted in the navy, where he spent the next four years. He returned in 1946 and shared third base with several others but was replaced in 1947 by rookie Spider Jorgensen. Lavagetto played against the Yankees in two World Series (1941 and 1947) and in 1947's Game Four had the most famous pinch-hit in World Series history. He pinch-hit in a similar situation the next day but struck out. It was Lavagetto's final major league at-bat. He returned to Oakland in 1948 and had three more productive seasons with the Pacific Coast League Oaks.

December 4, 1936: Traded Shortstop Lonny Frey to the Chicago Cubs for Shortstop Woody English and Pitcher Roy Henshaw

The same day the Dodgers traded with Pittsburgh for second baseman Harry Lavagetto, they traded their shortstop, Lonny Frey, to Chicago to get the Cubs' shortstop, Woody English. The Cubs tossed in pitcher Roy Henshaw to secure Frey.

"The Brooklyn club's immediate need was a shortstop and second baseman, and I think the club will be strong in those spots next year," said manager Burleigh Grimes. "English is only 30 and not through as a headliner."[9]

English, who had been with the Cubs since 1927, had his best years in 1930 and 1931. He batted .335 and .319 with OPS+ of 125 and 115. They were the only season his OPS+ was above the league average. English finished fourth in MVP voting in 1931 but was no longer the player he had been five years earlier. He batted .238 for the 1937 Dodgers and was sold on waivers to the Cincinnati Reds in July 1938, shortly after playing his final major league game on July 1.

Why manager Grimes thought he was upgrading the shortstop position is difficult to discern. The left-handed-hitting Frey was only 26 and had batted .279 in 1936. His OPS+ of 99 that season was the only one below 100 he had in his four seasons with the Dodgers. His combined OPS+ with Brooklyn was 108, and his combined batting average was .278. Frey would play in the major leagues until 1948 but missed the 1944 and 1945 seasons serving in the army.

Roy Henshaw was a 25-year-old left-hander with a 21–11 record and a 106 ERA+ in three seasons with the Cubs. He was listed at 5'8" and 155 pounds, leading Grimes to predict he would be a better pitcher in 1937 because he was getting heavier.

Also in 1936:

Traded: Outfielder Ox Eckhardt to Indianapolis Indians of the American Association to complete 1935 trade in which First Baseman Dick Siebert and Cash went to Indianapolis for Pitcher Johnny Cooney and Second baseman Vince Sherlock

Purchased: Outfielder George Watkins from Philadelphia Phillies; Infielder Jack Radtke from Dayton (OH) Ducks of the Middle Atlantic League; Infielder Tom Malinosky from Pittsburgh Pirates

Sold: Catcher Wally Millies to Washington Senators; Outfielder Danny Taylor to Indianapolis Indians of the American Association

Signed Amateur Free Agents: Outfielder Bert Haas

Signed Free Agents: Outfielder Heinie Manush; Shortstop Ben Geraghty; Outfielder Freddie Lindstrom

Released: Pitcher Tom Zachary

1937

For the 1937 season, Burleigh Grimes replaced Casey Stengel as manager.

June 11, 1937: Traded Pitcher Tom Baker to the New York Giants for Pitcher Fred Fitzsimmons

In a classic youth-for-experience trade, the Dodgers sent 24-year-old right-hander Tom Baker to the New York Giants for 35-year-old right-hander Fred Fitzsimmons. Manager Burleigh Grimes replied to questions about parting with a young, promising pitcher for a veteran who was nearing the end of a brilliant and colorful career.

"With an experienced pitcher to round out our staff, I think we have a good chance of finishing in the first division" Grimes explained. "Baker, while promising, never came up to expectations. He is a strong young kid with possibilities, and he may develop later. Right now, however, he has been of little value to our club."[10]

Baker's record with the Dodgers had been a far from impressive 2–9. In 1936 he won only one game while losing eight. He was 0–1 this season with an 8.64 earned run average. Giants manager Bill Terry liked Baker for his ability to throw hard and felt he may yet come around and was worth a try. Baker was 1–0 in 15 games over parts of two seasons with Giants.

Meanwhile, Grimes felt Fitzsimmons would be a big benefit to his pitching staff. "I have been after an experienced pitcher for some time," he said. "And I got one in Fitzsimmons. I can depend on him. That I know. I will be able to start him in games and also use him as relief hurler. With the warm weather coming on, Freddie should hit his stride. Anyway, remember, with Fitz on our side now, we can't lose any more games to him." (Fitzsimmons had a 33–15 record against the Dodgers.)[11]

Fitzsimmons, whose best pitch was a "knuckle curve," had been the longest tenured Giant, having broken in under John McGraw in 1925. He had a 170–114 record and had 10 seasons of double-digit wins, including a 20-win season in 1928. In addition, he was an excellent fielding pitcher.

Grimes was correct in predicting what Fitzsimmons would bring to the Dodgers, but he was gone by 1940 when Fitzsimmons had his best season as a Dodger. His 16–2 record gave him a league-best .888 winning percentage, and he finished fifth in voting for the Most Valuable Player.

Fitzsimmons had a 6–1 record in the Dodgers pennant-winning year in 1941. He was pitching a shutout against the Yankees in Game Three of the World Series when a seventh-inning line drive by Yankees pitcher Marius Russo broke his kneecap. The Dodgers eventually lost, 2–1. Fitzsimmons won 47 and lost 32 with a 116 ERA+ in his seven seasons as a Dodger. The club released him in July 1943 so he could accept a job as manager of the Philadelphia Phillies.

August 6, 1937: Purchased Second Baseman Pete Coscarart from the Portland Beavers of the Pacific Coast League

Second baseman Harry Lavagetto was doing well in his first season with Brooklyn, so it came as a surprise when the club purchased second baseman Pete Coscarart from the Portland Beavers of the Pacific Coast League. Burleigh Grimes explained that reports on Coscarart were too favorable to ignore. The club gladly paid a reported $23,000 to get him and even included a catcher from their Knoxville farm team. Grimes said the 24-year-old Coscarart was batting over .300 (he would finish the season at .254) and his sensational fielding had been the talk of the league.

"We are out to secure players of class no matter what position they play," he said. "The team needs a lot of building up and wherever our scouts see a player who holds forth promise of being a real big-league star we are going to grab them. The reports on Coscarart were so glowing that we did not hesitate a minute in going through with the deal for him. You cannot have too many good men for any one position."[12]

September 10, 1937: Purchased Pitcher Tot Pressnell from the Cleveland Indians

Among several pitchers the Dodgers purchased this day was Forest "Tot" Pressnell a 31-year-old right-hander with the Milwaukee Brewers of the American Association. A year earlier they had purchased pitcher Luke Hamlin from Milwaukee, which was then a Detroit Tigers farm club but was now affiliated with the Cleveland Indians. Hamlin had been a success so far, and the Dodgers were hoping that Pressnell would yield a similar result.

Pressnell had eight seasons of minor league experience, with a record of 107–87, including six seasons of double-digit wins. He had been with the Brewers the last five seasons, winning 71 and losing 56. Pressnell won 11 games for Brooklyn in 1938, nine the following year, and six in 1940, with an ERA+ above 100 each season. He was sold to the St. Louis Cardinals in November 1940, having finished his three years in Brooklyn with a 26–26 record and a 3.76 earned run average. A month later the Cincinnati Reds purchased Pressnell from St. Louis, and two months after that the Chicago Cubs purchased him from Cincinnati.

October 4, 1937: Traded Pitcher Roy Henshaw, Third Baseman Joe Stripp, Infielder Jim Bucher, and Outfielder Johnny Cooney to the St. Louis Cardinals for Shortstop Leo Durocher

The initial reaction in Brooklyn to this trade was that the Dodgers had given up too much to get the weak-hitting Leo Durocher. Manager Burleigh Grimes disagreed. He now had a capable shortstop, he said, something he did not have this past season.

"While some baseball men disagree, I believe we gained by the deal," Grimes said. "I've finally gotten myself a real shortstop. The trade may look one-sided because of the four-for-one transaction, but I'm perfectly satisfied."[13]

"That Durocher was ticketed for departure from the Cards, was evident when the Cardinals reappointed Frankie Frisch manager for 1938," wrote Martin J. Haley of the *St. Louis Globe Democrat*. "Durocher at one time was reported in line to take Frisch's job as the team's manager. That did not set well with Frisch, so the word went around that if he stayed Durocher would leave."[14]

Durocher had been a fulltime major league shortstop since 1928, first with the Yankees, then the Cincinnati Reds, and for the past four seasons the Cardinals. He was the Cardinals' team captain and the sparkplug of the famed St. Louis Gashouse Gang. Durocher was never known for his hitting—he was coming off a .203 season—but Grimes thought because he was only 32, he had a few good seasons left. He did. Durocher was an All-Star in 1938 and finished eighth in MVP voting in 1939, as Brooklyn's player-manager.

President Larry MacPhail had appointed him team captain in 1938 and promoted him to manager in 1939. Durocher yielded the shortstop position to Pee Wee Reese in 1940, but continued as manager, and in 1941 led the Dodgers to their first pennant in 21 years. He managed the Dodgers through the 1946 season, was suspended in 1947, and returned for half a season in 1948.

As for the four men the Dodgers gave up, two, Roy Henshaw and Jim Bucher, were youngsters. Henshaw had won five games for the Dodgers (5–12) in 1937, his only season with them, and Bucher had not lived up to his earlier promise. After batting .302 in 1935, he had barely been above .250 the past two seasons.

At one time Joe Stripp was considered among the best third basemen in baseball, but he was now 34 years old and coming off the first season since 1929 that he failed to play in 100 games. It also had been his worst season as a batter since 1922, hitting only .243 in 90 games.

Johnny Cooney, 36, played two plus seasons in Brooklyn. He batted .282 in 130 games in 1936 and .293 in 120 games in 1937, but his OPS+ for those years were a dismal 74 and 85. The Cardinals released him before he ever played a game for them, whereupon Cooney signed as a free agent with the Boston Braves, the team he had played for from 1921 to 1930.

Also in 1937:
Traded: Outfielder Randy Moore to St. Louis Cardinals for Catcher Paul Chervinko; Pitcher Ralph Birkofer to Detroit Tigers for Shortstop Lindsay Brown and Cash; Third Baseman Frank Skaff to Washington Senators for First Baseman Jake Daniel; Shortstop Ben Geraghty and Infielder Jack Radtke to Washington Senators for Shortstop Fred Chapman; Catcher Ray Berres and Cash to Louisville Colonels of American Association for Outfielder Gibby Brack

Purchased: Pitcher Waite Hoyt from Pittsburgh Pirates; Catcher Roy Spencer from New York Giants; Pitcher Ben Cantwell from New York Giants; Pitcher Bill Posedel from Portland Beavers of the Pacific Coast League

Sold: Pitcher Ben Cantwell to Pittsburgh Pirates

Signed Amateur Free Agents: Pitcher Sam Nahem

Signed Free Agents: Pitcher Jim Lindsey

Released: Pitcher Watty Clark; Outfielder Freddie Lindstrom; Outfielder George Watkins

Granted Free Agency: Pitcher Harry Eisenstat

1938

In 1938, Steve McKeever died. His daughter, Dearie, and her husband James Mulvey inherited his 25 percent interest. Mulvey led a move for a new president and general manager, settling on Larry MacPhail.

March 6, 1938: Traded Outfielder Eddie Morgan and Cash to the Philadelphia Phillies for First Baseman Dolph Camilli

When new president Larry MacPhail arrived in 1938, he began immediately to revitalize the franchise. He began by spending hundreds of thousands of dollars provided by the Brooklyn Trust Company, owner of 51 percent of the team, to refurbish Ebbets Field. The Dodgers' 25-year-old ballpark had deteriorated over the years and become an unappealing place for fans to visit. On the field, he began bringing in players that would turn the Dodgers from perennial also-rans into a pennant contender.

MacPhail's first big move came during spring training when he acquired slugging first baseman Dolph Camilli from the Philadelphia Phillies. Manager Burleigh Grimes had been asking the club to get him a slugger, as the Dodgers had not had a legitimate long ball hitter since trading Babe Herman in 1932. In the left-handed hitting Camilli, who batted .339 with 27 home runs in 1937, Grimes finally got his man. Camilli also led the league in on-base percentage in 1937, and his .587 slugging percentage ranked third behind the Cardinals' Joe Medwick and Johnny Mize.

The 31-year-old Camilli hit 92 home runs over the past four seasons with the Phillies. His 27 home runs in 1937 were only ten fewer than those hit by the entire Brooklyn team. Nevertheless, the Phillies finished seventh and Camilli, who earned $11,500 last season, was asking for $15,000 this season. Getting rid of him at a very good return was something the Phillies could not pass up. In addition to Eddie Morgan, a player with just 66 at-bats in his major league career, which was now over, the Dodgers sent Philadelphia $45,000. That sum was thought to be the most the Brooklyn club had ever paid for a player. (Other estimates ranged as high as $75,000.)

April 15, 1938: Purchased Outfielder Ernie Koy from the New York Yankees

The Dodgers played their final spring training series with three games against the Yankees in New York. During the first game, played at Ebbets Field, the club announced they had purchased minor league outfielder Ernie Koy from the Yankees for $15,000.

Koy had been an All-America fullback and a track star at the University of Texas, who upon graduation was signed by Yankees scout Eddie Herr. The six-foot, 200-pound Koy combined power and speed, but had been buried in New York's farm system for five years. A right-handed batter, he was said to have a weakness against a good right-hander's curve.

Four days later, on Opening Day at Philadelphia, Koy made his Dodgers debut a memorable one. He hit a home run off left-hander

Wayne LaMaster in his first major league at-bat and had three hits in a 12–5 win.

April 15, 1938; Signed Free Agent Shortstop Pete Reiser

The St. Louis Cardinals signed hometown boy Pete Reiser when he was 15 years old. Three years later, in 1937, Reiser began his professional career, batting .285 for the Newport (AR) Cardinals of the Northeast Arkansas League. After the season, Commissioner Kenesaw Landis discovered the Cardinals farm system, under president Branch Rickey, controlled so many young players that it went against the best interests of baseball and freed seventy-two of them.

One was Reiser, who signed with Larry MacPhail's Dodgers for $100, a deal Rickey silently and illegally arranged. As part of the arrangement, MacPhail would keep Reiser in the Dodgers minor league system for a few years and then trade him back to St. Louis. But Reiser's play in the minors and his sensational showing at spring training in 1939, made it unfeasible for MacPhail to trade him.

Observing Reiser that spring, Tommy Holmes wrote this about him. "Nobody is talking about anything else than Harold (Pete) Reiser, the most spectacular Class D kid ever to bust unexpectedly into a big-league training camp."[15] Reiser had spent the 1938 season with the Superior (WI) Blues of the Class D Northern League.

May 20, 1938: Purchased Pitcher Vito Tamulis from the St. Louis Browns

The Dodgers filled their need for a left-handed starter with the waiver purchase of 26-year-old Vito Tamulis from the St. Louis Browns. Tamulis began his career in 1930 when he signed with the New York Yankees out of high school. After working his way through the Yankees farm system, he reached New York late in the 1934 season. He earned the call-up after going 13–7 with a 2.74 earned run average for the International League's Newark Bears.

In 1935, his rookie season, Tamulis had a 10–5 record, including three shutouts, but that winter he came down with pleurisy and missed the first half of the 1936 season. Tamulis won seven and lost five for Newark in the second half and then went 18–6 for the league-champion Bears in 1937. The Yankees traded him to the Browns in December 1937.

Before his sale to Brooklyn, Tamulis made two starts for the Browns, lost both and lost a game in relief of Bobo Newsom.

July 11, 1938: Purchased Pitcher Whit Wyatt from the Milwaukee Brewers of the American Association

John McDonald, Brooklyn's road secretary, announced the club's purchase of 30-year-old right-hander Whit Wyatt, from the American Association's Milwaukee Brewers. "We gave Milwaukee $20,000 in cash [pitcher] Buck Marrow [two days earlier], and a player to be named later for Wyatt," McDonald said. "Several clubs were after him, but we outbid them."[16] Brooklyn wanted Wyatt for immediate delivery, but Milwaukee was fighting for the pennant and would keep him for the rest of the season.

Wyatt had nine years of major league experience, all in the American League: Detroit (1929–1933), Chicago (1933–1936), and Cleveland (1937). He had a combined record of 26 wins and 43 losses, including a 2–3 record with the 1937 Indians. With no room for him in 1938, Cleveland sent him to Milwaukee, a team with which they had a working agreement.

Wyatt lost his first three decisions with the Brewers, but won 12 of his next 14, with six shutouts. The addition of a changeup to go with an excellent fastball made Wyatt a much-improved pitcher. Remaining with the Brewers for all of 1938, he won the pitching Triple Crown, leading in wins (23), ERA (2.37), and strikeouts (208). He also led in complete games (26), shutouts (9), and innings pitched (254).

"I think Wyatt will prove a good pitcher for Brooklyn" Tom Sheehan who scouted him for the Dodgers said. "When he was in the American League, he had a sore arm and could never do himself justice. His arm is like whipcord today."[17]

October 4, 1938: Drafted Pitcher Hugh Casey from the Memphis Chicks of the Southern Association

Late in the 1932 season, 18-year-old Hugh Casey signed to play for his hometown team, the Atlanta Crackers of the Class A Southern Association. "I worked the 1932 season with them but never won a game," he recalled years later. "I lost three. Just a kid."[18] Pitching for the Class B

Charlotte Hornets of the Piedmont League in 1933, Casey won 19 games (19–9). That earned him a return to Atlanta, whose new president was Wilbert Robinson. The former Dodgers manager had taken a liking to Casey several years earlier. Casey was the kind of pitcher Robinson prized, big (6'1" and weighing more than 200 pounds), hard throwing, and mean and ornery on the mound.

The Chicago Cubs drafted Casey for the 1935 season; he spent the whole year with them, but manager Charlie Grimm used him in just 13 games, all out of the bullpen and mostly in non-crucial situations. It was back to the minor leagues in 1936, where Casey remained for the next three seasons, as a starter. An arm injury suffered while with the 1936 Los Angeles Angels, slowed down his fastball and forced him to come up with a new pitch, which was probably a spitball.

With his arm problems healed, Casey led the Southern Association with a 2.56 earned run average in 1937 as a member of the Birmingham Barons. The Dodgers selected him in the 1938 minor league draft following a 13–14 season with the Memphis Chicks. Casey was the third of the seventeen players chosen in the draft. Several of those drafted never made it to the big leagues. Among those that did, Casey, by far, had the most successful career.

"He has a head on him—and he has heart," said new manager Leo Durocher at training camp in 1939. "You won't see him flinch in a jam."[19] Although he did not make his first start until Memorial Day, Casey had an excellent first season, a 15–10 record, a 2.93 earned run average, and a 139 ERA+. He started 25 of the 40 games in which he appeared, and Durocher continued using him as a starter and a reliever in 1940 and 1941. But by the second half of the 1941 season, Casey was pitching almost always out of the bullpen. He pitched three time in relief in the World Series against the Yankees, with two losses, including the infamous "Mickey Owen game."

In 1942 Casey was a fulltime relief pitcher, starting in only two of his 50 appearances. His ERA that year was 2.25, and he led the National League with 13 saves. After three years in the navy, Casey returned in 1946, and for the next two seasons he solidified his reputation as the NL's best reliever. In the 1947 World Series, again against the Yankees, Casey set a major league record (since broken) by appearing in six of the seven games. He had a 2–0 record and an 0.87 earned run average.

The following spring, Casey reported to camp more overweight than usual, and he was drinking heavily. During that 1948 season, he missed two months after falling down a flight of stairs, and he also had an auto accident. He had pitched only 36 innings all season when the Dodgers released him on September 29. In his six years with Brooklyn,

Casey won 70, lost 41, with 49 saves and a 3.34 ERA. He had been the National League's best reliever during the 1940s and a memorable presence in two World Series against the Yankees.

December 13, 1938: Traded First Baseman Buddy Hassett and Outfielder Jimmy Outlaw to the Boston Bees for Outfielder Gene Moore and Pitcher Ira Hutchinson

Dodgers president Larry MacPhail made three deals this day at the winter meetings held at New York's Waldorf Astoria hotel. The first was a trade with the St. Louis Cardinals to get outfielder Jimmy Outlaw for use as part of the second trade. The Dodgers sent pitcher Lew Krausse from their Elmira, New York, farm team and $7,500 to St. Louis for Outlaw. They then traded Outlaw with first baseman Buddy Hassett to the Boston Bees for outfielder Gene Moore and pitcher Ira Hutchinson. Former Dodgers manager Burleigh Grimes thought his ex-club had gotten the better of the trade. "Moore and Hutchinson will be regulars in Brooklyn, while Hassett has to beat out Elbie Fletcher for the first base job," he said.[20]

Hassett spent three years with the Dodgers. He did well as a batter—a .304 average—but did not supply the power expected of a first baseman—a combined four home runs and 175 runs batted in. Hassett was the Dodgers first baseman in 1936 and 1937, but with the addition of slugging first baseman Dolph Camilli in 1938, they moved Hassett to the outfield. Going to Boston was perceived as a positive move for him, as he would be reunited with Bees manager Casey Stengel, who was his friend and who managed him in his first season in Brooklyn.

This past season, his second with Boston, Ira Hutchinson was 9–8 with a 2.74 earned run average. He had a 5–2 record and a 4.34 ERA with Brooklyn in 1939. The Dodgers sent him to the Montreal Royals in 1940, where he had a 1–7 record before being sold to the Cardinals in June.

Twenty-nine-year-old Gene Moore, a left-handed power hitter and outstanding defensive outfielder, was the player the Dodgers were after in this deal. Moore batted .290 in 151 games for Boston in 1936, with 38 doubles, 12 triples, and 13 home runs. He was even better in 1937, a .283 average in 148 games, with 29 doubles, 10 triples, and 16 home runs. An injured knee limited him to 54 games in 1938. However, MacPhail said Brooklyn scout Ted McGrew had gone to Texas to check on Moore and reported that his knee had healed, and he was in shape to play. Moore batted .225 for the 1939 Dodgers and was sold back to Boston on May 29, 1940.

December 13, 1938: Traded Pitcher Fred Frankhouse to the Boston Bees for Third Baseman Joe Stripp

When Larry MacPhail obtained Ira Hutchinson from the Boston Bees earlier in the day, it increased the already large number of pitchers on Brooklyn's reserve list. MacPhail had been planning to give Fred Frankhouse his unconditional release. But when he spotted Bob Quinn, the president of the Bees with whom he made the earlier trade, he said: "What will you give me for Frankhouse, Bob?" "I'll give you Stripp," said Quinn. "It's a trade," said MacPhail.[21]

Frankhouse was not the pitcher in Brooklyn he had been in Boston. In his three seasons with the Dodgers, he had a 26–28 record with a 3.94 earned run average. The Bees felt he would regain his old form by returning to Braves Field, where the dimensions were more favorable to pitchers than at Ebbets Field. The 35-year-old Frankhouse appeared in 23 games with the Bees in 1939, all in relief, losing his only two decisions. Boston released him in January 1940, ending his major league career.

For Joe Stripp, also 35, his professional career ended when the Dodgers released him in February 1939.

Also in 1938:

Traded: Catcher Paul Chervinko, Outfielder Art Parks, and Cash to Montreal Royals of International League for Catcher Gilly Campbell; Minor League Outfielder Willie Duke and Cash to Cleveland Indians for Catcher Greek George; Pitcher Johnnie Chambers to Boston Red Sox for Pitcher Lee Rogers; Player to be Named and Cash to Washington Senators for Outfielder Fred Sington; Outfielder Gibby Brack to Philadelphia Phillies for Outfielder Tuck Stainback

Purchased: Pitcher Wayne LaMaster from Philadelphia Phillies; Pitcher Jim Winford from St. Louis Cardinals; Catcher Ray Hayworth from Detroit Tigers; Third Baseman Don Ross from Detroit Tigers; Pitcher Johnnie Ray from St. Louis Cardinals

Sold: Outfielder Heinie Manush to Pittsburgh Pirates; Pitcher Max Butcher to Philadelphia Phillies: Shortstop Woody English to Cincinnati Reds; Outfielder Tom Winsett to New York Giants; Catcher Buck Marrow to Cleveland Indians; Catcher Gilly Campbell to Seattle Rainiers of the Pacific Coast League

Signed Free Agents: Outfielder Kiki Cuyler; Second Baseman Tony Lazzeri; Pitcher Dykes Potter; Catcher Ray Thomas; Catcher Merv Shea
Chosen in Major League Draft: Pitcher Red Evans
Released: Pitcher Waite Hoyt; Pitcher Jim Lindsey Third Baseman Nick Polly; Catcher Roy Spencer; Catcher Merv Shea

1939

For the 1939 season, Leo Durocher replaced Burleigh Grimes as manager.

July 18, 1939: Traded Three Players, Cash, and Two Players to be Named to the Boston Red Sox for Shortstop Pee Wee Reese

As a 19-year-old with the Louisville Colonels in 1938, Harold "Pee Wee" Reese, gained recognition as the best shortstop in the American Association and one of the best prospects in all the minor leagues. Tom Yawkey, the owner of the Boston Red Sox, purchased an interest in the Louisville Club in part to assure that Reese eventually would be Boston's next shortstop. At the time, the Red Sox had All-Star Joe Cronin as their shortstop. The 32-year-old Cronin was also their manager.

Many clubs were after Reese, however Brooklyn's Larry MacPhail, who was in Kansas City to see him compete in the American Association's All-Star game, was able to make the deal. MacPhail called Reese the most instinctive base runner he had ever seen. He had sent scouts Ted McGrew and Andy Hight to watch the young shortstop; both turned in glowing reports. At the time of his trade to Brooklyn, the 5'10" Reese was batting .278 and had stolen 25 bases. MacPhail agreed to leave him in Louisville for the remainder of the 1939 season and have him report to the Dodgers in 1940.

Reese had hoped to go to Boston and was disappointed at going to Brooklyn, a team that had finished in the second division for years. He would later call being sold to the Dodgers the best thing that ever happened to him in baseball. Described as "the most popular player ever to wear a Louisville uniform," he would earn a similar distinction with Brooklyn.[22]

When a reporter asked Donie Bush to describe Reese as a fielder, he replied: "There isn't anything to describe," said Bush, a former big-league shortstop and manager for 30 years. "He simply races over to a ground ball, picks it up and gets it away as fast as Durocher ever did. He has sure hands, great instinct, and the finest throwing arm I've ever seen. In fact, this kid is the greatest shortstop I've ever seen."[23]

This turned out to be one of the best purchases the Dodgers ever made. Pee Wee Reese starred for them beginning in Brooklyn in 1940 and ending in Los Angeles in 1958. (He missed the 1943–1945 seasons while serving in the navy.) He was the captain and the team leader for most of that time. Reese was also the longest-serving member of the team to make the move to California. He was an outstanding defensive shortstop, and paired with second basemen Billy Herman, Eddie Stanky, Jackie Robinson, and Jim Gilliam to give the Dodgers a consistently strong double play combination.

Reese retired after the 1958 season. He is the club's all-time leader in runs and walks, and in the top ten in games (3), at-bats (2), hits (2), runs batted in (7), doubles (4), triples (8), extra-base hits (8) total bases (5), and stolen bases (10). Reese was inducted into the Hall of Fame in 1984. "He was the heart and soul of the 'Boys of Summer,'" said Dodgers longtime broadcaster Vince Scully.[24]

[The deal was reported in different ways by different newspapers. Along with the one shown, there were reports of two players and more cash, and even no players with even more cash. We do know the players to be named as going to Boston were pitcher Red Evans, who went on September 1, 1939, and outfielder Art Parks who went on February 24, 1940.]

July 24, 1939: Purchased Outfielder Dixie Walker from the Detroit Tigers on Waivers

A May 1933 article in The Sporting News, said the New York Yankees thought Dixie Walker, their 22-year-old rookie outfielder, might be the eventual replacement for Babe Ruth. In June, Walker replaced a slumping Earle Combs in center field. Playing in 98 games, the 6'1" left-handed-hitter batted .274 with 15 home runs and was *The Sporting News's* right fielder on its unofficial American League rookie team. However, a series of serious injuries and a trip to the minor leagues limited him to a total of 57 games with the Yankees from 1934 to 1936.

Walker returned to fulltime action with the 1937 Chicago White Sox, batting .302 with a league-leading 16 triples in 154 games. Chicago traded him to the Detroit Tigers that December; he batted .308 for the 1938 Tigers and was batting .305 in 43 games in 1939 when the Tigers put him on waivers.

Walker had made a favorable impression on new manager Leo Durocher when he hit well against the Dodger during spring training. Larry MacPhail had gathered up several outfielders in hopes of finding a good one. Now he had succeeded.

"Walker's presence should help the weak-hitting Dodgers at this time," wrote the *Brooklyn Citizen*. "He figures to help relieve the terrible outfield situation, which has been a miserable flop. Walker's big bat should pound out the hits that have been sadly lacking in these past few weeks. If he does hit, and he figures to, he'll be most welcomed by skipper Durocher. Ernie Koy, Tuck Stainback, Mel Almada and Gene Moore have been big disappointments."[25]

September 7, 1939: Purchased Pitcher Max Macon from the St. Louis Cardinals

Max Macon, a 6'3" left-hander had not lived up to the promise he had shown as a 21-year-old with the 1937 Columbus (OH) Redbirds of the American Association. Pitching for the St. Louis Cardinals top farm club, Macon won 21 while losing 12 with a 3.46 earned run average. He spent all of 1938 with St. Louis but won only four games while losing 11, with a 4.11 ERA. Macon started this season with Columbus, before the Cardinals sent him to the Newark Bears of the International League. Although the Bears were a New York Yankees farm team, Macon remained the property of the Cardinals. He would finish the season with Newark and report to Brooklyn in 1940.

Macon pitched for Brooklyn in 1940, 1942, and 1943. (He spent the 1941 season with the Montreal Royals.) He won 13 and lost eight, with a 4.09 ERA. In November 1943 he was drafted by the Boston Braves in the rule 5 draft.

Also in 1939:

Traded: Pitcher Bill Posedel to Boston Bees for Catcher Al Todd; Pitcher Johnnie Chambers as Player to be Named to Washington Senators to complete trade for Outfielder Fred Sington; Catcher Ray Hayworth to New York Giants for Outfielder Jimmy Ripple; Catcher Al Todd to Chicago Cubs for Catcher Gus Mancuso and Pitcher Newt Kimball

Purchased: Pitcher Kemp Wicker from New York Yankees; Catcher Chris Hartje from New York Yankees; Pitcher Boots Poffenberger from

Detroit Tigers; Shortstop Lyn Lary from Cleveland Indians; Outfielder Mel Almada from St. Louis Browns; Outfielder Gene Schott from Philadelphia Phillies; Pitcher Al Hollingsworth from New York Yankees; Pitcher Carl Doyle from Memphis Chicks of the Southern Association

Sold: Outfielder Fred Sington to Boston Red Sox; Shortstop Lyn Lary to St. Louis Cardinals

Signed Amateur Free Agents: Stan Rojek

Signed Free Agents: Outfielder Charlie Gilbert

Released: Third Baseman Joe Stripp; Second Baseman Tony Lazzeri

CHAPTER ELEVEN

1940–1944

1940

June 12, 1940: Traded Outfielder Ernie Koy, Outfielder–First Baseman Bert Haas, Pitcher Carl Doyle, Pitcher Sam Nahem, and Cash to the St. Louis Cardinals for Outfielder Joe Medwick and Pitcher Curt Davis

A third-place finish in 1939 had Brooklyn fans hoping 1940 would bring them their first pennant in 20 years. The acquisition of outfielder Joe Medwick and pitcher Curt Davis removed all doubt—the first-place Dodgers were legitimate pennant contenders.

Medwick had been with St. Louis for seven full seasons, with an above .300 batting average in each of them. He was the most feared right-handed batter in the National League, having led the NL in runs batted in, total bases, and doubles three times each, in hits twice, and had 200 hits or more four times. In 1937 Medwick won the National League's Triple Crown, and its Most Valuable Player Award.

"You can say this is the biggest deal that has ever been pulled in the National League," said Dodgers team president Larry MacPhail. "We may go broke trying to pay for this fellow, but he is the man we wanted, and he is the player who is needed in Brooklyn to give us the strongest sort of pennant contending club, which is what I promised the fans when I came to Brooklyn."[1]

The cash going to St. Louis was estimated at somewhere between $150,000 and $200,000. Manager Leo Durocher was thrilled about the addition of the 28-year-old Medwick, with whom he had been friends when they were teammates on the Cardinals.

In addition to Medwick, the Dodgers received veteran right-hander

Curt Davis. A side-arm sinker-ball pitcher who had been with the Phillies and Cubs before the Cardinals, Davis had a lifetime record of 92–77. He won 22 games for the Cardinals in 1939 but was off to an 0–4 start this season. Although he was already 36 years old when Brooklyn got him, Davis went 13–7 for the 1941 pennant winners, 15–6 in 1942, and won 10 games in each of the following three seasons. He appeared in one game in 1946 before the Dodgers released him on May 1.

The Dodgers were losing only one established major leaguer, Ernie Koy, 30, whose batting averages of .299 in 1938 and .278 in 1939 were the highest of all Brooklyn outfielders.

Bert Haas, 26, appeared briefly for the Dodgers in 1937 and 1938. He was considered a good prospect but was presently in the minor leagues.

Pitcher Carl Doyle, a 27-year-old American League castoff, was 1–2 in 1939 and had appeared in just three games this season.

Pitcher Sam Nahem, 24, started and won in his only game for the 1938 Dodgers.

November 11, 1940: Traded Pitcher Vito Tamulis, Pitcher Bill Crouch, Minor League Catcher Mickey Livingston, and Cash to the Philadelphia Phillies for Pitcher Kirby Higbe

Larry MacPhail continued his strengthening of the Dodgers by acquiring Philadelphia's Kirby Higbe, whom he called the best pitcher available. "You can't rate anyone except [Cincinnati's Paul] Derringer and [Bucky] Walters better than this fellow," MacPhail said. "And when you consider that neither of them is available on the market and that both of them are years older and have years more of experience, you must admit that we got the best buy there was around. Taking Higbe's age into consideration, he's only 25, I don't think I'd trade him for any pitcher in the league."[2]

MacPhail added that he had been working with Phillies owner Gerry Nugent for two months to bring Higbe to Brooklyn. "When you come right down to it, we would have no excuse if we hadn't made this deal. The proposition was there for a pitcher who's bound to improve our ball club, make Brooklyn a pennant contender in 1941. The fans of this town make this a great baseball franchise because they are sold on the idea that we are doing everything in our power to build up a flag winner."[3]

Higbe, a right-hander, led the National League with 137 strikeouts in 1940, while winning 14 and losing 19 for the last-place Phillies. He immediately became the Dodgers ace going into the 1941 season. He cost the Dodgers a reported $100,000 and three players—pitchers Vito Tamulis and Bill Crouch and minor league catcher Mickey Livingston—who had no place the team's future. Following the acquisitions of Dolph Camilli, Pee Wee Reese, and Joe Medwick, Higbe was the fourth player MacPhail had spent highly for since taking over the club in 1938.

December 4, 1940: Traded Catcher Gus Mancuso, Minor League Pitcher John Pintar, and Cash to the St. Louis Cardinals for Catcher Mickey Owen

When 21-year-old Mickey Owen joined the St. Louis Cardinals in 1937, Cardinals president Branch Rickey called him the greatest catching prospect since Mickey Cochrane. Owen had fallen far short of Cochrane's level, but he had been a good, solid catcher for his four seasons with St. Louis, and he was still only 25 years old.

Owen would be the Dodgers' catcher until 1945, when he jumped to the Mexican League. He had a combined .258 batting average with Brooklyn, was selected to the All-Star game in each of his four full seasons (1941–1944), and in 1942 finished fourth in voting for the Most Valuable Player. And while he is unfortunately remembered for the Hugh Casey spitball that got away from him in the 1941 World Series, he was a very important part of the strong Dodger teams of 1941–1943. Cardinals president Sam Breadon had no qualms about trading Owen, feeling he had a more than adequate replacement in rookie Walker Cooper. He was right.

Gus Mancuso, the 35-year-old catcher going to St. Louis, batted .229 in 60 games in his one season with the Dodgers. He would play another five seasons in the National League.

John Pintar was a 26-year-old right-hander who had been in the minor leagues since 1936 and would remain there through 1946.

The Dodgers also sent $65,000 to St. Louis, as MacPhail continued to spend big for quality players.

Also in 1940:

Traded: Outfielder Roy Cullenbine to St. Louis Browns for Outfielder Joe Gallagher; Second Baseman Boze Berger to New York Yankees for Minor League First Baseman Jack Graham; Second Baseman Pep Young to Cincinnati Reds for Third Baseman Lew Riggs

Purchased: Catcher Herman Franks from St. Louis Cardinals;

Pitcher Lee Grissom from New York Yankees; Pitcher Lou Fette from Boston Bees; Pitcher Wes Flowers from Boston Red Sox; Outfielder Joe Vosmik from Boston Red Sox; Outfielder–First Baseman Jimmy Wasdell from Washington Senators; Catcher Tony Giuliani from Washington Senators; Second Baseman Alex Kampouris from New York Yankees; Pitcher Tex Carleton from Milwaukee Brewers of the American Association

Sold: Pitcher Jim Winford to St. Louis Cardinals; Outfielder Tuck Stainback to Detroit Tigers; Pitcher Ira Hutchinson to St. Louis Cardinals; Outfielder Jimmy Ripple to Cincinnati Reds: Outfielder Goody Rosen to Pittsburgh Pirates; Pitcher Newt Kimball to St. Louis Cardinals; Second Baseman Woody Williams to Cincinnati Reds; Outfielder Mel Almada to St. Louis Cardinals; Outfielder Gene Moore to Boston Bees; Pitcher Tot Pressnell to St. Louis Cardinals: Pitcher Al Hollingsworth to Washington Senators (returned to Dodgers this season); Pitcher Al Hollingsworth to St. Louis Cardinals; Pitcher Wayne LaMaster to Montreal Royals of the American Association

Signed Amateur Free Agents: Al Campanis; Bob Ramazzotti; Ben Wade, Chuck Connors

Signed Free Agents: Pitcher Wes Ferrell; Pitcher Ed Albosta; Pitcher Steve Rachunok; Outfielder Roy Cullenbine; Outfielder Tommy Tatum; First Baseman Gus Suhr

Chosen in Major League Draft: Pitcher Bill Swift; Second Baseman Pep Young

Released: Pitcher Wes Ferrell

1941

Before the 1941 season, the Dodgers Obtained Outfielder Carl Furillo from the Reading (PA) Chicks of the Interstate League

Larry MacPhail's purchase of the Class B Reading (PA) Chicks included the players, the uniforms, and the team bus. The best of those players was 19-year-old Carl Furillo, who batted .313 for Reading (renamed the Brooks) in 1941, and .281 for the Montreal Royals in 1942. The next three years were spent in the army, with Furillo making the club out of spring training in 1946.

A right-handed hitter and an excellent fielder with a legendary throwing arm, Furillo was a fixture in the Brooklyn outfield before injuries and age slowed him in 1959. He had played in eight games in 1960 when the Dodgers released him on May 17 of that year. It was a messy business involving lost salary and pension money, a lawsuit, and Furillo's belief that the Dodgers had blackballed his attempts to get a job in baseball.

"I've been betrayed," Furillo said. "I did everything the Dodgers asked of me. They just didn't have to do it this way."[4] He charged the club with waiting until all the other teams had reached the final cutdown so he could not catch on with any of them.

Furillo, the 1953 National League batting champion, finished his 15-year career, all with the Dodgers, with a .299 batting average, 1,910 hits, 1,058 runs batted in, and a 112 OPS+. He played on seven pennant-winning teams and received MVP consideration in eight seasons, including a sixth-place finish in 1949.

May 6, 1941: Traded Second Baseman Johnny Hudson, Outfielder Charlie Gilbert, and $65,000 to the Chicago Cubs for Second Baseman Billy Herman

This deal was made while Chicago was in New York playing the Giants. New Cubs general manager Jim Gallagher was having drinks and talking trades with Larry MacPhail in Gallagher's room at Manhattan's Commodore Hotel. At 3:28 a.m. the meeting concluded with Brooklyn sending second baseman Johnny Hudson and outfielder Charlie Gilbert, both of whom were with the Montreal Royals, and $65,000 to Chicago for second baseman Billy Herman.

Hudson played for the Dodgers briefly in 1936 and 1937, was their second baseman in 1938, and a backup at second base and shortstop in 1939 and 1940. Gilbert came to the Dodgers from Nashville as a rookie in the Spring of 1940 and played 57 games (43 in center field), hitting .246. With the aid of the cash, provided by the Brooklyn Trust Company, MacPhail had engineered an extremely one-sided trade.

In July 1945 MacPhail, then running the Yankees, sold Hank Borowy, the team's best pitcher, to Chicago for approximately $100,000. Adding Borowy was a huge factor in the Cubs preventing St. Louis from winning a fourth consecutive NL pennant. He had an 11–2 record with a league-leading 2.13 earned run average for the pennant-winning Cubs.

Many years later, a plausible explanation surfaced for the Yankees seemingly inexplicable sale of Borowy to the Cubs. It was, the theory went, MacPhail's repayment to Jim Gallagher, still Chicago's general manager, for the 1941 deal that brought Billy Herman to Brooklyn.

Acquiring Herman, the best second baseman in the National League and a future Hall of Famer, was the final piece in MacPhail's promise to give Brooklyn a championship team. Herman had a .309 batting average and a 112 OPS+ in his 11 seasons with the Cubs. He had been an All-Star for the past seven seasons and would be again this season.

The 31-year-old Herman was batting just .194, but the move from last-place Chicago to the pennant-contending Dodgers revitalized him immediately. After being notified of the trade, he said goodbye to his Cubs' teammates at the Commodore and crossed the East River to Brooklyn. Herman arrived at Ebbets Field at 12:30 in the afternoon and made his Dodgers' debut by going 4-for-4 in a 7–3 win over the Pirates. He went on to bat .291 in 133 games for the pennant-winning Dodgers.

Herman's average dropped to .256 in 1942, but he rebounded with a .330 mark and a career high 100 RBIs in 1943, scoring a fourth-place finish in the MVP voting. He spent the next two years in the navy and was batting .288 after 47 games on June 15, 1946, when the Dodgers traded him to the Boston Braves. Brooklyn received Stew Hofferth, a part-time catcher for the past three seasons with Boston. Hofferth would never play for the Dodgers—or any other major league team.

July 31, 1941: Purchased Pitcher Johnny Allen from the St. Louis Browns

Three and a half months into the 1941 season, the Dodgers and the St. Louis Cardinals continued to battle for first place. Currently, St. Louis had a two-game lead, which sent Larry MacPhail to the waiver wire to add another pitcher. He selected Johnny Allen, a 36-year-old right-hander, from the St. Louis Browns.

Allen was a 10-year veteran with an excellent record and a well-deserved reputation for being hot-tempered. Prior to this season, where he had won two and lost five for the Browns, he had starred for the New York Yankees and the Cleveland Indians. In four seasons with New York, he had a 50–19 record, including a 17–4 mark and a league-leading .810 winning percentage as a rookie in 1932. He won 67 and lost 34 in five seasons with Cleveland, and in 1937 he again led the league with a 15–1 record and a .938 winning percentage.

August 20, 1941: Purchased Pitcher Larry French from the Chicago Cubs

After going 7–5 as a rookie with the Pittsburgh Pirates in 1929, Larry French had double-digit win totals in each of the next 11 seasons—five with the Pirates and six with the Cubs. He had slipped badly this season, a 5–14 record with a 4.63 earned run average. At 33, French's career seemed over, but Larry MacPhail and Leo Durocher were desperate for an experienced left-handed pitcher and hoped French would be their man. Making him even more desirable was his history of success against the St. Louis Cardinals, Brooklyn's chief competitor for the National League pennant. The Dodgers had no other left-handers on the roster, and three of the Cardinals best hitters—Johnny Mize, Enos Slaughter, and Johnny Hopp—batted left-handed. In September, they would bring up another left-handed hitter, 20-year-old Stan Musial.

Cubs manager Jimmie Wilson woke French with a phone call to tell him he had been traded. "I don't know how to tell you this after being with the club all these years," Wilson said. "I just had to do it. You're going with a good club though, the Dodgers."[5]

French was pleased with the trade and believed he could help the Brooklyn club down the stretch. His first game as a Dodger was in relief against St. Louis, where he allowed four earned runs in five innings. In his second, also against the Cardinals, he pitched one inning and struck out the side. Overall, French made six appearances, without a decision. His 1942 season, however, was among the greatest comeback seasons ever. French won 15 games, lost only four, had a 1.83 earned run average, and gathered MVP votes for the first time since 1933.

"This fellow is truly a great pitcher," said Durocher. "The knuckle ball he developed this season (which he learned from teammate Freddie Fitzsimmons) has increased his effectiveness tremendously. He goes fine in relief roles because he's smart and can throw the ball where he wants."[6]

But 1942 would be French's final season. In January 1943, he enlisted in the navy, where he spent the next 27 years, rising to the rank of captain. Among pitchers with at least 75 innings in their final year, French's ERA+ of 180 in 1942 is second only to Sandy Koufax's 190 in 1966.

August 24, 1941: Traded Mace Brown and Cash to the Chicago Cubs for Outfielder Augie Galan

Brooklyn had purchased right-hander Mace Brown from the Pittsburgh Pirates on April 22, 1941. The 32-year-old Brown had appeared in one game for Pittsburgh, without a decision. A member of the Pirates since 1935, he had been primarily a relief pitcher, with an overall record of 55–45 and an ERA+ of 106. Brown was the National League's saves leader in 1937 and 1940, both times with seven. He also led the NL in games in 1938, with 51. Though he made only two starts, he was involved in 24 decisions, winning 15 of them.

Brown had a 3–2 record with a 3.16 ERA with Brooklyn this season. The Dodgers were, in effect, "lending" Brown to the Cubs, who sent him to their Los Angeles Angels farm club in the Pacific Coast League. In December they returned Brown to the Dodgers, who then sold him to the Boston Red Sox.

Augie Galan, 29, was a speedy switch-hitting outfielder who had twice led the National League in stolen bases. In his eight years in Chicago, he had a combined .277 batting average and a 107 OPS+. Galan's best season was for the 1935 pennant-winning Cubs. He batted .314 with an OPS+ of 131, had a league-leading 133 runs scored, and finished ninth in the voting for the Most Valuable Player Award.

A knee injury sustained when he crashed into a wall in Philadelphia limited Galan to just 68 games in 1940, and he was struggling this season. The Cubs sold him to the Pacific Coast League Angels, but when Galan refused to go, the Dodgers signed him and sent $2,500 and Brown to the Cubs.

During the 1941 season, Larry MacPhail made three separate deals with the Cubs that brought Billy Herman, Larry French, and Augie Galan to Brooklyn. All would help the Dodgers hold off the St. Louis Cardinals to win their first pennant since 1920. The Cubs received next to nothing in return.

December 4, 1941: Traded Pitcher Van Mungo and Catcher Tony Giuliani to the Minneapolis Millers of the American Association for Minor League Pitcher Joe Hatten

When 20-year-old Van Mungo joined the Robins in 1931, he was the youngest player in the National League. Expectations were extremely high for the hard-throwing right-hander. Manager Wilbert Robinson thought Mungo could be another Walter Johnson and predicted he would win 20 to 25 games a season for a long time. Mungo proved to be a very good pitcher, but not a great one. He never won more than 18 games, prevented from doing so by his eccentricities, bad temper, injuries and illnesses, and a drinking problem.

Managers Robinson, Max Carey, Casey Stengel, Burleigh Grimes, and now Leo Durocher all had difficulty dealing with Mungo. "Mungo and I get along fine. I just tell him I won't stand for no nonsense, and then I duck," said Stengel.[7]

When he was pitching well, his managers worked around it, but Mungo was now nearing the end of his career. Early in the 1941 season Durocher sent him to the Montreal Royals, Brooklyn's top farm team.

Mungo had double-digit win seasons from 1932 to 1936 but tailed off after that. In all, he had a 102–99 record and a 3.41 earned run average with the Dodgers. He led the league in games started twice, and in strikeouts and shutouts once each. True to form, Mungo balked at the trade. The South Carolina native said he would not go to Minneapolis because it was "too cold up there." He eventually did and was 11–3 for the Millers when the New York Giants purchased him in late July.

The Dodgers purchased Tony Giuliani from the Washington Senators in April 1940. He had played two years each with Washington and the St. Louis Browns. Giuliani spent the 1940 and 1941 seasons in the minors, with brief appearances in Brooklyn. He appeared in one game for the Dodgers in 1940 and three in 1941.

Joe Hatten was a 25-year-old left-hander who, in 1939, pitching for the Crookston (MN) Pirates, led the Class D Northern League with 299 strikeouts. Based on that, Larry MacPhail called him a definite big-league prospect.

December 12, 1941: Traded Second Baseman Pete Coscarart, Pitcher Luke Hamlin, Catcher Babe Phelps, and Outfielder Jimmy Wasdell to the Pittsburgh Pirates for Shortstop Arky Vaughan

Larry MacPhail announced he was after two star players at the National League winter meeting in Chicago—first baseman Johnny Mize of the St. Louis Cardinals and shortstop Arky Vaughan of the Pittsburgh Pirates. The Cardinals traded Mize to the New York Giants, but MacPhail finally persuaded Pirates president Bill Benswanger and manager Frankie Frisch to surrender Vaughan.

America's entry into the war the previous week had made the draft status of players a prime consideration in all trade negotiations, Players they could go after, as well as players they might lose, were now major factors. Vaughan, who was 30 and married, was not likely to be called for military service. He had been a shortstop his entire career, but third baseman Harry Lavagetto had joined the navy, and MacPhail and manager Leo Durocher planned for Vaughn to replace Lavagetto. Or he would replace Pee Wee Reese at shortstop if Reese, who had a 1-A classification, was drafted.

Vaughan had been with Pittsburgh for ten years. He batted above .300 in each one and had a lifetime batting average of .324 and an OPS+ of 141. The left-hand-hitting Vaughan had his best season in 1935, when he won the National League batting championship with a .385 average and led the league in on-base average and slugging percentage. Vaughan twice finished third in MVP voting and had been an All-Star in each of the last eight seasons. He slugged two home runs in the 1941 game, the first National Leaguer to do so.

Vaughan was the best shortstop in the National League and was expected to add firepower to Brooklyn's offense. Nevertheless, he did have one negative. He was beaned in an exhibition game this past season that resulted in recurring headaches and limited him to 106 games. Vaughan felt ready to play, but manager Frisch kept him on the bench far more often than Vaughan felt was necessary leading to several clashes between the two men.

In return for Vaughan the Pirates received second baseman Pete Coscarart, pitcher Luke Hamlin, catcher Babe Phelps and outfielder Jimmy Wasdell, none of whom figured in Brooklyn's plans for 1942.

The arrival of Billy Herman from the Cubs in May made Coscarart expendable. The Dodgers tried to waive him out of the league, but the New York Giants blocked the move. Coscarart was used mainly as backup and pinch-hitter the rest of the season, batting .129. He got into three games in the World Series, going hitless in seven at-bats. Overall, he batted .240 in four seasons with the Dodgers. Coscarart would be a regular in the Pittsburgh infield for the next four seasons.

Luke Hamlin came to Brooklyn from the Detroit Tigers organization in 1936. He won 60 games and lost 57 over the next five seasons, including a 20-win season in 1939. His record in 1941 was 8–8 with a 4.24 earned run average.

"Hamlin was of no value," wrote Lee Scott in the *Brooklyn Citizen*. "Whenever he was called upon to pitch in critical games, he fell down badly. The strain and tension proved too much for him. He was unable to pitch under the terrific pressure."[8] In addition, MacPhail found Hamlin's tendency to give up home runs infuriating.

Phelps was the oldest player in point of service on the club, having spent seven years with the Dodgers, compiling a .315 batting average and a 125 OPS+. His contributions to the club during the 1941 season were limited by a series of injuries, a fear of flying, and obsessive attention to his health. It all led to ongoing disputes with the club that began on the first day of spring training. Phelps finally left the team in June and later went on the inactive list. He appeared in just 16 games with a .233 batting average.

Twenty-seven-year-old Jimmy Wasdell was the most valuable member of the foursome that was leaving. Purchased from the Washington Senators in May 1940, Wasdell had a fine season in 1941, batting .298 in 94 games. He alternated between left and right field and subbed for Dolph Camilli at first base.

Frisch put a positive spin on his new acquisitions. "We're going to need Phelps. What if something happens to [Al] Lopez? Phelps will hit that ball into the rightfield stands for us and he's a good receiver," he said. "Coscarart is a swell defensive man, and he can fill in at several positions. Wasdell is good both on defense and offense. I'd like to think of Hamlin as a starting pitcher and if he can win 10 games for us, we're going to be all right. Baseball is a funny business, and these trades are all part of the game."[9]

Vaughan batted .277 while playing third base for the 1942 Dodgers. With Pee Wee Reese in the navy, Durocher moved Vaughan to shortstop in 1943, where he had his last outstanding season, batting .305 and leading the league in runs scored (112) and stolen bases (20). He retired after the season, but after missing three years returned to play for the Dodgers in 1947 and 1948. The Dodgers released him following the 1948 season.

Also in 1941:

Traded: First Baseman Gus Suhr, Outfielder Arnie Moser, and Cash to Milwaukee Brewers of the American Association for Shortstop Claude Corbitt; Pitcher Lee Grissom to Philadelphia Phillies for Pitcher Vito Tamulis; Pitcher Vito Tamulis to Nashville Vols of the Southern Association for Outfielder Tommy Tatum and Pitcher Tom Drake; Catcher Joe Becker, Outfielder George Staller, Minor League Second Baseman Sammy Bell, and Minor League Pitcher Ray Roche to the Baltimore Orioles of the International League for Catcher Homer "Dixie" Howell; Pitcher Kemp Wicker, Minor League Infielder Jack Burman, and Cash to St. Louis Cardinals for Catcher Don Padgett

Purchased: Pitcher Newt Kimball from St. Louis Cardinals; Pitcher Bob Chipman from Atlanta Crackers of the Southern Association; Outfielder Johnny Rizzo from Philadelphia Phillies

Sold: Pitcher Bill Swift to Saint Paul Saints of the American Association; Pitcher Mace Brown to Boston Red Sox

Signed Amateur Free Agents: Hank Behrman; Bruce Edwards; Hal Gregg; Spider Jorgensen; Vic Lombardi; Paul Minner; Marv Rackley; Ed Stevens

Signed Free Agents: Gene Hermanski; Paul Waner
Chosen in Major League Draft: Pitcher Les Webber
Released: Outfielder Paul Waner; Outfielder Joe Vosmik

1942

March 23, 1942: Purchased Outfielder Frenchy Bordagaray from the New York Yankees

Frenchy Bordagaray was returning to Brooklyn where he batted .282 and .315 as a Dodgers regular in 1935 and 1936. Traded to the St. Louis Cardinals following the 1936 season, he batted a combined .289 in two seasons as a part-timer with the Cardinals, but then batted a paltry .197 for the National League champion Cincinnati Reds in 1939.

The Reds traded Bordagaray to the New York Yankees in 1940, who sent him to their Kansas City farm team. He had a spectacular year with the Blues, batting .358 and leading the American Association with 214 hits. Playing for the Yankees in 1941, Bordagaray batted .260 in 36 games, but although he was not likely to be drafted, at age 32, Yankees manager Joe McCarthy had no place for him on the 1942 club.

Bordagaray spent the four World War II seasons with Brooklyn as an outfielder and a third baseman, the best of which was 1943, when he batted .302 with a 120 OPS+. The Dodgers released him in March 1946. He was 36 years old, and Brooklyn had a multitude of young players reporting to spring training.

August 31, 1942: Purchased Pitcher Bobo Newsom from the Washington Senators

As he watched the St. Louis Cardinals steadily reduce the big lead the Dodgers once had in the National League pennant race, Larry MacPhail made a move. He sent $25,000 to the Washington Senators for 35-year-old right-hander Bobo Newsom. The 6'3" Newsom was coming back to Brooklyn. He broke into the major leagues as a 21-year-old in 1929, going 0–3 with Wilbert Robinson's Robins.

Since then, Newsom had been with the Chicago Cubs, the Boston Red Sox, the St. Louis Browns (twice), the Detroit Tigers, and was currently in his second stint with Washington. Newsom's overall record of 144–139, included three 20-win seasons and two wins for the Tigers against the Cincinnati Reds in the 1940 World Series. His record with the Senators this season was 11–17 with a 4.93 earned run average.

A garrulous self-promoter, Newsom told the press, "It looks like them Dodgers need a little help and I'm just the man. I'm gonna bear down and give them all I got, and we'll clinch that pennant alright. No need to worry." After learning of the sale, he sent a telegram to Dodgers manager Leo Durocher stating: "I want to congratulate you on buying pennant insurance. I'm still a good pitcher."[10]

October 1, 1942: Purchased Outfielder Luis Olmo from the Richmond (VA) Colts of the Piedmont League

Luis Olmo batted .311 in 1941, his first full season with the Richmond (VA) Colts of the Class B Piedmont League. The 5'11" right-handed batter did even better in 1942. At age 22, Olmo led the Piedmont League in batting (.338), runs batted in (92), hits (170) triples (19) and tied for the lead in home runs (10). The Puerto Rico-born Olmo was sold for an undisclosed price, but in mid-season Colts owner Eddie Mooers had placed a $15,000 price tag on him.

According to those who scouted him, Olmo's chief weakness at the plate was an awkward stance and a desire to chase bad balls. Colts manager Ben Chapman, a former major league outfielder, did a lot to cure Olmo of his awkwardness at the plate but was unable to keep him from swinging at bad pitches. Olmo's defensive ability was said to have improved greatly under Chapman's tutelage.

December 12, 1942: Traded Pitcher Johnny Allen and Cash to the Philadelphia Phillies for Pitcher Rube Melton

Branch Rickey, named Brooklyn's president and general manager on October 29, 1942, completed his first major transaction when he traded pitcher Johnny Allen to the Philadelphia Phillies for pitcher Rube Melton. The Phillies also received a reported $30,000 in the deal.

The Dodgers purchased Allen from the St. Louis Browns in late July 1941. He contributed three victories without a loss in Brooklyn's successful pennant pursuit. He appeared in three games in the World Series, all in relief, holding the Yankees scoreless in 3 2/3 innings. Allen was 10–6 with a 3.20 earned run average this past season. However, he remained a problem for management, including his suspension by Larry MacPhail for breaking club rules during spring training in Havana.

Both men in this trade were difficult to handle. Nevertheless, Rickey was effusive in his praise for his new pitcher. "Rube Melton can throw a baseball as hard as any man living, and with his great fastball he also owns a beautiful curve. His trouble has been his wildness; but at his age this is a fault that's entirely correctible," he said. "In other words, I think we've got a man who can develop into one of the game's great pitchers. To me, his physical equipment and some of his mental equipment as well suggest a combination of Flint Rhem, Dizzy Dean, and Paul Derringer," Rickey, said citing some of the outstanding but troublesome pitchers he had when he ran the St. Louis Cardinals.[11]

When Rickey spoke of Melton's wildness, he was referring to both his difficulty in throwing strikes—he led the NL in walks with 115 this past season—as well as his antics off the field. The 6'5", 200-pound Melton had pitched in the Cardinals farm system, and Rickey was familiar with the soon to be 26-year-old's wildness.

Philadelphia had drafted him after his strong season with the Columbus (OH) Redbirds in 1940, He was 1–5 for the Phillies in 1941 and 9–20 in 1942, with a combined ERA+ of 85. But the Dodgers needed pitching, and Melton, with a wife and two children, seemed unlikely to be drafted into the military. He had a combined 13–21 record for the 1943–1944 Dodgers and after his draft status was reclassified as 1-A, he spent the 1945 season in the army. Returning in 1946, Melton won six and lost three with an ERA+ of 171. Arm surgery performed during spring training in 1947 adversely affected his fast ball, and after four appearances, the Dodgers released him.

Also in 1942:

Purchased: Catcher Ferrell Anderson from New York Yankees; Outfielder Gene Moore from New York Yankees; Catcher Billy Sullivan from Detroit Tigers; Pitcher Schoolboy Rowe from Detroit Tigers; First Baseman Babe Dahlgren from Chicago Cubs; Outfielder Hal Peck from Chicago Cubs

Sold: Outfielder Gene Moore to Washington Senators

Signed Amateur Free Agents: Cal Abrams; Dick Whitman

Chosen in Major League Draft: Catcher Dee Moore

Released: Pitcher Freddie Fitzsimmons

1943

In 1943, Branch Rickey replaced Larry MacPhail as club's president and general manager. MacPhail had left in October 1942 to accept a commission in the army.

March 24, 1943: Traded Major League Pitcher Jack Kraus and Cash to the Philadelphia Phillies for Shortstop Bobby Bragan

Branch Rickey was with the Dodgers at their training camp in Bear Mountain, New York, when he engineered a trade for Bobby Bragan. (Wartime travel restrictions prevented teams from going south for spring training.) Bragan, a 25-year-old right-handed batter had been the Philadelphia Phillies shortstop in his first two seasons (1940–1941), before being tried as a catcher for 22 games in 1942.

Bragan was a weak hitter, who batted .233 with an OPS + of 66 in his three seasons in Philadelphia. Nevertheless, Rickey saw in him that rare player who could be used at both shortstop and behind the plate. He tried to have him included in several negotiations with Philadelphia, including the trade that brought Rube Melton to Brooklyn.

Leo Durocher used Bragan at both positions in 1943 and 1944, as well as at second base and third base. Following army service in 1945 and 1946, Bragan returned to a role as a third-string catcher in 1947 and early 1948. Overall, he batted .259 with a 79 OPS+ in 202 games with Brooklyn. In June 1948 Bragan accepted a position as the manager of the Fort Worth Cats, the Dodgers farm team in the American Association, which led to a long career as a big-league manager.

Jack Kraus, 25, was a 6'4" left-hander with no big-league experience. He had a 12–9 record with the 1942 Montreal Royals and would have a 9–15 record with a 106 ERA+ for the 1943 Phillies.

April 16, 1943: Purchased Pitcher Johnny Allen and Pitcher George Washburn from the Philadelphia Phillies

Four months after selling veteran pitcher Johnny Allen to Philadelphia, the Dodgers bought him back when Allen refused to sign with the

Phillies. The war had some impact on baseball rosters in 1942, including the loss of Cleveland's Bob Feller, Detroit's Hank Greenberg, and Washington's Cecil Travis. But 1943 would see each team losing multiple players to the military. While most general managers had avoided signing young players because of the uncertainty of the draft, Branch Rickey had taken the opposite tack. He had his scouts scouring the country for young talent, and while some went to war and others never worked out, many of the players he signed would contribute greatly to Brooklyn's postwar success. In 1943 alone, the Dodgers signed teenagers Gil Hodges, Duke Snider, Ralph Branca, and Rex Barney.

The Dodgers had let Johnny Allen go because he was a difficult man who had infuriated Larry MacPhail and Leo Durocher. But MacPhail was now in the army, and with just days before the season-opener Durocher was desperate for pitching help. And even at age 38, Allen was still a legitimate major league pitcher.

George Washburn was a 28-year-old righthander with one big league game to his credit. Pitching for the 1941 New York Yankees he started against Detroit on May 4 and was the losing pitcher. It would be his only major league appearance. The Dodgers sent him to the minor leagues, where he would remain through 1951.

July 15, 1943: Traded Pitcher Bobo Newsom to the St. Louis Browns for Pitcher Fritz Ostermueller and Pitcher Archie McKain

On July 9, 1943, Dodgers manager Leo Durocher suspended pitcher Bobo Newsom for insubordination after the two argued about a pitch thrown to Pittsburgh's Vince DiMaggio. Arky Vaughan believed Durocher had lied to the press in describing his reasons for Newsom's suspension. In the locker room before the game the next day, Vaughan handed his uniform to Durocher, told him what he could do with it and threw it in his face.

Almost all the Dodgers' players opposed Durocher's suspension of Newsom and threatened to not take the field for that afternoon's game. What made a terrible situation even worse, it was Kitchen Fat Day at Ebbets Field. In addition to the 8,748 paying customers, there were more than 4,000 women who had been granted free admission for bringing a pound or more of household fats to the park. Also in the crowd were 930 servicemen and 441 blood donors. Ballplayers striking in the middle of a war would have been a public relations nightmare for the Brooklyn club.

Finally Branch Rickey intervened, while Durocher, more worried about a forfeit, said he would take no disciplinary action against Vaughan and convinced his players to call off their strike. Five days later Rickey traded Newsom to the Browns. "A manager must be fired or supported, there is no middle ground," he said. Durocher was pleased to still have his job as the Dodgers stumbled along. "I felt all along that I did no wrong in this incident. This was something that pertained to the discipline of a ball player. I'll make a million mistakes; I've made plenty of them in the past, but I don't think I made one here."[12]

Newsom had pitched well this season, a 9–4 record and a 3.02 earned run average. But he was so upset at the news of the trade, he said he would quit baseball rather than join the Browns. "I got the worst and rawest deal ever handed to a baseball player," Newsom said. "I have no intention of reporting to the Browns and will quit the game before I do. Sure, I'll hang around here for a few days and then I'm going home."[13] This was the usual idle threat. Newsom reported to the Browns and had a 1–6 record when they traded him to Washington on August 31.

Ostermueller, 35, and McKain, 32, were both left-handers. Ostermueller had a 62–71 record in his 10 big league seasons, seven with the Boston Red Sox and three with the Browns. McKain had pitched the past six seasons for the Red Sox, the Tigers, and the Browns, winning 26 and losing 21. The trade to Brooklyn ended McKain's major league career.

July 16, 1943: Sold Outfielder Joe Medwick to the New York Giants

When the Dodgers traded for the Cardinals' Joe Medwick in June 1940, they hoped he would help lead them to a pennant. Unfortunately, a week later, in the second meeting between Brooklyn and St. Louis after the trade, Cardinals pitcher Bob Bowman beaned Medwick, nearly killing him. Medwick recovered and batted .301 for the season, but the Dodgers finished second. A year later, in 1941, Medwick was a key player in Brooklyn's first pennant-winning season in 21 years, batting .318 with 18 home runs and 88 runs batted in. He followed up with another strong season in 1942, but in 48 games this season, Medwick had failed to hit a home run and had only 25 runs batted in.

A few days before his sale to the Giants, Medwick was told to remain in Brooklyn when the Dodgers traveled to Boston. "This may be another move to restore complete harmony on the team," reported the *Brooklyn Citizen*. "Medwick is not liked by the Dodgers. Some of the players have accused him of not hustling. They were also peeved at Durocher for not acting when Medwick's performance in the field was below par."[14]

His departure from Brooklyn pleased Medwick as much as it did the Dodgers. "It's one of the best things that ever happened to me," he said when told the Giants had bought him at the waiver price. (By virtue of their team being in last place, the Giants had first crack at Medwick.) President Horace Stoneham and manager Mel Ott agreed it was the best thing that has happened to the Giants in quite a while, and that Medwick would be a big help to their club.

July 31, 1943: Traded First Baseman Dolph Camilli and Pitcher Johnny Allen to the New York Giants for Pitcher Bill Sayles, Pitcher Bill Lohrman, and First Baseman Joe Orengo

Larry MacPhail began his transformation of the Dodgers during spring training of 1938 when he acquired Dolph Camilli from the Philadelphia Phillies. Camilli had been everything the Dodgers hoped he would be. So much so, that he received MVP votes in five of his six seasons with them. Camilli's best season was 1941, when Brooklyn won its first pennant since 1920. He led the National League in home runs and runs batted in and was the league's Most Valuable Player.

"[Camilli] was only 5 feet 10 inches and 185 pounds, but he had a ferocious swing that in seasons to come would swat balls over Ebbets Field's right-field screen onto Bedford Avenue," Richard Goldstein wrote in Camilli's *New York Times* obituary.[15]

Camilli drove in more than 100 runs in four of his five full seasons as a Dodger and 96 in the other. He had 139 home runs and an OPS+ greater than 100 in each of his six seasons, with a composite OPS+ of 143.

On July 31, 1943, Branch Rickey, MacPhail's replacement as president, was in the process of his own transformation. Since taking over he had gotten rid of five older players (and their larger salaries). In addition to Camilli and Johnny Allen, he had traded Bobo Newsom, sold Joe Medwick, and released Freddie Fitzsimmons. The 36-year-old Camilli, the team captain, was part of that process, but the move outraged Brooklyn fans. Camilli, meanwhile, accepted it as part of the game.

"I don't think I'll report to the Giants because I don't think I can help them," he said. "I don't want to take money under false pretenses."[16] He went home to California to play for the Oakland Oaks but returned to the major league for a half season with the 1945 Boston Red Sox.

Camilli's teammates were equally upset at his departure. Manager Durocher, not known for his sentimentally, spoke for all of them. "I'd rather have told any 20 other players they were through with us than to have to tell it to Dolph. It was the toughest assignment I ever had."[17]

Johnny Allen, who had been unimpressive this season despite his 5–1 record, said he would report to the Giants in Cincinnati as soon as possible.

Bill Lohrman, 30-year-old right-hander was in his seventh year with the Giants. He had a career record of 59–54 and had won five and lost six this season.

Bill Sayles, 25, was a right-handed rookie with a 1–3 record. He appeared in five games for the Dodgers without a decision.

Right-handed-hitting Joe Orengo, 28, was in his fourth major league season. He had a .218 batting average with six home runs in 83 games.

August 14, 1943: Traded Outfielder Joe Orengo, Pitcher Rube Melton, and Cash to the St. Paul Saints of the American Association for First Baseman Howie Schultz

Howie Schultz, a 6'6" right-handed-batter, was the man Rickey had in mind to be his new first baseman after trading Dolph Camilli two week earlier. Schultz, 21, had been a basketball star at Hamline University in Minnesota. His professional baseball experience was a season-and-a-half with the Grand Forks (ND) Chiefs, a Chicago White Sox affiliate in the Class C Northern League, before being promoted to St. Paul. This season he was batting .285 in 99 games with the Saints.

Schultz's height caused him to be rejected by the army and the navy, making him a prime target for several teams. Rickey won out by including veteran pitcher Rube Melton to help the Saints in their pennant race. Along with the recently acquired Orengo, who batted .200 in seven games, and Melton, Rickey sent a reported $40,000 to St. Paul.

Rickey had personally scouted Schultz on a recent tour of the midwest. "Schultz is not yet a finished hitter and his batting might be disappointing for a while," he said. "But he is still very young, and he will be a good hitter and before very long. I have hopes that our fans will like him immensely. He has exceptional speed, a strong arm, and is a natural athlete in every respect."[18]

Also in 1943:
Traded: First Baseman Babe Dahlgren to Philadelphia Phillies for Outfielder Lloyd Waner and Second Baseman Al Glossop; Outfielder Roberto Ortiz to Washington Senators for Outfielder Morrie Aderholt
Purchased: Outfielder Roberto Ortiz from Philadelphia Phillies
Sold: Pitcher Schoolboy Rowe to Philadelphia Phillies; Outfielder Hal Peck to Chicago Cubs; Second Baseman Alex Kampouris to Washington Senators; Pitcher Newt Kimball to Philadelphia Phillies; Catcher Dee Moore to Philadelphia Phillies; Second Baseman Al Glossop to Chicago Cubs
Signed Amateur Free Agents: Rex Barney; Ralph Branca; Gil Hodges; Gene Mauch; Duke Snider
Signed Free Agents: Pitcher Freddie Fitzsimmons; Catcher Ray Hayworth; Pitcher Johnny Cooney; Outfielder Paul Waner
Chosen in Major League Draft: Third Baseman Gil English
Released: Pitcher Freddie Fitzsimmons; Catcher Ray Hayworth

1944

Branch Rickey, club attorney Walter O'Malley, and Brooklyn insurance man Andrew Schmitz purchased the 25 percent of the team owned by Ed McKeever's heirs.

May 30, 1944: Traded Pitcher Bill Lohrman, Pitcher Fritz Ostermueller, and Cash to the Syracuse Chiefs of the American Association for Outfielder Goody Rosen

This would be Toronto native Goody Rosen's second tour of duty with the Dodgers. The first had been from 1937 to 1939. Rosen's only full season was 1938, when he batted .281 in 138 games. The Dodgers sold him to Pittsburgh in May 1940, but he never played for the Pirates. He had spent the last four seasons in the minor leagues, almost all with Syracuse of the American Association. The Chiefs were now an affiliate of the Cincinnati Reds.

The 31-year-old Rosen, a 5'9", 160-pound outfielder, was brought back to share center field with Luis Olmo. The right-handed-hitting

Olmo was having trouble with right-handed pitchers, a problem manager Leo Durocher hoped to solve by using the left-handed-hitting Rosen against right-handers. At the time of the trade, Rosen had a .295 batting average with the Chiefs, with a .422 on-base average and a .457 slugging percentage.

Ostermueller was 3–2 in 17 games over parts of the last two seasons with the Dodgers. Lohrman was 0–2 over nine games during that same period. The money going to Syracuse was said to be $18,000.

As the Dodgers' center fielder, Rosen batted .261 in 89 games, but followed with his career year in 1945. He batted a team-high .325, with 197 hits and a 134 OPS+. But he was 33 and the Dodgers had many young outfielders looking for jobs in 1946. Rookie Carl Furillo replaced him in center field, and after playing in three games, a bitterly disappointed Rosen was sold to the Giants.

June 6, 1944: Traded Pitcher Bob Chipman to the Chicago Cubs for Second Baseman Eddie Stanky

Billy Herman, the Dodgers' second baseman for the past few seasons was now in the navy, and the club had targeted the Chicago Cubs' Eddie Stanky as his replacement. The 5'8" Stanky joined the Cubs in 1943, following a sensational 1942 season with the Milwaukee Brewers, where he led the American Association with a .342 batting average and was named the league's most valuable player.

Stanky was a disappointment as a rookie, batting .245, and his .240 mark this season led Cubs manager Charlie Grimm to bench him. The 28-year-old Stanky asked to be traded, and on June 6, he got his wish. It followed weeks of negotiations between Chicago general manager Jim Gallagher and Brooklyn's Branch Rickey. Gallagher had asked for Dodgers catcher Mickey Owen or two pitchers. He finally agreed to take left-hander Bob Chipman in exchange for Stanky. In their new second baseman, the Dodgers were getting a hard-nosed, aggressive player, much like Leo Durocher, his new manager.

Chipman, 25, was in his fourth season with Brooklyn, though he had a total of just four appearances in the first three. He had been in 11 games this season, all but three in relief, and had a 3–1 record.

Also in 1944:

Traded: Minor League Second Baseman Frank Drews to Boston Braves for catcher Mike Sandlock and Cash; Pitcher Clyde King to

Richmond (VA) Pilots of the Piedmont League for Pitcher-Outfielder Ben Chapman

Purchased: Pitcher Charlie Fuchs from the St. Louis Browns

Signed Amateur Free Agents: Jack Banta; Tommy Brown; Clyde King; Clem Labine; Steve Lembo; Cal McLish; Eddie Miksis; Bobby Morgan; George Shuba; Preston Ward

Chosen in Major League Draft: Pitcher Lee Pfund; Pitcher Tom Seats

Released: Pitcher Johnny Cooney; Outfielder Paul Waner; Outfielder Lloyd Waner

Chapter Twelve

1945–1949

1945

Branch Rickey, Walter O'Malley, and Brooklyn industrialist John Smith bought out the Charles Ebbets heirs' 50 percent and also Andrew Schmitz's holdings. Each owned 25 percent, but they voted as a bloc in board decisions.

March 28, 1945: Sold Pitcher Whit Wyatt to the Philadelphia Phillies

In July 1938, when the Dodgers purchased Whit Wyatt from the Milwaukee Brewers of the American Association, scout Tom Sheehan predicted Wyatt would prove to be a good pitcher for Brooklyn. Wyatt proved to be much more. Manager Leo Durocher used him repeatedly for the big games in the 1941 and 1942 pennant races, particularly against St. Louis, and he mostly came through with a win.

Wyatt's 22 wins in 1941 tied teammate Kirby Higbe for the league high. He also led in shutouts, with seven, and had an earned run average of 2.34. He finished third in voting for the Most Valuable Player Award, behind teammates Dolph Camilli and Pete Reiser. Wyatt had a 78–39 record for his first five years as a Dodger, before falling off to a 2–6 mark and a 7.17 ERA in 1944. That, along with a persistent sore arm and his age, 37, made him expendable, and Branch Rickey was glad to send him to the Philadelphia Phillies in return for $20,000.

Phillies manager Freddie Fitzsimmons, Wyatt's teammate during his glory days in Brooklyn, thought he might still be an effective pitcher. As usual, Rickey was right. Wyatt appeared in 10 games in 1945, all starts and finished 0–7 with a 5.26 earned run average. Philadelphia released him before the start of the 1946 season.

October 23, 1945: Signed Free Agent Shortstop Jackie Robinson

Branch Rickey may not have been the only baseball man aware of the great pool of untapped talent in the Negro leagues, but he was the only one willing to recruit that talent. Signing Jackie Robinson was a bold move, opposed almost unanimously by the other clubs, but Rickey went ahead. He decided Robinson was the man to break baseball's color barrier. The 26-year-old shortstop for the Kansas City Monarchs of the Negro American League batted .375 in 34 games this season. Robinson had been a four-letter man at UCLA and an army officer during the war.

After getting endorsements for Robinson's abilities from scouts Tom Greenwade, George Sisler, and Clyde Sukeforth, Rickey met with Robinson at the Dodgers office in Brooklyn to judge Robinson's character. As a result of that meeting, Rickey signed him to a contract with the International League's Montreal Royals, the Dodgers top farm team. Aware that opposition to Robinson would come not only from other owners and players, but also from some on his own team, Rickey's son, Branch Jr. said this,

"Mr. Racine (Hector Racine was the principal owner of the Royals) and my father will undoubtedly be severely criticized in some sections of the country where racial prejudice is rampant, but they won't avoid it if it comes. Robinson is a fine type of young man, intelligent and college bred." The younger Rickey admitted the move might cause the Dodgers to lose several ball players. "Some of them, particularly those who come from certain sections of the South, will steer away from a club with a Negro player on its roster. Some players now with us may even quit, but they'll be back in baseball after they work a year or two in a cotton mill."[1]

Racine said he expected no opposition from the International League or from the Montreal fans. "Negroes fought alongside whites and shared the foxhole dangers" he said, "and they should get a fair trial in baseball."[2]

Also in 1945:

Traded: Pitcher-Outfielder Ben Chapman to Philadelphia Phillies for Catcher Johnny Peacock

Sold: Outfielder Carden Gillenwater to Boston Braves; Outfielder Morrie Aderholt to Boston Braves; Catcher Stan Andrews to Philadelphia Phillies; Catcher Johnny Peacock to New Orleans Pelicans of the American Association

Signed Amateur Free Agents: Don Lund; Erv Palica

Released: Catcher Clyde Sukeforth; Catcher Ray Hayworth

1946

April 4, 1946: Signed Free Agent Catcher Roy Campanella

Branch Rickey followed up his October 1945 signing of Jackie Robinson by signing two more Negro league stars on April 4, 1946. Just as Robinson was preparing for his season with the Montreal Royals, Rickey signed catcher Roy Campanella and pitcher Don Newcombe as free agents. Although both had played at a high level in the Negro leagues, Rickey assigned them to the Nashua (NH) Dodgers of the Class B New England League. "Our club is anxious to give these boys every opportunity to make good in organized baseball," said Nashua president, Fred Dobens.[3]

The Pittsburgh Pirates had passed on Campanella in 1944, but the Dodgers had been interested in him since November 1945. The powerfully built 5'9", 190-pound Campanella began his career in the Negro National League as a 15-year-old in 1937. He spent eight years in the league, all with the Baltimore Elite Giants except for seven games. Powerfully built, Campanella could hit, hit for power, and was an excellent defender with a powerful throwing arm. Negro League statistics are incomplete, but what we have show Campanella with a batting average of .317 in 233 games. He won a batting title (.388) in 1944, and this past season batted .369 while leading the league in games played, runs batted in, runs scored, and doubles.

After playing for Nashua in 1946, Campanella played at Montreal in 1947. He was clearly ready for the major leagues in 1948, but Rickey sent him to the St. Paul Saints where he integrated the American Association. After batting .325, with 13 home runs in 35 games for the Saints, the now 26-year-old Campanella got the call to replace sore-armed Bruce Edwards in Brooklyn.

Despite his late start and the tragic accident that limited him to 10 seasons, Campanella had a Hall of Fame career and established himself as one of the game's greatest catchers. He was an All-Star in eight of his ten seasons and received Most Valuable Player Award votes in seven seasons. Three times his was the winner of the award.

July 2, 1946: Sold Pitcher Les Webber to the Cleveland Indians

Hopes for the 1946 season were high in Cleveland because of new owner Bill Veeck, Jr. After fifth place finishes the past two seasons, the Indians were expected to rise, led by a strong pitching staff. But on the morning of July 2, they were 31–38 and the only pitcher who had lived up to expectations was Bob Feller (13–5).

No one expected 31-year-old Les Webber, a relief pitcher, would turn things around but Veeck, perhaps in desperation, was doing what he could. The day before he had added another relief pitcher, 41-year-old Joe Berry from the Philadelphia Athletics.

Webber had been a serviceable pitcher for the Dodgers through the war years. After five years in the minor leagues, the last four with the Pacific Coast League's Seattle Rainiers, he came to Brooklyn in 1942. The next year he appeared in 54 games, all in relief, and led the National League with 10 saves. Overall, Webber appeared in 149 games for the Dodgers (126 in relief), with a 22–18 record and a 3.89 earned run average.

December 4, 1946: Traded Infielder-Outfielder Augie Galan to the Cincinnati Reds for Pitcher Ed Heusser

Versatile Augie Galan had played first base, third base, and the outfield since joining the Dodgers late in the 1941 season. He played with Brooklyn through 1946, with a composite .301 batting average and a 143 OPS+. Galan walked more than 100 times in each season from 1943 to 1945, leading the league in the first two of those years. His ability to draw walks contributed heavily to a spectacular .416 on-base average with the Dodgers.

Ed Heusser, a 37-year-old right-hander, had been in the big leagues on and off since 1935. A member of the Reds since 1943, he had by far his best season in 1944, when he led the National League with a 2.38 earned run average. The Dodgers sent him to Montreal, where with Roy Campanella as his catcher, he had a 19–3 record. The Phillies claimed Heusser before the 1948 season, which would be his final season in baseball.

Also in 1946:

Traded: Second Baseman Billy Herman to Boston Braves for Catcher Stew Hofferth; Shortstop Eddie Basinski to Pittsburgh Pirates for Pitcher Al Gerheauser

Purchased: Outfielder Otis Davis from St. Louis Cardinals; Pitcher George Dockins from St. Louis Cardinals; Outfielder Earl Naylor from St. Louis Cardinals

Sold: First Baseman Jack Graham to New York Giants; Shortstop Claude Corbitt to Cincinnati Reds; Catcher Don Padgett to Boston Braves; Outfielder Goody Rosen to New York Giants; Pitcher Art Herring to Pittsburgh Pirates; First Baseman Jack Bolling to Mobile Bears of the Southern Association

Signed Amateur Free Agents: Carl Erskine; Phil Haugstad; Bill Antonello; Ken Lehman; Bud Podbielan; Jim Romano; Chris Van Cuyk; Dee Fondy; Toby Atwell

Signed Free Agents: Pitcher Johnny Van Cuyk; Outfielder Joe Tepsic; Pitcher Ed Chandler; Outfielder Joe Medwick

Released: Pitcher Curt Davis; Outfielder Frenchy Bordagaray; Pitcher Tom Drake; Third Baseman Lew Riggs; Catcher Bobby Bragan; Outfielder Joe Medwick

1947

For the 1947 season, Burt Shotton replaced Leo Durocher as manager.

May 3, 1947: Traded Pitcher Kirby Higbe, Pitcher Hank Behrman, Pitcher Cal McLish, Infielder Gene Mauch, and Catcher Dixie Howell to the Pittsburgh Pirates for Outfielder Al Gionfriddo and Cash

Kirby Higbe was part of a group of players acquired by Larry MacPhail to bring a pennant to Brooklyn. Higbe, who came in a November 1940 trade with the Philadelphia Phillies, helped make that happen when he won 22 games for the 1941 pennant winners. His win total tied teammate Whit Wyatt for the most in the National League and earned him a seventh-place finish in the MVP voting.

Higbe followed with records of 16–11 in 1942 and 13–10 in 1943. After two years in the army, he returned to win 17 (17–8) in 1946. He was off to a 2–0 start in 1947, giving him a composite record of 70–38 as a Dodger. But Higbe, a South Carolinian, had been involved, though half-heartedly, in the opposition to Jackie Robinson's arrival, and Rickey chose to get rid of him. Moreover, it had always been Rickey's policy, in St. Louis and now in Brooklyn, to get rid of his veterans while there was still a market for them. Higbe's departure left only five players from the 1941 NL champions: Hugh Casey, Harry Lavagetto, Pee Wee Reese, Pete Reiser, and Dixie Walker.

Hank Behrman, a 26-year-old right-hander, had a fine rookie season in 1946. Pitching mostly in relief, he had an 11–6 record and a 2.93 earned run average. This season he had pitched poorly in spring training and in two regular-season games. Behrman had an 0–2 record for Pittsburgh when the Pirates returned him to the Dodgers on June 14. Overall, Behrman won five and lost three for the pennant-winning 1947 Dodgers and had a 5–4 record in 1948. In March 1949 the Dodgers sold him to the New York Giants.

The Dodgers signed 18-year-old right-handed pitcher Cal McLish as an amateur free agent in 1944. He had a 3–10 record and a 7.82 earned run average for the seventh-place Dodgers when he was called to army duty in August. McLish returned in August 1946 and pitched in one game, against St. Louis, allowing two runs without retiring a batter.

Gene Mauch was 17 when the Dodgers signed him as an amateur free agent in 1943. He was Brooklyn's opening day shortstop in 1944 and played in five games in April. The army called in May, and Mauch was assigned to the Army Air Corps, where he served the rest of 1944 and all of 1945. Discharged early in 1946, he spent the season playing shortstop for the St. Paul Saints of the American Association, batting .248 in 149 games.

Homer "Dixie" Howell, 26, batted .295 with the Montreal Royals in 1946. But the Dodgers had Bruce Edwards, coming off an excellent rookie season, behind the plate and Bobby Bragan and Gil Hodges as backups. They had no need for Howell.

The joke at the time was that Al Gionfriddo was included in the deal so he could hand deliver to Branch Rickey the reported $100,000 the Pirates were sending to Brooklyn. Gionfriddo, a 5'6", 25-year-old left-handed hitter, had a fine season for the 1945 Pirates but fell off some in 1946. He batted .177 in 37 games for Brooklyn, in what would be his final big-league season, although he would play in the minor leagues through 1956. He is best-remembered for his great catch at Yankee Stadium, robbing Joe DiMaggio of a potential three-run home run in Game Six of the 1947 World Series.

May 9, 1947: Sold First Baseman Howie Schultz to the Philadelphia Phillies

In addition to the threats and racial epithets rookie Jackie Robinson had to face in 1947, he had to learn a new position. Although he was best suited for second base, Brooklyn had Eddie Stanky at that position, and so Robinson was assigned to play first base. Despite a flawless performance in the season-opener, when the Dodgers took the field in the ninth inning Robinson remained on the bench. Acting manager Clyde Sukeforth had inserted veteran Howie Schultz as a defensive measure. But Branch Rickey and manager Burt Shotton, who had replaced the suspended Leo Durocher, soon realized Robinson was more than adequate defensively. Schultz played in only one more game, as a pinch hitter, before Brooklyn sold him to the Phillies for $50,000.

Schultz had joined the Dodgers in mid–August 1943 and was their full-time first baseman in 1944, batting .255 with 83 runs batted in. He split the position with Augie Galan and Ed Stevens in 1945 and was platooned with Stevens in 1946. Schultz had a .255 batting average and an 87 OPS+ in 314 games as a Dodger.

August 24, 1947: Purchased Pitcher Dan Bankhead from the Memphis Red Sox of the Negro American League

Brooklyn had a six-game lead on the Cardinals, but still felt a need to add pitching strength. On August 24 Branch Rickey announced the club had signed Dan Bankhead, a 27-year-old right-hander from the Memphis Red Sox of the Negro American League (NAL). Bankhead, the first black pitcher to reach the major leagues, had pitched in the NAL since 1940, with 1945 out for military service. When he was asked if he thought he would be nervous about breaking into organized white baseball at the very top level, Bankhead said he supposed he would.

"He should be really good," said Rickey. "I don't know how quickly he can acquire the feel of the major leagues. I do know that if he can pitch up here with the same poise and confidence that he showed me last week in Memphis, he is ready to help us right away.... He's fundamentally a fastball pitcher and there aren't many men who can throw harder than he can."[4]

Manager Shotton made use of his new pitcher almost immediately.

Bankhead made his Brooklyn debut on August 26, hitting a home run in his first at bat. His pitching, however, was poor. In 10 innings, spread over four games, his earned run average was 7.20. The Dodgers sent him to the minor leagues for the next two season, before bringing him back in 1950. He won nine and lost four despite a 5.50 earned run average. After seven games in 1951, Bankhead was returned to the minor leagues and went on to pitch in the Mexican Leagues until the mid–1960s.

November 14, 1947: Sold First Baseman Ed Stevens and Shortstop Stan Rojek to the Pittsburgh Pirates

Signed as an amateur free agent in 1941, Ed Stevens worked his way up through the Dodgers farm system before reaching the big-league club in August 1945, at age 20. The left-handed-hitting Stevens was platooned at first base with Howie Schultz in 1946 and expected he would do the same in 1947. But the arrival of rookie Jackie Robinson changed the Dodgers first base plans. Robinson's mastery of his new position, along with his ability to hit both left-handed and right-handed pitchers, made Schultz and Stevens expendable. Branch Rickey had traded Schultz to the Phillies in May and now Stevens was sent to the International League's Montreal Royals.

According to Stevens, when he resisted the demotion, Rickey replied: "Well, I'm going to reward you if you'll do this for me, if you'll go down there and get in shape."[5] Stevens agreed, and he hit .290 with 27 home runs and 108 runs batted in for the Royals. Rickey sold him, nevertheless. In three years and 163 games with the Dodgers, Stevens batted .252 with a 111 OPS+.

Stan Rojek, 28, was signed as an amateur free agent in 1939. The Dodgers called him up late in 1942 after he batted .283 at Montreal and was named the International League's All-Star shortstop. Rojek had just one at-bat and then spent the next three years in the army air force. He returned in 1946 playing mostly as a backup to Pee Wee Reese. Rojek would have the best season of his career for the surprising 1948 Pirates, a .290 average in 156 games, and a tenth-place finish in the MVP balloting.

Rickey put a benevolent spin on the sale. "The transfer of Stevens and Rojek serves a double purpose—it makes our roster more flexible and gives two deserving boys an opportunity to play regularly in the major leagues."[6]

December 8, 1947: Traded Outfielder Dixie Walker, Pitcher Hal Gregg, and Pitcher Vic Lombardi to the Pittsburgh Pirates for Pitcher Preacher Roe, Shortstop Billy Cox, and Infielder Gene Mauch

Rumors that Branch Rickey was going to trade 37-year-old Dixie Walker began in spring training and resumed shortly after the 1947 World Series. "Rickey might peddle Dixie Walker, but the People's Choice holds a peculiar spot in the hearts of the Flatbush fans," wrote Harold C. Burr. "He's become a Brooklyn institution and resentment might run high if he was disposed of summarily in cold blood. Rickey would have to feel out public sentiment first."[7]

Yet Burr knew as well as anyone that Rickey did not pay any attention to public sentiment; that he had a long history of trading or selling veteran players while they still had market value. Tommy Holmes, Burr's associate at the *Brooklyn Eagle*, offered a more accurate reading of Rickey. "The fact that the customers would like to see Walker patrol right field until a wheelchair becomes an essential part of his equipment cuts no ice with Mr. Rickey who likes to talk as though baseball were a sport but always acts as though it were a business."[8]

In early December, Branch Rickey, Jr., confirmed that the Dodgers had offered Walker the chance to manage the St. Paul Saints, at a salary of $15,000. Dixie turned it down because he wanted to stay in the big leagues and, perhaps more importantly, he did not want to take the steep cut in salary. "The fact that we offered Walker a place in our organization," said Rickey Jr., "indicates, doesn't it, that we no longer consider him a topflight ball player."[9]

The trade of Dixie Walker from Brooklyn to Pittsburgh was announced on December 8, 1947. Along with Walker the Pirates received pitchers Vic Lombardi and Hal Gregg. Coming to the Dodgers were left-handed pitcher Preacher Roe, shortstop Billy Cox, and utility infielder Gene Mauch. Al Abrams, sports editor of the *Pittsburgh Post-Gazette*, believed Pittsburgh had gotten the better of the trade.

Given all that had transpired at spring training in Havana, many people jumped to the conclusion that Rickey was trading Walker because of his early opposition to Jackie Robinson. That false perception exists to this day. True, Walker had asked for a trade during spring training, but he later changed his mind, as Rickey knew.

Rickey had a well-deserved reputation for parsimony, and Walker, the 1947 team leader in batting average and runs batted in, was seeking a substantial raise for 1948. Dixie's excellent 1947 season, at age 37, allowed Rickey to exercise one of his guiding principles in trading players. It was better to get rid of them a year too early rather than a year too late. Moreover, the Dodgers were loaded with young outfielders, including Duke Snider, Carl Furillo, Gene Hermanski, and George Shuba.

Jackie Robinson wrote in 1955 that Walker made $30,000 in 1947 and did not want his salary cut in half to manage at St. Paul. Rickey engineered the deal with Pittsburgh so that Dixie would receive the same $30,000 salary. Knowing the Pirates were willing to pay Walker $20,000, Rickey put him on waivers, allowing the Pirates, who finished last in 1947, to claim him for one dollar. The Pirates then added the $10,000 waiver price to bring Walker's 1948 salary up to $30,000. This was covered up at the time and made to seem that Walker was part of the trade for Roe and Cox.[10]

Walker was home in Birmingham, Alabama, when Pirates general manager Roy Hamey called to tell him of the trade. "Naturally, I regret leaving Brooklyn, but I cannot say I am unhappy over going to Pittsburgh," he said. "In nine years with the Dodgers I've made many close friends. I love those Brooklyn people." Walker said that for the past nine years he had played before "the finest and most sincere group of people a man could ever hope to play before."[11]

Walker batted .300 or better in seven of his eight full seasons as a Dodger, missing only 1942 when he batted .290. He was the National League's batting champion (.357) in 1944 and its runs batted in leader (124) in 1945. He was an All-Star in five seasons and drew MVP votes in seven, finishing third in 1944 and second in 1946. His overall OPS+ as a Dodger was 129. Walker batted .316 as the Pirates full-time right fielder in 1948 and .282 as a part-time player in 1949, his final season.

Brooklyn signed Hal Gregg as an amateur free agent in 1941. The 6'3" right-hander made his debut in 1943, at age 21. His best season was in 1945, when he won 18 games. His career record with the Dodgers was 37–41 with an ERA+ of 82. Chronic back problems and a history of squabbles with Leo Durocher, who would be returning to manage the team in 1948, likely contributed to Gregg's departure.

Like Gregg, the Dodgers had signed Vic Lombardi as an amateur free agent in 1941. That's where the similarity ended. Lombardi was a 5'7" left-hander. He reached the major leagues in 1945 and won the hearts of Brooklyn fans by winning four games against the New York Giants without a loss. He would eventually stretch that streak to nine. In his three years in Brooklyn, Lombardi had a 35–32 record with a 122 ERA+.

Preacher Roe, 31, won 13 games for the 1944 Pirates and 14 in 1945. Roe's ERA+ for those two seasons was 120 and 128, and his 148 strikeouts in 1945 led the National League. He was coming off a 4–15 season for a bad Pittsburgh team, but Rickey knew he was a much better pitcher than that. And, of course, he was. Roe was the Dodgers best left-hander throughout the late 1940s and early 1950s, compiling a spectacular 93–37 record with a 124 ERA+. His best season was 1951, a 22–3 record and a league-leading .880 winning percentage.

Roe had a 2–1 record in three World Series, all against the Yankees, including a 1–0 shutout in Game Two of the 1949 Series. The Dodgers traded Roe and Billy Cox to the Baltimore Orioles after the 1954 season, but Roe chose to retire.

Billy Cox made his major league debut as a 21-year-old playing 10 games for the 1941 Pirates. He spent the next four years in the army, returning home with, what in retrospect, was a case of post-traumatic stress disorder (PTSD). Nevertheless, he had two fine seasons as the Pirates shortstop, batting .290 and .274. The Dodgers had Pee Wee Reese at shortstop, but some in the press thought the right-handed-hitting Cox might replace or platoon with the incumbent third baseman, left-handed-hitting Spider Jorgensen.

The Dodgers had traded Gene Mauch to Pittsburgh this past May. He played 16 games for the Pirates and 58 for the Indianapolis Indians of the American Association. Mauch appeared in 12 games for the Dodgers in 1948 before they sold him on waivers to the Chicago Cubs in June.

Also in 1947:

Sold: Tommy Tatum to Cincinnati Reds; Pitcher Rube Melton to Montreal Royals of the International League

Signed Amateur Free Agents: Jim Baxes; Rocky Bridges; Joe Landrum; Don Hoak; Bob Milliken; Ray Moore; Dick Teed; Johnny Rutherford; Dick Williams; Tim Thompson

Chosen in Minor League Draft: Pitcher Pete Wojey; Outfielder Bob Addis

Released: Catcher Billy Sullivan Pitcher Rube Melton

1948

For the 1948 season, Leo Durocher replaced Burt Shotton as manager.

March 6, 1948: Traded Second Baseman Eddie Stanky and a Player to be Named to the Boston Braves for Outfielder Bama Rowell, First Baseman Ray Sanders, a Player to be Named, and Cash

A few days after signing his 1948 contract at the Dodgers spring training camp in the Dominican Republic, Eddie Stanky learned he had been traded to the Boston Braves. "It was a wrench to let Stanky go," Branch Rickey said. "I'm fond of the boy and he can have a job in our organization any time he asks for it after he is through as a player.... I don't know what the fan reaction will be, but sometimes they are a year behind in realizing the wisdom of a move."[12]

Stanky's aggressive style of play had made him a favorite of Leo Durocher, who was returning to manage the club after his one-year suspension. But Durocher seemed less than upset at the trade. "Eddie Miksis is my second baseman," he announced, speaking of his 21-year-old infielder. "He has more power and runs faster than Stanky. I think he would have taken the job away from Stanky by May 30 anyway, and Stanky isn't the type to sit on the bench." Yet the real reason for the trade, was to allow Jackie Robinson to move from first base to second base, his best position. Rickey said as much. "The best second baseman in the world, but don't ask me who he is ... at present is playing first base." Stanky was philosophical about the trade. "It's baseball. I've made a lot of friends in Brooklyn, and I regret leaving 'em."[13]

And the Brooklyn fans regretted seeing him go. He had been a big part of their success in his stay there. In 1945 he led the National League in runs (128) and in walks, with a league record 148, since broken. The next year he again led in walks (137) and in on-base percentage (.436).

Stanky, who had been a holdout, was less philosophical about the trade a week later, admitting that it was a shock. "Ever since I started playing for $125-a-month I've given everything I had. Pee Wee Reese and I gave the Dodgers a good double-play combination. I think Alvin Dark, and I can do the same thing for the Braves." During Stanky's holdout, Durocher said he was not worth what he was asking.

"Leo's statement was unjustified," Stanky said. "I battled for him and never said anything about his $60,000 salary. And I played 145 games last year when he wasn't even there, so how did he know what I was worth? In short, he knifed me in the back. He really put the skids under me."[14]

Meanwhile, Braves manager Billy Southworth was enthusiastic about the trade. "Stanky is the best leadoff man in the National League.

And he's a good competitor—none better. He'll contribute a lot to any shortstop's success. Our shortstops are young, and he'll help them. He's a great double-play man, too," added Southworth, noting that for the last three years Stanky had led the league's second basemen in double plays.[15]

Ray Sanders, a 31-year-old left-handed hitter was the St. Louis Cardinals first baseman from 1942 to 1945, playing on three pennant winners (1942–1944). He batted .279 with a 118 OPS+ for St. Louis. The Cardinals sold him to the Braves in April 1946. On August 21 of that year, he was injured when Cardinals base runner Erv Dusak crashed into him at first base, breaking his left arm in three places. Sanders missed the rest of the 1946 season and all of 1947. He was supposedly fully recovered but it did not take long for the Dodgers to discover that was not the case. On April 18, they returned him to Boston, who paid the Dodgers $60,000. Sanders played five games for the Braves in 1948 and nine in 1949.

Bama Rowell was with the Braves from 1939 to 1941, and again in 1946 and 1947, after missing four years in the military. Rowell had a composite batting average of .279 and an OPS+ of 98 in those five years. The Dodgers had no use for the 32-year-old Rowell. Eleven days later they sold him to the Philadelphia Phillies, where Rowell played his final big-league season.

On July 17, 1948, Burt Shotton replaced Leo Durocher as manager.

December 15, 1948: Traded Outfielder Pete Reiser to the Boston Braves for Outfielder Mike McCormick and Infielder Nanny Fernandez

The 1941 season is remembered as the season of Joe DiMaggio's 56-game hitting streak and Ted Williams's .406 batting average. But the most exciting player in baseball in 1941 was Brooklyn's Pete Reiser. In his first full season, the 22-year-old Reiser led the National League in batting average (.343), slugging percentage (.558), OPS (.964), total bases (299), runs (117), doubles (39), and triples (17), and finished second in the MVP race to teammate Dolph Camilli.

Reiser was on his way to an even better year in 1942. He was batting .356 in mid–July when he crashed into a wall at Sportsman's Park in St. Louis, fracturing his skull. He returned to action too soon and played the rest of the season at less than full strength, finishing with a .310 average. After spending the next three seasons in the army, Reiser returned in 1946, but was never the player he had been. Still as reckless as ever, he almost died when he ran into a wall at Ebbets Field on June 4, 1947. (While in the hospital, he received the last rites of the Catholic Church.) This past season, Reiser appeared in just 64 games with a .236 batting average.

We will never know how good a player Pete Reiser was, and how good he might have been had he not played so recklessly. But many of those who saw him in 1941 said he had the potential to be among the greatest ever. "Maybe Pete Reiser was the purest ballplayer of all time," wrote sportswriter W.C. Heinz in 1958. "There is no exact way of measuring such a thing, but when a man of incomparable skills, with full knowledge of what he is doing, destroys those skills and puts his life on the line in the pursuit of his endeavor as no other man in his game ever has, perhaps he is the truest of them all."[16]

Leo Durocher managed Reiser and Willie Mays, ten years apart, and thought Reiser was as good as Mays. "There will never be a ballplayer as good as Willie Mays," Durocher wrote years later. "But Reiser was every bit as good as Mays. He might have been better. Pete Reiser might have been the best ball player I ever saw. He had more power than Willie. He could throw as good as Willie. You think Willie Mays could run in his hey-day? You think Mickey Mantle could run? Name whoever you want to, and Pete Reiser was faster. And he knew how to run the bases. Willie Mays had everything. Pete Reiser had, everything but luck."[17]

Heinz detailed that bad luck. "In two and a half years in the minors, three seasons of Army ball and ten years in the majors," he wrote, "Pete Reiser was carried off the field 11 times. Nine times he regained consciousness either in the clubhouse or in hospitals. He broke a bone in his right elbow, throwing. He broke both ankles, tore a cartilage in his left knee, ripped the muscles in his left leg, sliding. Seven times he crashed into outfield walls, dislocating his left shoulder, breaking his right collarbone and, five times, ending up in an unconscious heap on the ground. Twice he was beaned."[18]

"Reiser is a great ball player, as great as Stan Musial or any of the rest of 'em," said Dodgers manager Burt Shotton after the trade. "But he wasn't doing anything for me on the bench. I wanted a right-handed-hitting outfielder, and I got him in [Mike] McCormick."[19]

Billy Southworth would not agree to the deal until he had talked personally to Reiser, who flew in from St. Louis and satisfied the Braves' manager that he would undergo a rejuvenation at Boston. Southworth also checked with Eddie Stanky, a teammate of Reiser's in Brooklyn, and Stanky was all in favor.

McCormick, 32, spent five seasons with Cincinnati and the last three with the Braves. His two best seasons were as a Reds rookie in 1940 and this past season with the Braves. He twice suffered a broken ankle, one with the Reds in 1942 and once with the Braves in 1946. McCormick batted .209 for the 1949 Dodgers and was released after the season.

Nanny Fernandez was traded to Pittsburgh in May 1949, without ever playing for the Dodgers.

Also in 1948:

Sold: Outfielder Don Lund to St. Louis Browns; Infielder Gene Mauch to Chicago Cubs; Pitcher Ed Heusser to Philadelphia Phillies

Signed Amateur Free Agents: Billy Hunter; Billy Loes; Walt Moryn; Joe Pignatano

Signed Free Agents: Outfielder Sam Jethroe

Chosen in Minor League Draft: Pitcher Tom Lasorda

Released: Outfielder Arky Vaughan; Pitcher Hugh Casey; Third Baseman Harry Lavagetto

1949

October 13, 1949: Sold Pitcher Paul Minner and First Baseman Preston Ward to the Chicago Cubs

Branch Rickey had several minor leaguers that he wanted to bring to Brooklyn in 1950, including infielders Bobby Morgan and Rocky Bridges, first baseman Dee Fondy, and catcher Steve Lembo. He set the stage for their arrival by selling off some players that were no longer needed. Over two days four would go, beginning with the sale of pitcher Paul Minner and first baseman Preston Ward to Chicago. The cost to the Cubs for Minner and Ward was $100,000.

The Dodgers signed Minner as a 17-year-old amateur free agent in 1941. He had a combined 19–2 record with a 2.33 earned run average pitching for two farm teams in 1942, before spending 1943–1945 in the army. Minner, a 6'5" left-hander, pitched mostly for the Mobile Bears of the Southern Association in 1946 and 1947, but spent the 1948 and 1949 seasons in Brooklyn, winning seven and losing four in 55 games, only three of which he started.

Ward was a left-handed hitter whom the Dodgers signed as an amateur free agent in 1944, when he was 16 years old. He was Brooklyn's opening day first baseman in 1948 but was batting .260 with only one home run in 42 games when manager Leo Durocher replaced him with converted catcher Gil Hodges. Ward spent the entire 1949 season with the Fort Worth Cats of the Texas League, batting .303 with 13 home runs and 112 runs batted in.

October 14, 1949: Sold Outfielder Marv Rackley to the Cincinnati Reds and Outfielder Dick Whitman to the Philadelphia Phillies

A day earlier Branch Rickey received $100,000 from the Cubs in exchange for pitcher Paul Minner and first baseman Preston Ward. On this day he received another $100,000 in separate sales of two 28-year-old left-handed-hitting outfielders. Marv Rackley went to the Cincinnati Reds for $60,000, and Dick Whitman went to the Philadelphia Phillies for $40,000.

In May, the Dodgers had traded Rackley to Pittsburgh for Johnny Hopp, but the trade was voided a month later. The Pirates claimed they had received damaged goods after Rackley reported with a sore throwing arm. In 169 games with Brooklyn (1947–1949), Rackley, a spray-hitter, batted .316 but hit only one home run. His big-league career ended after five games for the 1950 Reds.

Whitman had a .266 batting average in 191 games as a Dodger (1946–1949). He, too, lacked power—two home runs in 489 at bats. Whitman would be a substitute outfielder and pinch-hitter for the National League champion Phillies in 1950.

December 24, 1949: Traded Outfielder Luis Olmo to the Boston Braves for Outfielder Jim Russell, Outfielder Ed Sauer, and Cash

Three days after the Dodgers announced they had sold Luis Olmo to the Boston Braves, they revealed that in addition to money, they were receiving two players from the Braves. Olmo joined the Dodgers from their Montreal farm team in July 1943 and played through 1945. Leo Durocher used him mostly as an outfielder, but he was versatile enough to play the infield as well. Olmo's best season was 1945, when he batted .313, had 110 runs batted in, and led the league with 13 triples.

When the Dodgers did not meet his salary demands for 1946, Olmo jumped to the Mexican League, where Jorge Pasquel was handing out large salaries to attract major league players. Those who chose to play in Mexico were banned from organized baseball for five years, but Commissioner Happy Chandler lifted the ban in June 1949. Olmo returned to Brooklyn as a backup outfielder and batted .305 in 38 games.

Jim Russell was a 31-year-old switch-hitter who played for Pittsburgh from 1942 to 1947 and for Boston the last two seasons. He had his best years for the 1944–1946 Pirates. Russell was in the center of much of the dissension that plagued the 1949 Braves, so his trade came as no surprise. He batted .229 for the 1950 Dodgers and was 0-for-13 in 1951.

Ed Sauer, also 31, played three seasons with the Cubs (1943–1945) and split the 1949 season between the Cardinals and the Braves. He had a lifetime batting average of .256 in 189 games. Sauer was assigned to the minor leagues and never played for Brooklyn or any other major league team.

This deal was rumored to be the forerunner of a major trade between the two teams. Brooklyn would get 32-year-old right-hander Johnny Sain, one of the top pitchers in the game, and 33-year-old left-handed-hitting outfielder Tommy Holmes, who in 1945 finished second to Phil Cavarretta in the voting for the Most Valuable Player Award. Going to Boston would be pitcher Carl Erskine, 23, second baseman Eddie Miksis, 23, and outfielder Gene Hermanski, 30.

Fortunately for the Dodgers, this rumored trade never happened. If it had, they would have lost one of the best and most popular pitchers in their long history. Carl Erskine was a member of the Dodgers beginning in 1948 in Brooklyn and continuing through 1959 in Los Angeles, finishing with a record of 122–78. His best season was 1953, when he led the NL with a .769 winning percentage (20–6). He topped it off by striking out 14 New York Yankees in Game Three of the World Series to set a major league record, since broken. Erskine also pitched two no-hitters at Ebbets Field, against the Cubs in 1952 and the Giants in 1956.

Also in 1949:

Traded: Infielder Bob Ramazzotti to Chicago Cubs for Infielder Hank Schenz; Minor League Outfielder Sam Jethroe and Minor League Outfielder Bob Addis to Boston Braves for Outfielder Don Thompson, Pitcher Al Epperly, and Infielder Dee Phillips

Purchased: Catcher Mickey Livingston from the Boston Braves

Sold: Pitcher Hank Behrman to New York Giants; Pitcher Elmer Sexauer to Philadelphia Phillies; Catcher Mickey Owen to Chicago Cubs; Infielder Hank Schenz to Pittsburgh Pirates

Signed Amateur Free Agents: Ed Roebuck; Wayne Belardi; Gino Cimoli; Don Zimmer; Ron Negray
Chosen in Major League Draft: Pitcher Mal Mallette
Released: Outfielder Mike McCormick

CHAPTER THIRTEEN

1950–1954

1950

May 10, 1950: Sold Pitcher Willie Ramsdell to the Cincinnati Reds

Manager Luke Sewell and general manager Warren Giles of the last-place Cincinnati Reds made three deals this day. In addition to trading catcher Walker Cooper to the Boston Braves for infielder Connie Ryan and selling infielder Jimmy Bloodworth to the Philadelphia Phillies, the Reds purchased right-hander Willie Ramsdell from Brooklyn for an estimated $25,000.

Ramsdell, a 34-year-old knuckleballer, began his career with the Big Spring (TX) Barons of the Class D West Texas–New Mexico League in 1938. He pitched for the Dodgers in 1947, 1948, and this season. Overall, Ramsdell appeared in 34 games, 33 in relief, and had a 6–7 record and a 5.01 earned run average. Sewell was expected to use Ramsdell as a starter, which he did. Ramsdell started 53 games for Cincinnati in 1950–1951.

May 17, 1950: Sold Third Baseman Spider Jorgensen to the New York Giants

When Jackie Robinson made his major league debut on Opening Day in 1947, across the diamond, at third base, 27-year-old John "Spider" Jorgensen was doing the same. Signed by Brooklyn as an amateur free agent in 1941, Jorgensen, a 5'9" left-handed-hitter, was sent to the Santa Barbara Saints of the Class C California League. He batted .332 and led the league with 184 hits. After spending the next four years in the army air force, Jorgensen played the 1946 season with the Montreal Royals, where he was a teammate of Robinson.

Injuries to Arky Vaughan and Cookie Lavagetto had allowed Jorgensen to win the third base job. The rookie batted .274 in 129 games in 1947, but injured his shoulder during the winter and reinjured it during spring training in 1948. Newly acquired Billy Cox replaced him at third base, as Jorgensen played only 31 games that year and 53 in 1949. He had been in only two games this season before he was sold to the Giants for a reported $20,000. Jorgensen's totals for Brooklyn were a .276 batting average and a 103 OPS+ in 215 games.

Giants manager Leo Durocher was glad to have Jorgensen, whom he managed in Brooklyn in 1948. "I've wanted him for a long time," Durocher said. "He's an ideal pinch hitter for us since he pulls the ball to right field." The Polo Grounds ought to be right up his alley. "We've needed another lefty on the bench."[1]

Also in 1950:

Traded: Pitcher Glenn Moulder to St. Louis Cardinals for Outfielder Johnny Lindell; Traded First Baseman Dee Fondy and First Baseman Chuck Connors to Chicago Cubs for Outfielder Hank Edwards

Purchased: Pitcher Ben Wade from Chicago Cubs

Signed Amateur Free Agents: Roger Craig; Bert Hamric; Glenn Mickens; Charlie Neal; Norm Sherry; Bob Wilson

Chosen in Minor League Draft: Pitcher Earl Mossor

1951

For the 1951 season, Walter O'Malley bought Branch Rickey's shares in the club and replaced him as president. Buzzie Bavasi replaced Branch Rickey as general manager.

Charlie Dressen replaced Burt Shotton as manager.

June 8, 1951: Traded Outfielder Tommy Brown to the Philadelphia Phillies for Outfielder Dick Whitman and Cash

The Dodgers trade of Tommy Brown to the Philadelphia Phillies for Dick Whitman and a reported $20,000 came about in an unusual way. Dick Williams, an outfielder with Brooklyn's Texas League team, the

Fort Worth Cats, had recently been discharged from the army because of an injured knee and placed on the National Defense List. But the baseball ruling was that such a player must be kept by the parent club for the rest of the year if waivers on him could not be obtained. The Dodgers could not get waivers on Williams, giving them one too many outfielders. One had to go, and new manager Charlie Dressen chose Brown as the one. He found a taker in Phillies manager Eddie Sawyer, who needed a right-handed-hitting outfielder.

Brown was only 16—too young for the military draft—when he joined the Dodgers as a shortstop in 1944. He made history on August 20, 1945, when, at age 17, he homered against Pittsburgh's Preacher Roe. Brown remains the youngest major leaguer to hit a home run. In 1946, when other players were coming home, Brown went the other way. He was drafted and missed the season, returning in 1947. Brown eventually transitioned from an in infielder to an outfielder but the 57 games he played in 1945 were his high as a Dodger. Overall, he played in 272 games in his seven years in Brooklyn, with a .237 batting average and a 67 OPS+.

Whitman was a Dodger from 1946 to 1949 before he was traded to Philadelphia. After two seasons with the Phillies, they sent Whitman to the minor leagues, where he played successfully through the 1957 season.

June 15, 1951: Traded Pitcher Joe Hatten, Catcher Bruce Edwards, Infielder Eddie Miksis, and Outfielder Gene Hermanski to the Chicago Cubs for Pitcher Johnny Schmitz, Catcher Rube Walker, Second Baseman Wayne Terwilliger, and Outfielder Andy Pafko

On the morning of June 15, the trading deadline, the Dodgers had a six-game lead over the second-place New York Giants. Already the clear favorites to win the pennant, they took a huge step in that direction by acquiring Chicago Cubs outfielder Andy Pafko in an eight-player trade. The trade had a symmetry about it, as the teams swapped catchers, infielders, outfielders, and left-handed pitchers.

"The big man in the swap for us is Pafko," said Dodgers manager Charlie Dressen, stating the obvious. "I'm going to play Pafko in left and with Snider in center and Furillo in right that will give us a pretty slick outfield." Dressen also assessed the rest of the trade. "I gave up Miksis, who hasn't been playing, and Edwards, who hasn't been catching, and Hermanski, who plays only against right-handers." (He didn't mention Hatten, whom he had used sparingly.) "I think I'll get some winning starts out of Schmitz, and I like Walker as a receiver."

The Cubs offered Smoky Burgess, their third string catcher, and $50,000 in place of Walker, but Dressen and vice president Buzzie Bavasi did not want money and insisted on Walker. Dressen also revealed he would have preferred right-hander Bob Rush instead of Schmitz. "I wanted Bob Rush and Pafko—and would still let 'em have our four," he confessed.[2]

Andy Pafko, a 30-year-old right-handed batter, joined the Cubs at the tail end of the 1943 season. Although the Dodgers had him slated for left field, he had been the Cubs' center fielder all his years in Chicago, except for 1948 when he was their third baseman. Pafko was a five-time All-Star, and finished fourth in the MVP voting in 1945, the Cubs pennant-winning year. In 960 games with the Cubs, he had a .294 batting average, 126 home runs, 584 runs batted in, and an OPS+ of 126.

Johnny Schmitz had been with the Cubs since 1941, except for 1943–1945 when he was in the navy. Schmitz's best season was 1948, when he went 18–13 with a 147 ERA+ and led the league in hits allowed per nine innings, giving up an average of only 6.92. He also was third in the league in wins and complete games, fifth in ERA, and sixth in games started. Schmitz's career record with the Cubs was 69–80 with a 108 ERA+. That 18 of those 69 wins had come against Brooklyn made him even more enticing. Schmitz was 1–2 with an 8.00 ERA at the time of the trade.

Wayne Terwilliger, 26, saw combat duty throughout the Pacific as a marine in World War II. He began his professional career in 1948 and made his major league debut with the Cubs on August 6, 1949. The next year he was Chicago's regular second baseman, but contributed little offensively, batting .242 with a 77 OPS+. In 50 games this season, his average was .214 and his OPS+ was 52. He did surprisingly well for Brooklyn, batting .280 in 37 games in 1951 and was batting .312 in 77 games for St. Paul in 1952 when the Dodgers sold him to the Washington Senators on September 23.

Left-hand-hitting Rube Walker batted .275 with 26 runs batted in as a 22-year-old rookie in 1948. He never topped those marks with the Cubs, nor would he in his eight years with the Dodgers. Walker was the only new Dodger in this trade that was not traded within a year or two. He served through 1957 as a backup to Roy Campanella.

Walker was a member of the team that went to Los Angeles in 1958 but was released in June. He batted .214 in 362 games for the Dodgers, with a 59 OPS+. He was behind the plate on October 3, 1951, when Bobby Thomson's pennant-winning home run sailed over the head of left fielder Andy Pafko.

Chapter Thirteen: 1950–1954

The Dodgers acquired Joe Hatten from the Minneapolis Millers of the American Association in a December 1941 trade that sent Van Mungo to Minneapolis. Hatten started the 1942 season with Brooklyn's Montreal farm team. He had a 4–2 record in May before spending the rest of that season and the next three seasons in the navy. Hatten returned in 1946 and had a 14–11 record as a 29-year-old rookie. He was a double-digit winner in each of his first four seasons. By 1950 the Dodgers had greatly strengthened their pitching staff, and Hatten was used primarily in relief that season and this. Hatten had a 59–39 record and a 107 ERA+ in 197 games as a Dodger.

Bruce Edwards signed with Brooklyn as a 17-year-old amateur free agent in 1941. He played the 1941 and 1942 seasons in the low minors and served in the navy in 1943–1945. Edwards started the 1946 season with the Mobile Bears of the Southern Association. He was batting .332 after 62 games, when the Dodgers, unhappy with catcher Ferrell Anderson, called him up in June. Edwards was a big improvement over Anderson, defensively and offensively, and earned some MVP votes. He was even better in 1947, batting .295 with 80 runs batted in and a 105 OPS+. His fourth-place finish in the MVP voting was the highest of any member of the pennant-winning Dodgers.

That was the peak of Edwards's career. The Dodgers brought Roy Campanella to the team in 1948, relegating Edwards to the role of backup catcher and part-time third baseman and left fielder for the rest of his stay in Brooklyn. His career totals for his 449 games as a Dodger were a .263 batting average and a 97 OPS+.

The Dodgers signed 17-year-old Eddie Miksis as an amateur free agent in 1944. After starting the season in the minors, Miksis was called up and got into 26 games. He served in the navy in 1945 and a good part of 1946. Branch Rickey and Leo Durocher had high expectations for Miksis, but he spent his Brooklyn career primarily as a backup infielder. (He did play 11 games in left field in 1947.)

The highlight of Miksis's time as a Dodger was in Game Four of the 1947 World Series. Pinch running for Pete Reiser in the ninth inning, he scored the winning run when Harry Lavagetto doubled off Bill Bevens, driving home two runs and ending the Yankees' pitcher's bid for a no-hitter. Miksis appeared in 300 games as a Dodger, with a .222 batting average and a 55 OPS+.

Gene Hermanski appeared briefly for the Dodgers in the wartime season of 1943. He rejoined the Dodgers in 1946 after spending 1944 and 1945 in the Coast Guard. A powerfully built left-handed hitter, Hermanski had his best season in 1948—a .290 batting average, 15 home runs, 60 runs batted in, and a 134 OPS+ as Brooklyn's right fielder.

When Duke Snider took over in center field in 1949, Carl Furillo moved from center to right, and Hermanski moved to left, a position he shared with several others. Weakness defensively hindered Hermanski's career, but he could always hit. He had a .282 average and a 119 OPS+ in 506 games with Brooklyn.

Manager Frankie Frisch of the seventh-place Cubs called it a good trade for both clubs. "The way we were going, I had to do something. I like Edwards under the bat, and I've seen Hatten pitch. I'm going to make Miksis my regular second baseman and bat Hermanski cleanup."[3]

Giants manager Leo Durocher, who was with his team in Pittsburgh, was clearly upset at the news. "I can't believe it," he said. "Why Pafko alone is worth all the four players Brooklyn sent to the Cubs. I offered Frisch three times what the Dodgers gave him, and the Cubs wouldn't listen. Somebody must be out of his mind."[4]

"The Dodgers will win the pennant by 20 games instead of 10," predicted one Giants player, while St. Louis Cardinal president Fred Saigh simply said: "I think it is bad for the league."[5]

Also in 1951:
Traded: Minor League Third Baseman Hector Rodriguez to the Chicago White Sox for First Baseman Rocky Nelson; Traded Catcher Toby Atwell to Chicago Cubs for Outfielder Carmen Mauro

Purchased: Pitcher Joe Black from the Baltimore Elite Giants of the Negro National League; Purchased Second Baseman Jim Gilliam from the Baltimore Elite Giants of the Negro National League

Sold: Outfielder Hank Edwards to the Cincinnati Reds

Signed Amateur Free Agents: Chico Fernandez; Bob Lillis; Johnny Podres; Karl Spooner; Maury Wills; Ed Palmquist; Bill Harris; Hector Rodriguez

Released: Catcher Mickey Livingston

1952

June 8, 1952: Traded Outfielder Cal Abrams to the Cincinnati Reds for a Player to be Named and Cash

Cal Abrams was drafted as an amateur free agent in 1942. The Dodgers sent him to the Olean (NY) Oilers of the Class D Pennsylvania-

Ontario–New York League, where he batted .327 in 19 games. The next three years were spent in the army. Abrams, now 22, returned in 1946 and spent the next five seasons as an outstanding minor league hitter. He compiled batting averages of .331, .345, .337, .336, and .333, as he worked his way up Brooklyn's extensive farm system.

The left-handed-hitting Abrams could not duplicate that success with the 1949 and 1950 Dodgers. He got off to an excellent start in 1951 (he was batting .470 at the end of May) but after cooling off, he could never secure a spot as the Dodgers every-day left fielder. Never a favorite of manager Charlie Dressen, he had appeared in only 10 games this season when he was traded. Playing in 123 games over four seasons for Brooklyn, Abrams had a .241 batting average and a 91 OPS+.

The player to be named turned out to be Rudy Rufer, a 25-year-old shortstop with the Tulsa Oilers of the Texas League. Rufer's only big-league experience was a combined 22 games with the 1949–1950 New York Giants, in which he batted .077. The Dodgers sent Rufer to the minor leagues, where he remained until 1957, his final professional season.

June 15, 1952: Traded Pitcher Bud Podbielan to the Cincinnati Reds for Pitcher Bud Byerly and Cash

The Dodgers had a verbal agreement with Tommy Holmes to sign the former Boston Braves outfielder as a free agent in the next few days. Trading pitcher Bud Podbielan to the Cincinnati Reds allowed general manager Buzzie Bavasi to create room on the roster for Holmes. The Reds made room for Podbielan by selling pitcher Bud Byerly to Brooklyn's St. Paul Saints farm team.

Podbielan, a 28-year-old right-hander, signed with Brooklyn as an amateur free agent in 1946. He had pitched for the Dodgers as a reliever and spot starter since 1949, splitting 14 decisions with a 90 ERA+. Byerly, a 32-year-old right-hander, would never pitch for the Dodgers.

June 17, 1952: Signed Free Agent Outfielder Tommy Holmes

As expected, the Dodgers signed Tommy Holmes to shore up their left-handed pinch-hitting corps. The 35-year-old Holmes spent 10 years with the Boston Braves, with a combined batting average of .302 and an

OPS+ of 122. The Brooklyn native had his greatest season in 1945. He batted .352 and led the National League in hits (224), doubles (47), home runs (28) total bases (367), slugging percentage (.577) and OPS+ (175). His 37-game hitting streak that year was the post–1900 National League record until Pete Rose broke it in 1978.

Holmes had a 48–47 record as the Braves' manager after replacing Billy Southworth in 1951, but he was fired after starting the 1952 season 13–22 and replaced by Charlie Grimm. Holmes batted .111 in 31 games for the 1952 Dodgers, with an OPS+ of -5. He was released after the season.

August 1, 1952: Sold Pitcher Johnny Schmitz to the New York Yankees

For the fourth consecutive year, Yankees manager Casey Stengel fortified his club for the stretch drive by adding a veteran named Johnny who had been waived out of the National League. In 1949, it was first baseman Johnny Mize from the Giants; in 1950, outfielder-first baseman Johnny Hopp from Pittsburgh; and in 1951, pitcher Johnny Sain from Boston. This year it was 31-year-old left-hander Johnny Schmitz from Brooklyn.

Schmitz came to Brooklyn with Andy Pafko in June 1951 in the trade that was supposed to assure the Dodgers of the pennant. But Schmitz won only one game the rest of the season, while losing four, and the Dodgers did not win the pennant. His record with the Dodgers this season was one win and one loss.

In addition to sending Brooklyn the $10,000 waiver price, the Yankees transferred 26-year-old righthander Wally Hood from their American Association team in Kansas City to the Dodgers' Texas League's Fort Worth Cats. Hood had pitched in two games for the Yanks in 1949, which would be his only major league action.

As many pitchers had before and after him, Schmitz complained about the way Charlie Dressen had used him. "With the Dodgers the last half of last season and up till two weeks ago this season I don't think I got a chance to show what I could do," Schmitz said. "I made only three starts this season. The third day of the season I beat Boston, 8–2. Then I didn't start until three weeks later and then I wasn't used for another three weeks. I have nothing against anybody over in Brooklyn, but I'd get a kick out of getting into a World Series and beating them."[6] Schmitz's Yankees did face Brooklyn in the World Series in 1952, but Stengel never used him.

October 10, 1952: Traded Pitcher Clyde King to the Cincinnati Reds for Catcher Dixie Howell and Cash

Looking to make room for new faces in 1953, the Dodgers traded right-handed pitcher Clyde King to the Cincinnati Reds for Homer "Dixie" Howell, a 32-year-old catcher, and cash. Brooklyn had sent Howell, then a minor leaguer with the Montreal Royals, to Pittsburgh in the May 1947 trade that sent Kirby Higbe to the Pirates. He had been with the Reds since 1949, but the Dodgers had no room for him on their roster and assigned him to the Saint Paul Saints. He would play for the Saints and Royals through the 1958 season, with brief stays in Brooklyn, amounting to 24 games, in 1953, 1955, and 1956.

The Dodgers signed the 6'1" King out of the University of North Carolina in 1944 and brought him directly to the big leagues. The 20-year-old rookie appeared in 14 games, winning two and losing one with a 3.09 earned run average. He was 5–5 in 1945 with a much heavier workload, 42 games, all but two in relief.

King bounced between the Dodgers and their farm teams for the rest of his seven-year career in Brooklyn. He had his best season in 1951, when pitching mainly in relief (45 of his 48 appearances), he had a 14–7 record. In all, he pitched in 165 games for the Dodgers with a 29–19 record and a 3.94 ERA. King's 1953 season with the Reds was his last as a major leaguer. He went on to be a minor and major league manager and executive.

December 2, 1952: Selected Pitcher Don Bessent from the New York Yankees in the Minor League Draft

In the fall of 1952, the Dodgers lost the World Series to the New York Yankees; in December they felt they outsmarted the Yanks by drafting Don Bessent. "We drafted Fred Bessent (Don was his middle name) from the [Yankees] Binghamton farm team in the Eastern League," said Dodgers vice president Fresco Thompson. "The boy had a great record in the minors, winning 22 and losing seven for LaGrange in the Georgia-Alabama League in 1950 and hung up an 11–2 won-and-lost mark the next year with Norfolk in the Piedmont [League]. He underwent a back operation and was out of baseball last year. He cost us the $5,000 waiver price and we're sending him to St Paul. Of course, he's a gamble. We are betting the five grand his back has come around."[7] It was an excellent bet. Bessent had been unable to pitch in 1952 because of a spinal condition. The Yankees gave up on him, but his condition was corrected by bone graft surgery.

Bessent spent two-and-a-half seasons with St. Paul before the Dodgers called him up in July 1955. The 24-year-old right-hander went 8–1 that year to help the Dodgers win the pennant and their first World Series. Despite his late start, he finished third in Rookie of the Year voting. Injuries over the next three seasons prevented Bessent from duplicating his rookie success. In his four years with the Dodgers, he appeared in 108 games, all in relief except for two starts he made in 1955. He had a 14–7 record and a 123 ERA+.

Also in 1952:
   Sold: Second Baseman Wayne Terwilliger to Washington Senators
   Signed Amateur Free Agents: Sandy Amorós, Jim Gentile, Dick Gray, Ralph Mauriello; John Roseboro
   Signed Free Agents: Pitcher Danny McDevitt

1953

January 17, 1953: Traded Outfielder Andy Pafko to the Boston Braves for Second Baseman Roy Hartsfield and Cash

The Dodgers were an aging team. Catcher Roy Campanella and right-fielder Carl Furillo were 31, shortstop Pee Wee Reese and third basement Billy Cox were 33, and second baseman Jackie Robinson would turn 34 in two weeks. Only center-fielder Duke Snider, 26, and first baseman Gil Hodges, who would turn 29 in April, were under 30.

"We can't sit still and watch the team collapse of old age," said Dodgers vice president Buzzie Bavasi in announcing the club had sent 32-year-old Andy Pafko to the Boston Braves for second baseman Roy Hartsfield. Bavasi added that Hartsfield would be sent to the Montreal Royals (which ended his big-league career), giving Brooklyn room for another player on their roster.

Pafko came to the Dodgers in June 1951 in an eight-player deal with the Chicago Cubs. He had been their left fielder ever since. In 150 games in 1952, he batted .287, with 19 home runs and 85 run batted in. Pafko would never play a regular season game for the BOSTON Braves. In March 1953, while they were at spring training, the Braves announced they were relocating the franchise to Milwaukee.

With Pafko gone, Bavasi said the Dodgers' left-field job would be wide open. George Shuba and Dick Williams were the leading contenders, but the team would also look at Sandy Amorós, Jim Pendleton, Bill Antonello, Gino Cimoli, Bill Sharman, Carmen Mauro, Walt Moryn and Don Thompson.

The player Brooklyn added to its roster would be 24-year-old second base man Jim Gilliam, who hit .301 for Montreal in 1952 and was the International League's Most Valuable Player. Gilliam, a switch-hitter, would be the National League's Rookie of the Year in 1953 and a key member of the Dodgers for 14 seasons, at second base, third base, and the outfield. He played in 1,956 games, the fifth most in Dodgers history, with a .266 batting average. Gilliam is in the Dodgers top-ten in walks, hits, doubles, and total bases. He was released following the 1966 season.

February 16, 1953: Traded Infielder Rocky Bridges and Minor League Shortstop Jim Pendleton to the Boston Braves for Pitcher Russ Meyer

The Dodgers had been rebuffed at the winter meetings in trying to obtain Philadelphia Phillies right-hander Russ Meyer when the Phillies demanded third baseman Billy Cox in return. Brooklyn finally got their man, but it took a four-team trade to do it. Philadelphia traded the 29-year-old Meyer to the Boston Braves for first baseman Earl Torgeson and cash. The Braves, a month away from relocating to Milwaukee, then traded Meyer to Brooklyn for utility infielder Rocky Bridges, 25, and rookie outfielder Jim Pendleton, 27. The Braves kept Pendleton but traded Bridges and cash to the Cincinnati Reds for outfielder-first baseman Joe Adcock.

Meyer was a talented pitcher. He had a 60–54 record in seven seasons with the Chicago Cubs and Phillies, including a 17–8 season and a 127 ERA+ with Philadelphia in 1949. But he was hot-tempered and often uncontrollable, on and off the field, including a notorious near riotous incident with Jackie Robinson.

"He's a good pitcher, with a real good curve ball," said Dodgers manager Charlie Dressen. "And we're giving up two guys we didn't use last year." When he was asked about Meyer's reputation as a hothead,

Dressen said: "That's all right, I think I'll be able to handle him. And maybe with a better club behind him, he won't have as much reason to blow his top during a game."[8]

Meyer was overjoyed about coming to the defending National League champions. He promised "to win 18 games for the Dodgers this year or hang up my glove. Any pitcher who can't win 18 games with that ball club behind him ought to quit and try some other business."[9] Recalling problems he had with Robinson and other Dodgers, Meyer assured the club they had made a good deal.

Rocky Bridges batted .237 in 114 games as a Dodger, serving as a backup at second base, shortstop, and third base. His spirited style of play was sure to appeal to his new manager at Cincinnati, Rogers Hornsby. Bridges' chances for a full-time position were much improved now that he no longer had to compete with Jackie Robinson, Pee Wee Reese, and Billy Cox. The Reds were set at shortstop and third base with Roy McMillan and Bobby Adams, so his best chance would be at second base, where the competition was veteran Grady Hatton and rookie Johnny Temple. (Bridges won that competition and was the Reds' second baseman in 1953.)

Jim Pendleton played with the Chicago American Giants of the Negro American League in 1948 and was signed by the Dodgers in 1949. He did extremely well at St. Paul in 1950 and 1951, and he was the International League's All-Star shortstop playing for Montreal in 1952. However, the Dodgers had Reese at shortstop. Pendleton's opportunities would be much better with the Braves, where weak-hitting Jack Dittmer was the competition. (Dittmer retained the position in 1953, while the Braves moved Pendleton to the outfield.)

July 10, 1953: Sold Pitcher Ralph Branca to the Detroit Tigers on Waivers

Because the Dodgers had put Ralph Branca on waivers a few days earlier, for the third time this season, they could not recall him when the Detroit Tigers claimed him for the $10,000 waiver price. Branca, the son-in-law of James Mulvey, one of the Dodgers vice presidents and directors, was disappointed at leaving the team. "I'm sorry to leave Brooklyn," he said, "but I guess it's for the best. It seems like I'm a rookie all over again. At 27."[10]

Signed as an amateur free agent out of New York University in 1943, Branca made his Dodgers debut at age 18 in 1944. He had an 8–9 record over the next three seasons but blossomed in 1947. The

21-year-old right-hander won 21 games (21–12) and had an ERA+ of 154. He was the ace of the pennant-winning Dodgers and was the starter in the first game of the World Series against the Yankees. In July 1948, the 6'3" Branca was the National League's starting pitcher in the All-Star game.

Branca started a total of 55 games in 1948–1949, winning 27 and losing 14. His .722 winning percentage in 1949 led the NL, but beginning in 1950, manager Burt Shotton started using him more in relief. New manager Charlie Dressen continued doing so in 1951. It was in that role that Branca, in relief of Don Newcombe, surrendered Bobby Thomson's pennant-winning home run on October 3.

A spring training injury, when he fell off a chair, limited Branca to just 16 games in 1952. This season he had just seven relief appearances with no decisions. But in 11 innings, he had allowed 12 runs, 15 hits, and four home runs. Branca's 10-year Brooklyn record was 80–58 with a 107 ERA+ in 282 games. (He would return in 1956 to pitch two innings in one game for the Dodgers.)

Branca was told to report to the Tigers in Detroit the next day, July 11. On July 12, Fred Hutchinson, his new manager, started him against the St. Louis Browns. Branca allowed three earned runs in five innings and was the losing pitcher. On July 19, he pitched a complete game against the Philadelphia Athletics for his first American League win. "Boy, that really felt good," Branca said. "It was my first victory since June 27, 1952, and that one was in relief. I can't remember the last time I went the distance to win."[11]

Also in 1953:

Traded: Outfielder Carmen Mauro to Washington Senators for Outfielder Ken Wood; First Baseman Rocky Nelson to Cleveland Indians for Pitcher Bill Abernathy and Cash; Pitcher Bud Byerly to New York Giants for Minor League Pitcher Norman Fox

Signed Amateur Free Agents: Don Demeter; Fred Kipp; Bob Darnell; Larry Sherry; Dick Scott; Dick Tracewski; Sparky Anderson

1954

For the 1954 season, Walter Alston replaced Charlie Dressen as manager.

March 28, 1954: Traded Infielder Bobby Morgan to the Philadelphia Phillies for Second Baseman Dick Young and Cash

In discussing this trade, new Dodgers manager Walt Alston said veteran Billy Cox would again be the team's regular third baseman in 1954. Alston also announced he had chosen rookie Don Hoak over Bobby Morgan to be Cox's backup. The Dodgers believed that while Hoak, 26, did not have the 27-year-old Morgan's power, he was a better third baseman, faster, and a better base runner.

After Morgan led the International League in batting (.337) and winning the league's Most Valuable Player Award with the 1949 Montreal Royals, he was considered the eventual replacement for shortstop Pee Wee Reese. But replacing Reese or anyone else in that Brooklyn infield was beyond Morgan's ability. In three years with the Dodgers, Morgan, who signed as an amateur free agent in 1944, had a .241 batting average, 21 home runs, and a 104 OPS+.

While exclusively a utility player with the Dodgers, the Phillies were expected to use him as a replacement for Willie Jones at third base. But Jones retained his position, while Morgan replaced shortstop Ted Kazanski, who was now in the army.

In return for Morgan, the Dodgers got Dick Young and a reported $50,000. Young had spent almost all of the past three seasons at Triple A. He played briefly with the Phillies in 1951 and 1952, getting 18 hits in 81 at-bats. The Dodgers sold him to Montreal, and he continued to play in the minor leagues through 1960.

August 6, 1954: Sold Pitcher Ben Wade to the St. Louis Cardinals

Ben Wade, a 6'3" right-hander, debuted with the Chicago Cubs in 1948, appearing in two games and losing his only decision. The Cubs sent him to the Nashville Vols of the Southern Association in 1949, where he won 18 and lost 8. The Dodgers bought Wade in the winter of 1950 and sent him to the Hollywood Stars of the Pacific Coast League. he spent two seasons with the Stars, winning 30 games and earning a promotion to Brooklyn.

Wade was in 37 games, 24 as a starter, and had an 11–9 record and a 102 ERA+ for the 1952 pennant-winning Dodgers. In 1953, manager Charlie Dressen moved him to the bullpen. In 32 appearances he had a 7–5 record and a 114 ERA+, as the Dodgers repeated as National

League champions. Wade continued to be a relief pitcher this season under new manager Walt Alston but had been mostly ineffective. When he was sold to St. Louis, Wade had an 8.20 earned run average and an ERA+ of 51. Moving him allowed the Dodgers, struggling to keep pace with the league-leading New York Giants, to bring up a pitcher from the minors. The two most likely candidates were right-hander Bob Darnell and left-hander Karl Spooner. They chose Darnell. In September they brought up Spooner.

December 13, 1954: Traded Pitcher Preacher Roe and Third Baseman Billy Cox to the Baltimore Orioles for Minor League Pitcher-Outfielder John Jancse, Minor League Infielder Harry Schwegman, and Cash

Seven years after they came to Brooklyn in a trade with the Pittsburgh Pirates, the Dodgers traded pitcher Preacher Roe and third baseman Billy Cox to the Baltimore Orioles. It was Brooklyn's first deal with the American League Orioles, the former St. Louis Browns who had relocated to Baltimore for the 1954 season.

Roe and Cox had been a big part of Brooklyn's success these past seven years. "All Brooklyn fans will appreciate the great job Preacher has done for us over the years, and we regard Cox as the greatest glove man we have ever had," said owner Walter O'Malley.[12] But while the fans appreciated them, both players had complaints about their lack of playing time under new manager Walter Alston.

Roe, 38, pitched only 63 innings in 15 games, with a record of 3–4. He thought he deserved more of a chance, given the magnificent 44–8 record he had compiled the past three seasons under manager Charley Dressen. Roe's overall record as a Dodger was 93–37, with a 124 ERA+. A four time All-Star, he led the National League with an .880 winning percentage (22–3) in 1951. Roy Campanella called him the best pitcher he ever caught. "He was a guy who knew what he was doing every second of every minute."[13] Roe never joined the Orioles, choosing to retire instead.

Alston had dropped the 35-year-old Cox to the role of third-string third baseman in 1954, behind rookie Don Hoak and Jackie Robinson. In his seven seasons in Brooklyn, Cox batted .259 with an 82 OPS+, while saving countless runs with his excellent defense. He played a nondescript season with Baltimore in 1955 and then retired.

The Dodgers received a reported $60,000 in the deal, which is all they got. Neither John Jancse nor Harry Schwegman ever reached the big leagues.

December 14, 1954: Signed Pitcher Sandy Koufax as an Amateur Free Agent

The Major Leagues' Bonus Rule had been in effect since 1947, but the Dodgers did not sign their first "bonus baby" until the closing days of 1954. Vice president Fresco Thompson had been reluctant to sign bonus players but explained that the Dodgers felt 19-year-old Sandy Koufax, from the University of Cincinnati, was too good a prospect to lose. And had he not acted, Koufax would have been lost. The Giants, Yankees, Pirates, Cubs, Indians, and Braves were all interested in signing him. The $14,000 signing bonus the Dodgers gave the Brooklyn native would result in their getting the most talent for the least money in team history.

The Bonus Rule stipulated that when a major league team signed a player to a contract in excess of $4,000, the team was required to keep that player on the 25-man roster for two full-seasons. Therefore, the Dodgers had to keep the 6'2" left-hander with them in 1955 and 1956. Koufax was erratic in those two seasons, but showed enough promise that he never would have to pitch in the minor leagues. He finally reached his full potential in 1961, the Dodgers fourth year in Los Angeles, winning 18 games (18–13) and leading the league with 269 strikeouts.

Koufax followed with five years (1962–1966) that are as good as any pitcher has ever had. His won-lost record was 111–34 and he led the league in wins three times and in winning percentage twice. He was the earned run average leader in each of those five seasons, and in three of them was the leader in shutouts and strikeouts.

Koufax was the National League's Most Valuable Player in 1963 and finished second in 1965 and 1966. In three of his last four seasons, he won the major league's Cy Young Award. (There was just one award covering both leagues until 1967.) Koufax pitched in four World Series, winning four and losing three, despite an earned run average of 0.95. In 57 World Series innings pitched, he struck out 61 batters.

An arthritic left elbow forced Koufax to retire at age 30, following the 1966 season. He was inducted into the Hall of Fame in 1972.

Also in 1954:

Traded: First Baseman Wayne Belardi to Detroit Tigers for Pitcher Ernie Nevel, Catcher Johnny Bucha, First Baseman Chuck Kress, and

Cash; Pitcher Ray Moore to Baltimore Orioles for Second Baseman Chico Garcia

Purchased: First Baseman Rocky Nelson from Cleveland Indians

Sold: First Baseman Chuck Kress to Toronto Maple Leafs of the International League; Sold Outfielder Dick Whitman to Portland Beavers of the Pacific Coast League

Signed Amateur Free Agents: Don Drysdale; Stan Williams; Don LeJohn

Chapter Fourteen

1955–1957

1955

March 17, 1955: Traded Pitcher Erv Palica to the Baltimore Orioles for First Baseman Frank Kellert and Cash

When Preacher Roe chose to retire rather than join the Baltimore Orioles as part of a December 1954 trade, the Orioles returned him to the Dodgers. By sending pitcher Erv Palica to Baltimore, the Brooklyn club fulfilled its obligation to Baltimore and picked up some cash as well as a player.

Frank Kellert, 30, had been in the minor leagues since 1949, except for two games with the 1953 St. Louis Browns and 10 games with the 1954 Orioles. Playing for the Texas League's San Antonio Missions in 1954, he batted .316 with 41 home runs and 146 runs batted in. Manager Walter Alston was pleased when several Dodgers, who played against Kellert in the minor leagues, told him Kellert was an excellent hitter and a good addition.

Seventeen-year-old Erv Palica got into two games in 1945, the year Dodgers scout Tom Downey signed him as an amateur free agent. In both games, he was a pinch-runner. The 6'1" right-hander spent the rest of the season, all of 1946, and all but three games in 1947 in the minor leagues. In 1948 he returned to Brooklyn full-time, under managers Leo Durocher and Burt Shotton.

Palica's best year was 1950, under Shotton. He won 13, lost eight, and had a 115 ERA+. Much was expected of him in 1951, but unfortunately for him, Charlie Dressen had replaced Shotton as the Dodgers' manager. Dressen is blamed for ruining several pitchers' careers by misusing them. He did the same with Palica. In addition to misusing him, he called Palica a hypochondriac and publicly questioned the 23-year-old's courage and commitment.

The once very promising young pitcher finished his Brooklyn career with a 32–33 record and a 97 ERA+. In two seasons with the second-division Orioles, he won nine games and lost 22.

June 9, 1955: Traded Pitcher Joe Black to the Cincinnati Redlegs for Cash and a Player to be Named

Joe Black had pitched for six seasons with the Baltimore Elite Giants of the Negro National League when the Dodgers bought him from Baltimore in 1951. As a 28-year-old rookie, the 6'2" right-hander played a major role in leading the 1952 Dodgers to the National League pennant. Black set a club record by appearing in 56 games, winning 15 (15–4) and saving 15 others. His performance earned him the National League's Rookie of the Year Award and a third-place finish in the voting for the Most Valuable Player Award. Manager Charlie Dressen started Black in two games just before the season ended and then chose him to pitch the opening game of the World Series. He defeated the Yankees, 4–2, but lost in two subsequent starts.

Dressen told Black he was considering making him a starter in 1953 and urged him to develop a third pitch. Black tried, without success. In the process of being told to change his stride, he lost the dominance he had in 1952, becoming yet another pitcher ruined by Charlie Dressen. Dressen used him sparingly in 1953 and almost never in clutch situations. New manager Walter Alston used him hardly at all in 1954, and with the addition of Ed Roebuck and the effectiveness of Jim Hughes and Clem Labine, Black had appeared in only six games this season.

Cincinnati paid a reported $15,000 for Black. On June 14 they sent 29-year-old outfielder Bob Borkowski to Brooklyn as the player to be named. Borkowski was a journeyman who had been in the league with the Chicago Cubs and the Reds since 1950. Brooklyn's original plan was to send Borkowski to the minor leagues and bring up Gino Cimoli from Montreal to use as a right-handed pinch hitter. But because Cimoli was more an everyday player rather than the bench-sitting, pinch-hitting type, Alston decided to hold Borkowski for the present.

Borkowski played in nine games for Brooklyn, with a .105 batting average.

October 11, 1955: Sold First Baseman Frank Kellert to the Chicago Cubs

A week after the Dodgers said they would not stand pat on the squad that won the 1955 World Series; they made their first change. They sold Frank Kellert to the Chicago Cubs for an estimated $15,000. Kellert, a combination first baseman and outfielder, was the Dodgers No. 1 right-handed pinch-hitter in 1955. He batted .325 with 19 RBIs in 39 games. He pinch-hit three times during the Series and had one single.

Kellert was the batter when Jackie Robinson stole home in the first game of the Series. Yankees catcher Yogi Berra vehemently disputed umpire Bill Summers's safe call, and according to Kellert, Berra was correct. Speaking from his home in Oklahoma City, he told the *Daily Oklahoman* Berra had tagged Robinson before he reached the plate.

December 6, 1955: Traded, Third Baseman Don Hoak and Outfielder Walt Moryn to the Chicago Cubs for Third Baseman Randy Jackson

Don Hoak and Jackie Robinson shared the third base position in 1955, but both had drawbacks. Hoak, 27, was a hard-nosed player with speed and a strong arm. However, his hitting was not what teams wanted in a third baseman. He had a .243 batting average in his two seasons in Brooklyn, with 12 home runs and 45 runs batted in. Hoak's style of play appealed to Cubs manager Stan Hack. "We need a spark plug on our club, and he has a chance to be it. He has aggressiveness and speed and that's what I'm looking for."[1]

The trade seemed to indicate Brooklyn did not expect much from Robinson in 1956. When vice president Buzzie Bavasi was asked about the team's plans for Robinson, who would turn 37 in two months, he was non-committal. "I don't know what Alston is going to do with him. He's still on the Dodgers. He can play some first base and some outfield."[2]

Robinson appeared unconcerned. When asked if he was worried about his third base job, he said: "No, I'm not. I'm just going down south next year and get in shape. I'll be all right." He called the trade good for both teams. "You can't help but improve your club when you get a fellow like Randy. He can hit that long ball. But it's tough to see a guy like Hoak go. You always hate to see a guy that's been with you a couple of years go. He's young and just starting to come."[3]

Walt Moryn, a 29-year-old outfielder, played in 48 games for the Dodgers in 1954 and 11 this past season. The 11 games were at the beginning and end of the season, the rest of which he spent at St. Paul. The 6'2" left-handed slugger hit 25 home runs and batted in 88 runs for the Saints. Moryn would hit 84 home runs for the Cubs over the next five seasons.

The right-handed-hitting Jackson, 29, was a slow runner and only an adequate fielder, but he was a good hitter, with power. He had 88 home runs since coming to Chicago late in the 1950 season. In 138 games for the 1955 Cubs, Jackson batted .265, with 21 home runs and 70 runs batted in. "He'll hit some home runs for us, especially at Ebbets Field," predicted Bavasi.[4]

Jackson had been criticized in the Chicago press for lacking hustle and motivation, which prompted New York sportswriter Bill Roeder to observe: "You can never pry a ballplayer away from another club unless the other club is at least slightly dissatisfied."[5]

Cubs general manager Wid Matthews raised interest when he announced there would be an addition to this transaction in the next week. Bavasi said it was not definite, but the Dodgers might sell a pitcher to Chicago.

December 9, 1955: Traded Pitcher Russ Meyer to the Chicago Cubs for Pitcher Don Elston and Cash

Three days after the Chicago's Wid Matthews announced there would be an addition to the Randy Jackson for Don Hoak and Walt Moryn trade, the Cubs acquired veteran right-hander Russ Meyer from the Dodgers. In return, Brooklyn received pitcher Don Elston and an estimated $20,000.

Meyer, 32, was returning to Chicago, where his major league career began in 1946. He came to the Dodgers from the Philadelphia Phillies as part of a four-team trade in February 1953. Meyer had a 15–5 record that year, an 11–6 mark in 1954, but slipped to just 6–2 in 1955. Despite his 32–13 record as a Dodger, his ERA+ was a below average 94. The numbers reflected why Meyer was so happy when he was traded to Brooklyn. "With the Dodgers, you can give up three or four runs and still win the game easily," he had said. "That's the thing I like about the Dodgers. They get their pitchers some runs."[6]

Elston, a 26-year-old right-hander, had pitched in only two major league games, with the 1953 Cubs. But he had been a very successful minor leaguer wherever he went. This past season he was 17–6 with a 3.05 earned run average for the Los Angeles Angels of the Pacific Coast League. Elston's career in Brooklyn would consist of one inning pitched in 1957. On May 23 of that year, he was traded back to the Cubs for pitchers Jackie Collum and Vito Valentinetti.

Collum appeared in five games for the 1957–1958 Dodgers, without a decision. Valentinetti was purchased by the Cleveland Indians in August 1957, without ever appearing in a game for the Dodgers.

Also in 1955:

Traded: Pitcher Ron Negray to the Philadelphia Phillies for Pitcher Dave Cole and Cash; Pitcher Pete Wojey to Detroit Tigers for Pitcher Leo Cristante and Cash
   Signed Amateur Free Agents: Jack Smith; Willard Hunter
   Chosen in Minor League Draft: Pitcher Ken Rowe

1956

May 14, 1956: Sold Pitcher Billy Loes to the Baltimore Orioles

Branch Rickey signed right-hander Billy Loes from a Queens, New York, high school in 1948. Rickey was not sure the slender pitcher had a major league fastball, but because other clubs were anxious to sign him, he reluctantly gave Loes a $21,000 bonus, the largest ever for a Dodger at that time. Loes filled out quickly and soon had a fast ball that was better than average. In 1952, at age 22, he became a regular in the Dodgers rotation, winning 50 and losing 25 over the next four seasons.

Loes had complained of arm problems even in his best years. The Dodgers may have been skeptical before but not this time. Tendinitis in his pitching arm had limited him to only one appearance this season, a start in which he allowed six earned runs in 1 1/3 innings.

The reported sales price ranged from $20,000 to $30,000, which constituted a gamble for a sore-armed pitcher with a history of zaniness. However, it was not the first gamble Orioles manager Paul Richards had taken with a Dodgers' pitcher. Two years earlier, he took a chance on another "alleged" Dodgers problem child, Erv Palica, and on a sore-armed Ray Moore. Both came cheaper than Loes and both were now members of Baltimore's starting rotation.

Loes was happy to leave the Dodgers. "I was always under a strain," he said. "I've been asking for two years to be traded and it's finally happened. I just could not be comfortable in Brooklyn."[7]

May 15, 1956: Sold Pitcher Jim Hughes to the Chicago Cubs on Waivers

Jim Hughes became part of the Dodgers' organization in 1949, when the team entered into a working agreement with the Hollywood Stars of the Pacific Coast League. Hughes, now 33, had been in five games in 1956 without a decision. In the previous four seasons, working strictly in relief, he had a 14–10 record. The 6'1" right-hander had his best seasons in 1954. Appearing in a league-leading 60 games, he won eight and lost four, and his 24 saves were the league's high. (The 60 games were a Dodgers record, equaled by Clem Labine in 1955.) His ERA+, which had been 124 in 48 games in 1953, was 128. Labine replaced Hughes as Brooklyn's top man in the bullpen in 1955, while Hughes, who had been so ineffective, was sent to St. Paul in August.

May 15, 1956: Purchased Pitcher Sal Maglie from the Cleveland Indians

The man who had tormented Brooklyn fans for most of this decade was now a Dodger. Pitching for the hated New York Giants, Sal Maglie had a 23–11 lifetime record against Brooklyn; from 1950 to 1954 he was 22–6 with five shutouts.

"We've got a lot of young pitchers. He has the experience that could be helpful to them and the club," vice president Buzzie Bavasi said in explaining the purchase. "He knows the league well for he hasn't been out of it long. He'll be spotted as a starter and a reliever."[8]

Maglie, a right-hander, had a 95–42 record with the Giants when he was sold to the Cleveland Indians on July 31, 1955. He had an 0–2 record with Cleveland and had appeared in just two games this season. However, he had impressed the Dodgers two weeks earlier in an exhibition game played at Roosevelt Field in Jersey City. The 39-year-old Maglie pitched four scoreless and hitless innings against the defending world champions. After the game, Pee Wee Reese said, "If he can still throw like that, I'm glad he's in the other league."[9]

June 25, 1956: Sold Outfielder Dick Williams to the Baltimore Orioles

In his five years with Brooklyn, right-handed-hitting outfielder Dick Williams bounced back-and-forth between the Dodgers and their farm clubs in Montreal, St. Paul, and Fort Worth. With Brooklyn, Williams played in 112 games with a .232 batting average and a 61 OPS+. The Dodgers used him in seven games this season, all as a pinch-hitter. While they had no room for the 27-year-old Williams, the Baltimore Orioles did. Manager Paul Richards said he would use him immediately as an outfielder, despite a separated shoulder, suffered in 1952 that limited his throwing ability.

"Yes, his arm isn't as strong as it once was," Richards conceded. "But he can still throw pretty well. He also has very good speed. Best of all, he's supposed to be a hitter. We don't think he'll hurt us on defense and are hoping he'll help our attack."[10]

Williams did help their attack. Playing in 87 games, mostly in center field, he batted .287 with 11 home runs, 37 runs batted in, and a 118 OPS+.

December 13, 1956: Traded Infielder Jackie Robinson to the New York Giants for Pitcher Dick Littlefield and Cash

That the Dodgers would trade Jackie Robinson, the face of the franchise for a decade, was a shock to their fans. That they would trade him to his and their archenemy, the Giants, and get so little in return, a journeyman pitcher and $30,000, compounded their shock. If they had not realized it earlier, Brooklyn fans were learning that baseball, a religion to them, was still a business. That lesson would be hammered home in less than a year when the team was moved to Los Angeles.

Sportswriter Dick Young, who covered Robinson's career from the beginning, gave the two major reasons why the Dodgers traded him. Foremost was his age—he would be 38 in January—and the club was trying to make over an aging team. Also, there was his often-contentious relationships with owner Walter O'Malley and manager Walter Alston.

According to Young, the Giants wanted Robinson to play first base in place of Bill White, who would be spending the 1957 season in the army, and to serve as a gate attraction.

At first, Robinson seemed undecided about playing for the Giants, said the team's vice president, Chub Feeney, but appeared to have changed his mind. "That's baseball," Robinson said. "I thought I might be traded a year ago but, after the good season I had this year, I thought I'd stay in Brooklyn. I'm sorry to be leaving a lot of nice guys; fellows like Pee Wee and Gil. I'll be out to beat them if I can, but if the Giants can't win the pennant, I'll be hoping the guys in Brooklyn do."[11]

Giants manager Bill Rigney said he expected Robinson to play two more seasons and as many as 120 games per season. "I'm hoping he fills the spot till White gets out of the service. Playing him at first base should lengthen his career."[12]

Robinson, the first Black player in the twentieth century, went on to have a Hall of Fame career. The most exciting player of his generation, or maybe ever, he batted .311 with a 132 OPS+ in his 10 seasons in Brooklyn. Robinson was the Rookie of the Year in 1947, the batting champion and the Most Valuable Player in 1949, a six-time All-Star, and the recipient of MVP votes in eight of his ten seasons.

Dick Littlefield, a 30-year-old left-hander, had a 31–50 record pitching for eight different major league teams in his seven-year career. "We took him on Al Campanis's say-so," said Buzzie Bavasi, explaining that Campanis, a Dodgers scout, managed Littlefield in Cuba. "Al says Littlefield developed a good changeup down there, but hardly ever used it up here. If we can get him to throw it, he may be at good pitcher."[13]

On January 14, 1957, Jackie Robinson formally announced his retirement, voiding the trade.

Also in 1956:

Traded: Catcher Tim Thompson to Kansas City Athletics for Pitcher Lee Wheat, Outfielder Tom Saffell, and Cash

Purchased: Outfielder Dale Mitchell from Cleveland Indians

Sold: Pitcher Tom Lasorda to Kansas City Athletics; First Baseman Rocky Nelson to St. Louis Cardinals

Signed Free Agents: Pitcher Ralph Branca

Signed Amateur Free Agents: Tommy Davis; Bob Aspromonte; Bob Giallombardo; Don Miles

1957

Walter O'Malley bought the 25 percent of the team owned by John Smith's widow. O'Malley now owned two-thirds of the franchise.

April 5, 1957: Traded Shortstop Chico Fernandez to the Philadelphia Phillies for Outfielder Elmer Valo, Pitcher Ron Negray, Minor League First Baseman Tim Harkness, Minor League Shortstop Melvin Geho, a Player to be Named, and Cash

Shortstop Chico Fernandez's brief reign as the "heir to Pee Wee Reese" ended when the Dodgers traded him to the Philadelphia Phillies. (He had replaced Don Zimmer, who now reclaimed that role.) Fernandez was signed by Dodgers scout Andy High as an 18-year-old in 1951. He had been in Brooklyn's farm system ever since, except for 34 games with the parent club in 1956. At spring training that year, he had become so discouraged, he told Buzzie Bavasi he was going to quit and return to his native Cuba. Bavasi sent Jackie Robinson to persuade Fernandez to stay. "Look Chico," Robinson said, "don't be stupid because Pee Wee has maybe one more year."[14]

Fernandez would play another seven major league seasons, with the Phillies, the Detroit Tigers, and briefly with the New York Mets. His defense kept him in the big leagues, as his career batting average was .240 and his OPS+ was 67.

Thirty-six-year-old Elmer Valo played 15 years for the Philadelphia/Kansas City Athletics, before Kansas City released him in May 1956. A few days later he signed with the Philadelphia Phillies as a free agent. In 98 games with the Phillies, he batted .289 and had a 118 OPS+. Valo, a left-handed hitter, played for the Dodgers in Brooklyn in 1957 and in Los Angeles in 1958, as a pinch hitter and part-time corner outfielder. He batted .263, with 40 runs batted in and a 91 OPS+ in 146 games. Los Angeles released him early in 1959.

Right-hander Ron Negray was returning to Brooklyn. Signed as an amateur free agent in 1949, he appeared in four games in 1952 without a decision. The Dodgers traded him to the Phillies in 1955 for pitcher Dave Cole and cash. Cole was sent to St. Paul and never pitched for Brooklyn, while Negray had a 6–6 record and a 100 ERA+ for the 1955–1956 Phillies. The Dodgers sent him to the minor leagues this season, but he returned to again pitch in four games without a decision for the 1958 Dodgers.

Tim Harkness, a 6'2" left-handed-hitting first baseman, was just 19 years old with one season of professional baseball experience. He played in 56 games for the 1956 Olean (NY) Oilers of the Class D Pennsylvania-Ontario–New York League, batting .251. The Dodgers would keep him in the minor leagues until 1961.

Melvin Geho, a 21-year-old shortstop, had spent three seasons in the minor leagues. The Dodgers would keep him there, and though he played through the 1961 season, he never made it to the major leagues.

In addition to the $80,000 the Dodgers received, the Phillies sent them Ben Flowers, on April 8, as the player to be named. The Dodgers sent Flowers, along with Negray, to the Los Angeles Angels of the Pacific Coast League. On May 24, they traded Flowers from the Angels to the New York Yankees for outfielder Jim Fridley, a former major leaguer now with their American Association farm team, the Denver Bears. Neither Flowers nor Fridley ever played for the Dodgers.

June 14, 1957: Sold Pitcher Ken Lehman to the Baltimore Orioles

Ken Lehman had been rumored on his way to Baltimore for more than a month. Orioles manager Paul Richards had been pleased with the recent work of two other former Dodgers, pitchers Ray Moore and Billy Loes, and was willing to spend a reported $30,000 on Lehman. Richards also let it be known he would be interested in anyone the Dodgers considered expendable. Lehman, a 29-year-old left-hander, had been in the Brooklyn organization since signing as an amateur free agent in 1946. He had been successful in several minor leagues, but never could make it at the major league level.

The Dodgers brought up Lehman at the end of the 1952 season, where he went 1–2 in four games. Pitching for Montreal the past three seasons, he had win totals of 13, 18, and 22. After his 22–9 mark in 1955, along with his International League-leading 241 innings pitched, Lehman seemed ready to finally succeed with the Dodgers. But he appeared in only 25 games in 1956, with 49 1/3 innings pitched and a 2–3 record. In three games this season, he had no decisions. Lehman did much better in Baltimore. In 30 games for the 1957 Orioles, all but three in relief, he had an 8–3 record with a 129 ERA+.

The Dodgers made several other moves this day. They promoted left-handed pitcher Danny McDevitt from St. Paul and catcher John Roseboro from Montreal, while little-used catcher Joe Pignatano was sent down to the Royals.

September 1, 1957: Sold Pitcher Sal Maglie to the New York Yankees

Despite being in third place, seven games behind the league-leading Milwaukee Braves, the Dodgers postponed the sale of Sal Maglie until the August 31 deadline for World Series eligibility had passed. They did not want to be confronted by their former longtime nemesis if they managed to overtake the Braves and face the Yankees in the World Series.

Maglie had just arrived at Ebbets Field for the Dodgers' Sunday afternoon game against the Giants when the club informed him he had been sold. He left quickly and was in the Bronx and in the Yankees' dugout in time for their game against Washington. When Yankee Stadium public address announcer Bob Sheppard told the crowd of Maglie's presence, the fans greeted him with a rousing ovation.

Casey Stengel, Maglie's new manager, was delighted with the acquisition. "I'm glad you are here," he told him. "The players are glad, my coaches are glad, and the front office is glad. He's been a pitcher and he's still a pitcher," Stengel told the press. "He knows how, and I think he can help me, especially in this big ballpark here."[15]

After being slowed by injuries earlier in the season, Maglie was in good shape. He had a 6–6 record for the Dodgers with a 2.93 earned run average. Following his acquisition from Cleveland in May 1956, Maglie went 13–5 and was a key factor in Brooklyn's edging Milwaukee by one game for the National League pennant. On September 25, he pitched the Brooklyn club's last no-hitter, against the Phillies. In the World Series, he was the winner in Game One, and the 2–0 loser in Don Larsen's perfect game in Game Five.

The Yankees had to wait until Maglie got waivers from every team in both leagues; a task made easier because of his age (40) and his relatively high salary ($27,500). Then they reportedly paid Brooklyn $37,500, while also agreeing to send two minor leaguers to the Dodgers in 1958.

By becoming a Yankee, Maglie joined a select group of those who had played for all three New York teams. The group consisted of Willie Keeler, Jack Doyle, Fred Merkle, Waite Hoyt, Lefty O'Doul, Burleigh Grimes, Tony Lazzeri, and Bobo Newsom. With the Dodgers having agreed to move to Los Angeles for the 1958 season Maglie would be the last.

Also in 1957:

Traded: Pitcher Don Elston to Chicago Cubs for Pitcher Vito Valentinetti and Pitcher Jackie Collum

Purchased: Outfielder Bob Kennedy from Chicago White Sox; Pitcher Tom Lasorda from New York Yankees; Pitcher Babe Birrer from Baltimore Orioles

Sold: Pitcher Vito Valentinetti to Cleveland Indians

Signed Amateur Free Agents: Larry Burright; Doug Camilli; Rod Miller; Ed Rakow; Charley Smith; Carl Warwick; Dick Smith

Released: Pitcher Dave Cole; Outfielder Bob Kennedy

The franchise relocated to Los Angeles for the 1958 season.

Chapter Notes

Chapter One

1. "Base Ball Notes," *New York Sun*, February 6, 1891.
2. "Manager Ward Home," *Brooklyn Citizen*, April 2, 1891.
3. "New Players," *Cincinnati Enquirer*, March 25, 1891.
4. "Brooklyns at New Haven," *Brooklyn Citizen*, April 10, 1891.
5. "Base-Ball Gossip," *Cincinnati Enquirer*, April 18, 1891.
6. "Dan Brouthers," B-R Bullpen (Baseball-Reference).
7. "A New Pitcher," *Brooklyn Citizen*, March 16, 1892.
8. "Richardson Will Play with the Brooklyns," *Brooklyn Standard Union*, February 20, 1893.
9. "Richardson Ultimatum," *New York Sun*, July 28, 1893.
10. "Beat Them 20 to 2," *Brooklyn Citizen*, July 28, 1893.
11. "Foutz's New Players," *Brooklyn Eagle*, January 2, 1894.
12. "Manager William Barnie's Idea," *Brooklyn Eagle*, January 24, 1894.
13. "Danny Is a Colonel," *Brooklyn Eagle*, March 16, 1894.

Chapter Two

1. "Baseball News," *Brooklyn Standard Union*, January 29, 1895.
2. "Byrne Lands the Prize," *Brooklyn Eagle*, November 24, 1895.
3. *Sporting Life*, October 10, 1896.
4. "Germany," *Cincinnati Enquirer*, November 14, 1896.
5. "The Deal for Tucker," *Brooklyn Eagle*, March 7, 1898.
6. "Tommy Tucker Gone," *Brooklyn Standard Union*, July 19, 1898.
7. Bready, *The Home Team*, 25.
8. Rich Eldridge, *Baseball's First Stars*, 94.
9. "Oriole Players Combine," *Brooklyn Eagle*, December 23, 1898.
10. "Keeler Talks of the Deal," *Brooklyn Eagle*, December 23, 1898.
11. Spatz, *Bad Bill Dahlen*, 61–62.
12. Jimmy Keenan, "Joe Kelley," SABRBioProject.
13. "Mike Griffin Sold," *Brooklyn Citizen*, March 12, 1899.
14. "Won a Slugging Match," *Brooklyn Eagle*, April 25, 1899.
15. "Another Big Deal Strengthens Team," *Brooklyn Eagle*, July 14, 1899.
16. "Another Big Deal Strengthens Team."
17. David Nemec, "Hughie Jennings," SABRBioProject.
18. "Big Deal Called Off on Hanlon's Demand," *Brooklyn Eagle*, August 5, 1899.

Chapter Three

1. "Lave Cross to Wear a Brooklyn Uniform," *Brooklyn Times Union*, May 15, 1900.
2. "Baseball Notes," *Brooklyn Citizen*, February 18, 1901.
3. Chris Rainey, "Doc Newton," SABRBioProject.
4. James, *The New Bill James Historical Baseball Abstract*, 79.
5. Bill Nowlin, "Doc Gessler," SABRBioProject.
6. *Brooklyn Eagle*, December 14, 1903.
7. "Jack Doyle Released," *Brooklyn Citizen*, April 27, 1904.

Chapter Four

1. "Sheckard Makes a Kick," *Brooklyn Citizen*, December 22, 1905.
2. "Burch Now a Superba," *Brooklyn Citizen*, July 2, 1907.
3. "World's Record Made by Southern Pitcher," *Brooklyn Eagle*, September 15, 1907. The paper reported the 59 innings was a professional record.
4. "Ebbets Gets Tommy Sheehan Through a Cash Purchase," *Brooklyn Citizen*, December 15, 1907.
5. "Lumley Still Trying to Nail Stricklett," *Brooklyn Eagle*, February 21, 1909.
6. *Sporting Life*, June 26, 1909.
7. Creamer, *Stengel*, 51.
8. Niese, *Zack Wheat*, 13.
9. "Zack Wheat," B-R Bullpen (Baseball-Reference).

Chapter Five

1. "McIntyre [*sic*] Goes to Cubs for Three Hard Hitters," *Brooklyn Standard Union*, April 10, 1910.
2. "Brooklyn Club Buys New Player," *Brooklyn Citizen*, June 16, 1910.
3. Thomas S. Rice, "Aitchison Turned Back," *Brooklyn Eagle*, December 10, 1915.
4. "Local Jottings," *Sporting Life*, July 20, 1912.
5. "Tooley for Newark: Kirkpatrick to Report," *Brooklyn Eagle*, August 20, 1912.
6. R.W. Lardner, "In the Wake of the News," *Chicago Tribune*, August 6, 1913.
7. Thomas S. Rice, "Indians Defeat Superbas 5–1," *Brooklyn Eagle*, October 10, 1920.

Chapter Six

1. "Jack Coombs Declares He Will Report in Condition," *Brooklyn Times Union*, January 19, 1915.
2. "Egan Sold to the Braves to Brace Weak Infield," *Brooklyn Eagle*, April 24, 1915.
3. "The Superbas Are Off to the West in Second Place," *Brooklyn Eagle*, September 10, 1915.
4. "Cheney Goes to Brooklyn; Schultz a Cub," *Chicago Tribune*, August 30, 1915.
5. *Sporting Life*, November 25, 1916.
6. "Hickman is No Hick Player, But a First Class Prospect," *Brooklyn Times Union*, February 29, 1916.
7. "Merkle Will Help Robins," *Brooklyn Times Union*, August 26, 1916.
8. "Stengel and Cutshaw Traded for Mamaux, Grimes, and Ward," *Brooklyn Times*, January 9, 1918.
9. Thomas S. Rice, "Ebbets Waxes Enthusiastic Over Trade with Pittsburgh," *Brooklyn Eagle*, January 11, 1918.
10. "Al Mamaux Says He's Glad to Be with the Superbas," *Brooklyn Eagle*, January 11, 1918.
11. Thomas S. Rice, "Ebbets Waxes Enthusiastic Over Trade with Pittsburgh," *Brooklyn Eagle*, January 11, 1918.
12. "Mamaux Goes with Ward and Grimes," *Pittsburgh Post-Gazette*, January 10, 1918.
13. *Indianapolis Star*, January 9, 1915.
14. "Dodgers Whet Fans' Appetites," *Brooklyn Times*, April 19, 1919.
15. Thomas S. Rice, "Robbie Will Manage Superbas Next Year," *Brooklyn Eagle*, September 24, 1919.

Chapter Seven

1. "Marquard's Days with Robins Ended," *New York Times*, October 13, 1920.
2. Graham, *The Brooklyn Dodgers*, 87.
3. Thomas S. Rice, "Departure of Smith to Cleveland Club is Much Regretted," *Brooklyn Eagle*, September 19, 1922.
4. Ben Rosenberg, "Sherry Smith Goes to Indians via Waivers," *Brooklyn Times Union*, September 19, 1922.
5. *Washington Post*, February 16, 1923.
6. "Fournier Balks at Trade; Won't Leave St. Louis," *Brooklyn Eagle*, February 16, 1923.
7. Charles Segar, "Robbie Pleased by Latest Deal with Indianapolis; Bailey and Jones to Go," *Brooklyn Citizen*, June 5, 1924.
8. "Ruether Passes to the Washington Senators for Cash Consideration," *Brooklyn Standard Union*, December 18, 1924.

Chapter Eight

1. Thomas W. Meany, "McKeever Brothers Place No Restrictions on Man-

ager Robby's Trades," *Brooklyn Times Union*, April 27, 1925.
2. Thomas W. Meany, "Dodgers Beat Reds, 5–3," *Brooklyn Times Union*, May 10, 1925.
3. Thomas W. Meany, "Hot Stove Embers," *Brooklyn Eagle*, February 5, 1926.
4. "Iron Man Stunt Earned Clark Chance with Robins," *Brooklyn Eagle*, August 8, 1926.
5. "Carey in Robins Uniform Should Speed Up Team," *Brooklyn Eagle*, August 19, 1926.
6. John Bennett, "Max Carey," SABR-BioProject.
7. Daniel M. Daniel, "Walter (Butch) Henline Greatest of All Brooklyn Catchers in Dodger History," *Yonkers* (New York) *Herald*, February 8, 1927.
8. Thomas W. Meany, "Butch Henline, In Town to See Robby, Pleased with Deal," *Brooklyn Times Union*, February 5, 1927.
9. Thomas Holmes, "If Flowers Makes Good, He Will Strengthen Two Robin Posts," *Brooklyn Eagle*, April 29, 1927.
10. "Doak Thinks Lopez is a First Class Prospect—Catcher is Okayed by Rucker," *Brooklyn Standard Union*, August 28, 1927.
11. Thomas W. Meany, "Butler, Felix and Barrett Leave Brooklyn," *Brooklyn Times Union*, December 16, 1927.
12. Thomas Holmes, "Bressler Sure He'll Hit .300," *Brooklyn Eagle*, March 18, 1928.
13. Thomas Holmes, "Gooch Notable Addition to Robins 'Tennessee Colony,'" *Brooklyn Eagle*, June 12, 1928.
14. Holmes, "Gooch Notable Addition to Robins."
15. Wilbert Robinson, "Frederick, New Robin, May be Leadoff Batter," *Brooklyn Standard Union*, September 10, 1928.
16. Thomas Holmes, "Trade Pleases Wright but Petty's Chance to Collect Back Pay is Dim," *Brooklyn Eagle*, December 15, 1928.
17. Thomas Holmes, "Give Us Pitching Strength and Watch Us Go—Robbie," *Brooklyn Eagle*, April 21, 1929.
18. Thomas Holmes, "New Brooklyn Player Won Twenty Games; 'Mashes the Potato,'" *Brooklyn Eagle*, October 26, 1929.

Chapter Nine

1. Thomas Holmes, "Gordon Slade and Neal Finn Come to Robins in $50,000 Deal," *Brooklyn Eagle*, February 11, 1930.
2. Thomas Holmes, "New Robin Infielder Picked Brooklyn as His Preferred Team," *Brooklyn Eagle*, February 13, 1930.
3. Henry Richards, "Purchase of Boone Fails to Enthuse Flatbush Club," *Brooklyn Standard Union*, July 1, 1930.
4. Arch Ward, "Mungo in Eclipse as Dodgers Sun Rises," *Sporting News*, July 4, 1940.
5. Stan Baumgartner, "Stars Couldn't Win for Us, Says Burt Shotton," *Philadelphia Inquirer*, October 15, 1930.
6. "McCarthy Says Robins are Aided by Trade," *Brooklyn Eagle*, October 15, 1930.
7. "McCarthy Says Robins are Aided by Trade."
8. Murray Robinson, "As You Like It," *Brooklyn Standard Union*, January 21, 1931.
9. Thomas Holmes, "Brooklyn Club Grabs Fanny Ward of Game as Its New Pitcher," *Brooklyn Eagle*, February 10, 1931.
10. Thomas Holmes, "Brooklyn Baseball Club Will Officially Nickname Them 'Dodgers,'" *Brooklyn Eagle*, January 23, 1932.
11. Thomas Holmes, "Dodgers Pay $50,000 for Hack Wilson in First Flag Drive Step," *Brooklyn Eagle*, January 24, 1932.
12. "New Dodger Jubilant, Sees Big Year Ahead," *Brooklyn Eagle*, January 24, 1932.
13. Jack Ryder, "Herman, Lombardi, and Gilbert Are to Come to Redlegs," *Cincinnati Enquirer*, March 15, 1932.
14. Murray Robinson, "As You Like It," *Brooklyn Times-Union*, March 15, 1932.
15. William McCullough, "Trade Makes Dodgers Serious Pennant Contenders, Says Carey," *Brooklyn Times-Union*, March 15, 1932.
16. William McCullough, "Dodgers Trade Finn, Warner, Moore for Benge," *Brooklyn Times-Union*, December 15, 1932.
17. Thomas Holmes, "Carey Believes Ray Benge Can Win Fifteen or Twenty

Games," *Brooklyn Eagle*, December 16, 1932.
  18. Lee Scott, "Dazzy Vance Registers First Kick Against Big Cut," *Brooklyn Citizen*, January 26, 1933.
  19. Thomas Holmes, "Owen Carroll's Youth Biggest Factor in Dodger-Cardinal Deal," *Brooklyn Eagle*, February 9, 1933.
  20. "Dodgers Trade O'Doul, Clark for Leslie, Giants' Utility First Sacker," *Brooklyn Eagle*, June 15, 1933.
  21. "Dodgers Trade O'Doul, Clark for Leslie."
  22. "Dodgers Trade O'Doul, Clark for Leslie."
  23. Lee Scott, "Emil 'Dutch' Leonard Impresses Carey with Fine Exhibition Against Cards," *Brooklyn Citizen*, September 1, 1933.
  24. Lee Scott, "Brooklyn Club Purchases Two More Promising Young Pitchers; Quinn Says Herring Will Win," *Brooklyn Eagle*, December 5, 1933.
  25. "Flock Buys Herring, St. Paul Pitcher," *Brooklyn Eagle*, August 13, 1944.
  26. Tommy Holmes, "Dodgers May Get Frenchy Bordagaray," *Brooklyn Eagle*, December 12, 1934.
  27. Bill McCullough, "Dodgers Give Frederick, Herring, and Cash in Deal for Bordagaray," *Brooklyn Times-Union*, December 26, 1934.

Chapter Ten

  1. Bill McCullough, "Dodgers Purchase George Earnshaw from White Sox at Waiver Price," *Brooklyn Times-Union*, May 15, 1935.
  2. Bill McCullough, "Other Players Involved Used as Mere Padding in Brandt-Lopez Trade," *Brooklyn Times-Union*, December 13, 1935.
  3. Tommy Holmes, "Dodgers Get Frankhouse in 2 for 1 Swap," *Brooklyn Eagle*, February 6, 1936.
  4. Bill McCullough, "Dodgers Acquire Frankhouse, Trading Gene Moore and Babich to Bees," *Brooklyn Times-Union*, February 6, 1936.
  5. Lou Niss, "Purchase of Hassett Seen as a Ten-Strike in Rebuilding of Dodgers," *Brooklyn Times Union*, February 21, 1936.
  6. Bill McCullough, "Dodgers May Prove Pennant Spoilers in Closing Stages of Drive," *Brooklyn Times-Union*, August 20, 1936.
  7. Bill McCullough, "Grimes, Happy Over Trades, Still Seeks Outfield Star," *Brooklyn Times-Union*, December 5, 1936.
  8. McCullough, "Grimes, Happy Over Trades."
  9. McCullough, "Grimes, Happy Over Trades."
  10. Lee Scott, "Manager Grimes Says Fitzsimmons' Ability Should Help Dodgers," *Brooklyn Citizen*, June 12, 1937.
  11. Scott, "Manager Grimes Says."
  12. "Dodgers Do Not seem to Take Kindly to Ball Games Under Arclights," *Brooklyn Citizen*, August 7, 1937.
  13. Lee Scott, "Grimes Satisfied with Trade That Brought Durocher to Dodgers," *Brooklyn Citizen*, October 6, 1937.
  14. Martin J. Haley, "Cards Trade Durocher to Dodgers," *St. Louis Globe-Democrat*, October 6, 1937.
  15. Tommy Holmes, "Reiser a Year Away; Durocher's Opinion," *Brooklyn Eagle*, March 24, 1939.
  16. "Dodgers Buy Hurler Wyatt," *Brooklyn Eagle*, July 11, 1938.
  17. "Dodgers Buy Hurler Wyatt."
  18. J. G. Taylor Spink, "Looping the Loops," *Sporting News*, June 11, 1947.
  19. Harold Parrott, "Big Hugh Casey, Dodgers' Legacy from Uncle Robbie, Watches His Diet in Effort to Weigh in with 20 Wins," *Sporting News*, March 28, 1940.
  20. Bill McCullough, "McPhail Leading Man in Waldorf Whirlesque," *Brooklyn Eagle*, December 15, 1938.
  21. Tommy Holmes, "Frankhouse-Stripp New High in Trading," *Brooklyn Eagle*, December 14, 1938.
  22. Tommy Fitzgerald, "Brooklyn in $75,000 Deal for Reese, who 'Didn't Want to Be a Dodger.'" *Sporting News*, July 27, 1939.
  23. Tommy Holmes, "Donie Bush Rates Harold Reese Best Shortstops He's Ever Seen," *Brooklyn Eagle*, July 23, 1939.
  24. "Pee Wee Reese," B-R Bullpen, https://www.baseball-reference.com/bullpen/Pee Wee Reese.
  25. "Veteran Fred 'Dixie' Walker Joins Crippled Dodgers in Chicago Today," *Brooklyn Citizen*, July 25, 1939.

Chapter Eleven

1. Harold Parrott, "Hang Up the Pennant! We've Got Medwick," *Brooklyn Eagle*, June 13, 1940.
2. Tommy Holmes, "Higbe Purchase Seen Big Stride to Pennant," *Brooklyn Eagle*, November 12, 1940.
3. Holmes, "Higbe Purchase Seen Big Stride."
4. "'Betrayed,' says Furillo; 'No Job Now'—Bavasi," *Independent* (Long Beach, CA), May 18, 1960.
5. "Elliott's Error Wrings Applause from Boro Fans," *Brooklyn Eagle*, August 21, 1941.
6. Tommy Devine, "Revenge, Bonus Drive Larry French to Role of Top Major League Pitcher," *Pittsburgh Post-Gazette*, July 18, 1942.
7. "Van Mungo," B-R Bullpen, https://www.baseball-reference.com/bullpen/Van_Mungo.
8. Lee Scott, "Arky Vaughan to Play Short if Pee Wee Reese is Inducted into Army," *Brooklyn Citizen*, December 13, 1941.
9. Lester Biederman, "Pirates Trade Vaughan to Brooklyn," *Pittsburgh Press*, December 14, 1941.
10. Tommy Holmes, "Newsom May Start for Flock in Cincy," *Brooklyn Eagle*, September 1, 1942.
11. Tommy Holmes, "Dodgers Buy Rube Melton from Phils," *Brooklyn Eagle*, December 13, 1942.
12. Tommy Holmes, "No Shakeup Looms as Bobo is Traded," *Brooklyn Eagle*, July 15, 1943.
13. "Rather Quit than Join Browns—Bobo," *Brooklyn Eagle*, July 15, 1943.
14. "Leaving Medwick Behind Another Move to Restore Harmony," *Brooklyn Citizen*, July 16, 1943.
15. Richard Goldstein, "Dolph Camilli, Who Led Dodgers to '41 Pennant, Dies at 90," *New York Times*, October 22, 1997.
16. Tommy Holmes, "Camilli Considers Retiring from Game," *Brooklyn Eagle*, August 1, 1943.
17. Holmes, "Camilli Considers Retiring from Game."
18. Tommy Holmes, "Dodgers Part With $40,000 for Schultz," *Brooklyn Eagle*, August 16, 1943.

Chapter Twelve

1. Harold C. Burr, "Negro Ace Standout Prospect," *Brooklyn Eagle*, October 24, 1945.
2. Burr, "Negro Ace Standout Prospect."
3. Ben Gould, "Dodgers Sign 2 Negro Aces for Nashua Farm," *Brooklyn Eagle*, April 4, 1946.
4. Tommy Holmes, "A Colored Pitcher Joins the Dodgers," *Brooklyn Eagle*, August 26, 1947.
5. Jim Kreuz, "Ed Stevens," SABRBio Project.
6. Harold C. Burr, "Stevens, Rojek Sold to Pirates Off Flock Shelf," *Brooklyn Eagle*, November 14, 1947.
7. Harold C. Burr, *Brooklyn Eagle*, October 16, 1947.
8. Tommy Holmes, *Brooklyn Eagle*, December 10, 1947.
9. *Brooklyn Eagle*, December 3, 1947.
10. Jackie Robinson, "Now I Know Why They Boo Me," *Look*, January 25, 1955.
11. *New York Times*, December 9, 1947.
12. Harold C. Burr, "Dodgers Send Stanky to Braves for Sanders, Rowell, and Cash," *Brooklyn Eagle*, March 7, 1948.
13. Burr, "Dodgers Send Stanky to Braves."
14. "'Knifed in the Back' by Lip, Stanky Charges," *Brooklyn Eagle*, March 15, 1948.
15. "Stanky Comes to Braves for Sanders, Rowell, and Cash," *Boston Globe*, March 7, 1948.
16. W. C. Heinz, "The Rocky Road of Pistol Pete," 162.
17. Creamer, *Baseball in '41*, 207–08.
18. W. C. Heinz, "The Rocky Road of Pistol Pete," 162.
19. Harold C. Burr, "Dodger Brass Happy About Boston Trade," *Brooklyn Eagle*, December 16, 1948.

Chapter Thirteen

1. "Giants Buy Jorgensen, Sell Mueller to Bucs," *New York Daily News*, May 18, 1950.
2. Harold C. Burr, "Pafko Solves Left Field Problem for Flock," *Brooklyn Eagle*, June 16, 1951.

3. Burr, "Pafko Solves Left Field Problem."
4. Jim McCulley, "Lippy Hollers Cop at Dodger Swap," *New York Daily News*, June 16, 1951.
5. "Dodgers' Pafko Deal Stuns Giants and Cards," *Binghamton (NY) Press and Sun-Bulletin*, June 16, 1951.
6. Dave Anderson, "Schmitz Thirsts for Revenge at Flock in Oct. Series," *Brooklyn Eagle*, August 15, 1952.
7. Harold C. Burr, "Junior Executive Shows Dodgers How It's Done," *Brooklyn Eagle*, December 18, 1952.
8. Dick Young, "Chuck Happy," *New York Daily News*, February 17, 1953.
9. Tommy Holmes, "Meyer is Likely Gamble for Dodgers," *Brooklyn Eagle*, February 17, 1953.
10. Dave Anderson, "Branca to Face Browns," *Brooklyn Eagle*, July 11, 1953.
11. "Branca Brilliant in First Win Since '52," *Brooklyn Eagle*, July 20, 1953.
12. Dave Anderson, "Flock Youth Movement in Full Swing," *Brooklyn Eagle*, December 15, 1954.
13. *Baltimore Afro-American*, August 7, 1965.

Chapter Fourteen

1. Dick Young, "Dodgers Get Cubs' Jackson in Swap for Hoak, Moryn," *New York Daily News*, December 7, 1955.
2. Young, "Dodgers Get Cubs' Jackson."
3. "Likes Swap," *New York Daily News*, December 7, 1955.
4. Young, "Dodgers Get Cubs' Jackson."
5. Bill Roeder, "Jackson Deal Seems No Threat at This Point," *New York World-Telegram and Sun*, December 15, 1955.
6. "Meyer Promises Flock 18 Victories," *Brooklyn Eagle*, February 17, 1953.
7. "Billy Loes Glad to be Departing from Brooklyn," *Troy (NY) Times Record*, May 16, 1956.
8. Dick Young, "Maglie Now Pitching for Flock," *New York Daily News*, May 16, 1956.
9. Young, "Maglie Now Pitching for Flock."
10. James Ellis, "Orioles Sell Harry Dorish to Red Sox," *Baltimore Evening Sun*, June 25, 1956.
11. Dick Young, "Robby Sold to Giants for Littlefield + 30G," *New York Daily News*, December 14, 1956.
12. Young, "Robby Sold to Giants."
13. "Li' Li'field," *New York Daily News*, December 14, 1956.
14. Bill Dow, "Fernandez Paved Way as Tigers' First Latin Position Player," *Detroit Free Press*. August 1, 2015.
15. "Yankee Dollars Obtain Maglie," *New York Daily News*, September 2, 1957.

Bibliography

Alexander, Charles. *John McGraw*. New York: Viking, 1988.

Alexander, Charles C. *Breaking the Slump: Baseball in the Depression Era*. New York: Columbia University Press, 2002.

Alexander, Charles C. *Our Game: An American Baseball History*. New York: Henry Holt, 1991.

Allen, Maury, with Susan Walker. *Dixie Walker of the Dodgers: The People's Choice*. Tuscaloosa: Fire Ant Books, 2010.

Anderson, Dave. *Pennant Races: Baseball at Its Best*. New York: Doubleday, 1994.

Armour, Mark L., and Daniel R. Levitt. *In Pursuit of Pennants: Baseball Operations from Deadball to Moneyball*. Lincoln: University of Nebraska Press, 2015.

Armour, Mark L., and Daniel R. Levitt. *Paths to Glory: How Great Baseball Teams Got That Way*. Dulles, VA: Brassey's, 2003.

Bailey, Judson. "New Players Put Brooklyn There—MacPhail." *Atlanta Constitution*, August 22, 1941.

Barber, Red. *1947—When All Hell Broke Loose in Baseball*. Garden City, NY: Doubleday, 1982.

Barber, Red, and Robert Creamer. *Rhubarb in the Catbird Seat*. Garden City, NY: Doubleday, 1968.

Barthel, Thomas. *The Fierce Fun of Ducky Medwick*. Lanham, MD: Scarecrow Press, 2003.

Bjarkman, Peter C., editor. *Encyclopedia of Major League Baseball Team Histories: National League*. Westport, CT: Meckler, 1991.

Bloodgood, Clifford. "The Abnormal Season of '46." *Baseball Magazine*, December 1946.

Boren, Stephen D., and Thomas Boren, "The 1942 Pennant Race." *The National Pastime*, Society for American Baseball Research, No. 15, 1995, 133–135.

Borst, Bill. "Showdown in St. Louis." *The National Pastime*, Society for American Baseball Research, No. 11, 1991, 63–64.

Boston, Talmage. *1939, Baseball's Pivotal Year*. Fort Worth: The Summit Group, 1994.

Bragan, Bobby, and Jeff Guinn. *You Can't Hit the Ball with the Bat on Your Shoulder: The Baseball Life and Times of Bobby Bragan*. Fort Worth: The Summit Group, 1992.

Bready, James H. *Baseball in Baltimore: The First 100 Years*. Baltimore: Johns Hopkins University Press, 1998.

Bready, James H. "Play Ball! The Legacy of Nineteenth-Century Baltimore Baseball." *Maryland Historical Magazine*, Volume 87, Summer 1992.

Broeg, Bob. "The '42 Cardinals." *Sport*, July 1963, p. 40 (7).

Broeg, Bob, and William J. Miller, Jr. *Baseball from a Different Angle*. South Bend, IN: Diamond Communications, 1988.

Cannon, Jimmy. "Leo Buttons His Lip." *Baseball Digest*, November 1946, 42 (2).

Cohen, Stanley. *Dodgers! The First 100 Years*. New York: Carrol Publishing Group, 1990.

Creamer, Robert W. *Baseball in '41: A Celebration of the Best Baseball Season Ever—in the Year America Went to War*. New York: The Penguin Group, 1991.

Bibliography

Creamer, Robert W. *Stengel: His Life and Times*. New York: Dell, 1984.

D'Antonio, Michael. *Forever Blue: The True Story of Walter O'Malley, Baseball's Most Controversial Owner, And the Dodgers of Brooklyn and Los Angeles*. New York: Riverhead Books, 2009.

Debs, Victor, Jr. *Missed It by That Much*. Jefferson, NC: McFarland, 1998.

Dewey, Donald, and Nicholas Acocella. *The Ball Clubs*. New York: HarperCollins, 1996.

Dewey, Donald, and Nicholas Acocella. *The Biographical History of Baseball*. New York: Carroll & Graf, 1995.

Dickson, Paul. *Leo Durocher*: Lincoln: University of Nebraska Press, 2017.

DiMaggio, Dom, with Bill Gilbert. *Real Grass, Real Heroes: Baseball's Historic 1941 Season*. New York: Kensington, 1990.

Dorinson, Joseph, and Joram Warmund, editors. *Jackie Robinson: Race, Sports, and the American Dream*. Armonk, NY: M.E. Sharpe, 1998.

Durocher, Leo. *The Dodgers and Me: The Inside Story*. Chicago: Ziff-Davis, 1948.

Durocher, Leo, with Ed Linn. *Nice Guys Finish Last*. New York: Simon & Schuster, 1975.

Eig, Jonathan. *Opening Day: The Story of Jackie Robinson's First Season*. New York: Simon & Schuster, 2007.

Eldridge, Larry. "Why Isn't Pee Wee Reese in the Hall of Fame." *Baseball Digest*, July 1978, 80 (4).

Erskine, Carl. *Tales from the Dodgers Dugout: A Collection of the Greatest Dodgers Stories*. New York: Sports Publishing, 2014.

Falkner, David. *Great Time Coming: The Life of Jackie Robinson, from Baseball to Birmingham*. New York: Simon & Schuster, 1995.

Figone, Al. "Larry MacPhail and Dolph Camilli." *The National Pastime*, Society for American Baseball Research, No. 14, 1994, 106–109.

Fimrite, Ron. "The Play That Beat the Bums." *Sports Illustrated*, October 20, 1997.

Freese, Mel R. *The St. Louis Cardinals in the 1940s*. Jefferson, NC: McFarland, 2007.

Frommer, Harvey. *New York City Baseball: The Last Golden Age: 1947–1957*. New York: Macmillan, 1980.

Frommer, Harvey. *Rickey and Robinson*. New York: Macmillan, 1982.

Gaven, Michael. "What a Load of Rhubarb." *Baseball Digest*, February 1958, 51 (12).

Goldblatt, Andrew. *The Giants and the Dodgers: Four Cities, Two Teams, One Rivalry*. Jefferson, NC: McFarland, 2003.

Goldstein, Richard. *Spartan Seasons: How Baseball Survived the Second World War*. New York: Macmillan, 1980.

Goldstein, Richard. *Superstars and Screwballs: 100 Years of Brooklyn Baseball*. New York: Dutton, 1991.

Golenbock, Peter. *Bums: An Oral History of the Brooklyn Dodgers*. New York: G.P. Putnam's Sons, 1984.

Gough, David. "A Tribute to Burt Shotton." *The National Pastime*, Society for American Baseball Research, No. 14, 1994, 99–101.

Graham, Frank. *The Brooklyn Dodgers: An Informal History*. New York: G.P. Putnam's Sons, 1945.

Graham, Frank., Jr "Greatest Fight on a Ballfield." *Baseball Digest*, June 1953, 45 (2).

Green, Paul. *Forgotten Fields*. Waupaca, WI: Parker Publications, 1984.

Green, Paul. "Whitlow Wyatt." *Sports Collectors Digest*, March 28, 1986, 172–220.

Harwell, Ernie, edited by Geoff Ward. *The Babe Signed My Shoe*. Lanham, MD: Diamond Communications, 1994.

Heinz, W.C. "The Rocky Road of Pistol Pete." In *The Baseball Reader: Favorites from The Fireside Books of Baseball*, edited by Charles Einstein, 162–176. New York: Lippincott & Crowell, 1980.

Helyar, John. *Lords of the Realm: The Real History of Baseball*. New York: Ballantine, 1994.

Higbe, Kirby, with Martin Quigley. *The High Hard One*. New York: Viking, 1967.

Hiltner, Judith R., and James R. Walker. *Red Barber: The Life and Legacy of a Broadcasting Legend*. Lincoln: University of Nebraska Press, 2022.

Holmes, Tommy. *The Dodgers*. New York: Macmillan, 1975.

Honig, Donald. *Baseball America: The

Bibliography

Heroes of the Game and the Times of Their Glory. New York: Macmillan, 1985.

Honig, Donald. *Baseball When the Grass Was Real: Baseball from the Twenties to the Forties Told by the Men Who Played It*. New York: Coward, McCann & Geoghegan, 1975.

Honig, Donald. *The Brooklyn Dodgers: An Illustrated Tribute*: New York: St. Martin's, 1981.

Hynd, Noel. *The Giants of the Polo Grounds: The Glorious Times of Baseball's New York Giants*. New York: Doubleday, 1988.

Ivor-Campbell, Frederick, Robert L. Tiemann, and Mark Rucker, editors. *Baseball's First Stars*. Cleveland: Society for American Baseball Research, 1996.

Jacobson, Sidney. *Pete Reiser: The Rough-and-Tumble Career of the Perfect Ballplayer*. Jefferson, NC: McFarland, 2004.

James, Bill. *The New Bill James Historical Baseball Abstract*. New York: Free Press, 2001.

Jones, David, editor. *Deadball Stars of the American League*. Dulles, VA: Potomac Books, 2006.

Kahn, Roger. *The Boys of Summer*. New York: Harper and Row, 1971.

Kahn, Roger. *The Era, 1947–1957: When the Yankees, the Giants, and the Dodgers Ruled the World*. New York: Ticknor & Fields, 1993.

Kahn, Roger. *Rickey & Robinson: The True, Untold Story of the Integration of Baseball*. New York: Rodale, 2014.

Kashatus, William. *Jackie & Campy: The Untold Story of Their Rocky Relationship and the Breaking of Baseball's Color Line*. Lincoln: University of Nebraska Press, 2014.

Kavanagh, Jack. "Dixie Walker." *Baseball Research Journal*, Society for American Baseball Research, No. 22, 1993, 80–83.

Kavanagh, Jack. "A Dodger Boyhood." *Baseball History* 3 (1990), 119–132.

Kavanagh, Jack, and Norman Macht. *Uncle Robbie*. Cleveland: Society for American Baseball Research, 1999.

Knight, Tom. "Uncle Robbie and Hugh Casey," *Baseball Research Journal*, Society for American Baseball Research, No. 22, 1993, 105–106.

Krell, David. *Our Bums: The Brooklyn Dodgers in History, Memory and Popular Culture*. Jefferson, NC: McFarland, 2015.

Langford, Walter M. *Legends of Baseball: An Oral History of The Game's Golden Age*. South Bend, IN: Diamond Communications, 1987.

Light, Jonathan F. *The Cultural Encyclopedia of Baseball*. Jefferson, NC: McFarland, 1997.

Liley, Thomas. "Whit Wyatt—The Dodgers' 1941 Ace," *The National Pastime*, Society for American Baseball Research, No. 11, 1991, 46–47.

Lowenfish, Lee. *Baseball's Endangered Species: Inside the Craft of Scouting by Those Who Lived It*. Lincoln: University of Nebraska Press, 2023.

Lowenfish, Lee. *Branch Rickey: Baseball's Ferocious Gentleman*. Lincoln: University of Nebraska Press, 2007.

Lowenfish, Lee. "The Gentlemen's Agreement and the Ferocious Gentleman Who Broke It." *Baseball Research Journal*, Society for American Baseball Research, Volume 38, Summer 2009, Number 1, 12–13.

Lowenfish, Lee. *The Imperfect Diamond: A History of Baseball's Labor Wars*. New York: Da Capo Press, 1991.

Lowry, Philip J. *Green Cathedrals: The Ultimate Celebration of Major League and Negro League Ballparks*. New York: Walker & Company, 2006.

Macht, Norman L. "Why Did Mickey Miss the Ball?" *The National Pastime*, Society for American Baseball Research, No. 11, 1991, 44–45.

MacPhail, Lee. "A Year to Remember Especially in Brooklyn." *The National Pastime*, Society for American Baseball Research, No. 11, 1991, 41–43.

Mann, Arthur. "The Truth About the Jackie Robinson Case," *Saturday Evening Post*, May 20, 1950.

Marshall, William. *Baseball's Pivotal Era, 1945–1951*. Lexington: University Press of Kentucky, 1999.

Marzano, Rudy. *The Brooklyn Dodgers in the 1940s: How Robinson, MacPhail, Reiser and Rickey Changed Baseball*. Jefferson, NC: McFarland, 2005.

McCue, Andy. *Mover & Shaker: Walter O'Malley, the Dodgers, & Baseball's Westward Expansion*. Lincoln: University of Nebraska Press, 2014.

McGee, Robert. *The Greatest Ballpark Ever: Ebbets Field and the Story of the Brooklyn Dodgers*. New Brunswick, NJ: Rivergate Books, 2005.

McGowen, Roscoe. "Boss of Bums but Not Bum Boss," *Baseball Magazine*, August 1947, 307 (4).

McKelvey, G. Richard. *The MacPhails: Baseball's First Family of the Front Office*. Jefferson, NC: McFarland, 2005.

McNeil, William F. *The Dodger Encyclopedia*. Champaign, IL: Sports Publishing, 1997.

Mead, William B. *Even The Browns: The Zany, True Story of Baseball in the Early Forties*. Chicago: Contemporary Books, 1978.

Meany, Tom. "Dixie Deal Strictly Business," *Baseball Digest*, March 1948, pages 55–56.

Meany, Tom. "Hugh Casey." *Sport*, May 1948, p. 27 (5).

Mele, Andrew Paul. *A Brooklyn Dodgers Reader*. Jefferson, NC: McFarland, 2004.

Miller, Patrick B., and David K. Wiggins, editors. *Sport and the Color Line: Black Athletes and Race Relations in Twentieth Century America*. New York: Routledge, 2004.

Moss, Robert A. "The Fireman." *NINE: A Journal of Baseball History and Culture*, University of Nebraska Press, Volume 21, Number 2, Spring 2013, pages 125–134.

Nack, William. "The Breakthrough." *Sports Illustrated*, May 5, 1997.

Nemec, David. *The Great Encyclopedia of 19th Century Major League Baseball*. New York: Donald I. Fine, 1997.

Nemec, David. *Major League Baseball Profiles, 1871–1900: The Ballplayers Who Built The Game*. Volume 1. Lincoln: University of Nebraska Press, 2011.

Nemec, David. *Major League Baseball Profiles, 1871–1900: The Ballplayers Who Built The Game*. Volume 2. Lincoln: University of Nebraska Press, 2011.

Neyer, Rob, and Eddie Epstein. *Baseball Dynasties: The Greatest Teams of All Time*. New York: W.W. Norton, 2000.

Niese, Joe. *Burleigh Grimes: Baseball's Last Legal Spitballer*. Jefferson, NC: McFarland, 2013.

Niese, Joe. *Zack Wheat: The Life of the Brooklyn Dodgers Hall of Famer*. Jefferson, NC: McFarland, 2021.

Oakley, J. Ronald. *Baseball's Last Golden Age, 1946–1960: The National Pastime in a Time of Glory and Change*. Jefferson, NC: McFarland, 1994.

Oliphant, Thomas. *Praying for Gil Hodges*. New York: St. Martin's, 2005.

Panaccio, Tim. "How It was During the War Years." *Baseball Digest*, January 1977, 68 (3).

Parker, Clifton Blue. *Big and Little Poison: Paul and Lloyd Waner, Baseball Brothers*. Jefferson, NC: McFarland, 2003.

Paxton, Harry T. "It's Raining Dollars in Pittsburgh." *Saturday Evening Post*, May 8, 1948, 20 (7).

Pietrusza, David, Matthew Silverman, and Michael Gershman, editors. *Baseball: The Biographical Encyclopedia*. Kingston, NY: Total/Sports Illustrated, 2000.

Porter, David L., editor. *Biographical Dictionary of American Sports: Baseball, Revised and Expanded Edition*. Westport, CT: Greenwood, 2000.

Powell, Larry. "Jackie Robinson and Dixie Walker: Myths of the Southern Baseball Player." *Southern Cultures*, Summer 2002, pages 56–70.

Prince, Carl E. *Brooklyn's Dodgers: The Bums, The Borough, and The Best of Baseball*. New York: Oxford University Press, 1996.

Rampersad, Arnold. *Jackie Robinson: A Biography*. New York: Ballantine, 1997.

Reed, Ted. *Carl Furillo: Brooklyn Dodgers All-Star*. Jefferson, NC: McFarland, 2011.

Reese, Pee Wee, with Tim Cohane. "Reese's Own Story." *Baseball Digest*, May 1954, 32 (8).

Rice, Damon. *Seasons Past*. New York: Praeger, 1976.

Ritter, Lawrence S. *East Side West Side: Tales of New York Sporting Life, 1910–1960*. New York: Total Sports, 1998.

Ritter, Lawrence S. *The Glory of Their Times: The Story of the Early Days of Baseball Told by the Men Who Played it*. New York: Macmillan, 1966.

Robinson, Jackie. *Baseball Has Done It*. Philadelphia: Lippincott, 1964.

Robinson, Jackie. "Now I Know Why They Boo Me." *Look*, January 25, 1955, pages 23–28.

Robinson, Jackie, as told to Alfred Duckett. *I Never Had it Made.* New York: G.P. Putnam's Sons, 1972.

Rosenthal, Harold. *The 10 Best Years of Baseball: An Informal History of the Fifties.* Chicago: Contemporary Books, 1979.

Seymour, Harold. *Baseball: The Early Years.* New York: Oxford University Press, 1960.

Seymour, Harold. *Baseball: The Golden Age.* New York: Oxford University Press, 1971.

Shapiro, Milton J. *Heroes of the Bullpen: Baseball's Greatest Relief Pitchers.* New York: Julian Messner, 1967.

Shatzkin, Mike. *The Ballplayers.* New York: William Morrow, 1990.

Silber, Irwin. *Press Box Red: The Story of Lester Rodney, the Communist Who Helped Break The Color Line in American Sports.* Philadelphia: Temple University Press, 2003.

Simon, Scott. *Jackie Robinson and the Integration of Baseball.* Hoboken: John Wiley & Sons, 2002.

Simon, Tom, editor. *Deadball Stars of the National League.* Washington, D.C.: Brassey's, 2004.

Smith, Ira. *Baseball's Famous Pitchers.* New York: A.S. Barnes, 1954.

Smith, Robert. *Baseball in the Afternoon: Tales from a Bygone Era.* New York: Simon & Schuster, 1993.

Snider, Duke, with Bill Gilbert. *The Duke of Flatbush.* New York: Kensington, 1988.

Snider, Duke, with Phil Pepe. *Few and Chosen: Defining Dodger Greatness Across the Eras.* Chicago: Triumph Books, 2006.

Solomon, Burt. *Where They Ain't: The Fabled Life and Untimely Death of the Original Baltimore Orioles, the Team that Gave Rise to Modern Baseball.* New York: Free Press, 1999.

Spatz, Lyle. *Bad Bill Dahlen: The Rollicking Life and Times of an Early Baseball Star.* Jefferson, NC: McFarland, 2004.

Spatz, Lyle. *Dixie Walker: A Life in Baseball.* Jefferson, NC: McFarland, 2011.

Spatz, Lyle. *Hugh Casey: The Triumphs and Tragedies of a Brooklyn Dodger.* Lanham, MD: Rowman & Littlefield, 2016.

Spatz, Lyle. "Three Georgia-Born Former Dodgers Lead the Crackers to a Pennant." *The National Pastime: Baseball in the Peach State,* Society for American Baseball Research, 2010, pages 69–71.

Spatz, Lyle. *Willie Keeler: From the Playgrounds of Brooklyn to the Hall of Fame.* Lanham, MD: Rowman & Littlefield, 2015.

Spatz, Lyle, editor. *The Team That Forever Changed Baseball and America: The 1947 Brooklyn Dodgers.* Lincoln: University of Nebraska Press and the Society for American Baseball Research, 2012.

Stevens, David. *Baseball's Radical for All Seasons: A Biography of John Montgomery Ward.* Lanham, MD: Scarecrow Press, 1998.

Stevens, Ed. *The Other Side of the Jackie Robinson Story.* Mustang, OK: Tate Publishing, 2009.

Thorn, John. *The Relief Pitcher: Baseball's New Hero.* New York: E.P. Dutton, 1979.

Tiemann, Robert L. *Dodger Classics.* St. Louis: Baseball Histories, 1983.

Tiemann, Robert L. "The National League in 1893." *Baseball Research Journal* (1993), 38–41.

Tiemann, Robert L., and Mark Rucker, editors. *Nineteenth Century Stars.* Kansas City, MO: The Society for American Baseball Research, 1989.

Tiller, Guy. "Prospect for Majors: Dixie Walker." *Baseball Digest,* October 1950.

Tygiel, Jules. *Baseball's Great Experiment: Jackie Robinson and His Legacy.* New York: Vintage Books, 1984.

Van Blair, Rick. *Dugout to Foxhole: Interviews with Baseball Players Whose Careers Were Affected by World War II.* Jefferson, NC: McFarland, 1995.

Vincent, Fay. *We Would Have Played for Nothing: Baseball Stars of the 1950s and 1960s Talk About the Game They Loved.* New York: Simon & Schuster, 2008.

Weintraub, Robert. *The Victory Season: The End of World War II and the Birth of Baseball's Golden Age.* New York: Little, Brown, 2013.

Woodward, Stanley. "In the Rickey Manner." *Baseball Digest,* July 1950, 23.

Zachter, Mort. *Gil Hodges: A Hall of Fame*

Life. Lincoln: University of Nebraska Press, 2015.

Zinn, John G. *Charles Ebbets: The Man Behind the Dodgers and Brooklyn's Beloved Ballpark.* Jefferson, NC: McFarland, 2019.

Newspapers

Baltimore Afro-American
Baltimore Evening Sun
Baltimore Sun
Boston Globe
Brooklyn Citizen
Brooklyn Eagle
Brooklyn Standard Union
Brooklyn Times
Brooklyn Times Union
Chicago Tribune
Cincinnati Enquirer
Detroit Free Press
Milwaukee Journal
New York Daily News
New York Sun
New York Times
New York World Telegram and Sun
Philadelphia Inquirer
Pittsburgh Post-Gazette
Pittsburgh Press
St. Louis Globe-Democrat
Sporting Life
Sporting News
Washington Post

Index

Abbey, Bert 17
Abbott, Spencer 105–6
Abell, Ferdinand 19–23, 50
Abernathy, Bill 221
Abrams, Cal 182, 215
Adams, Babe 110
Adams, Bobby 220
Adcock, Joe 219
Addis, Bob 201, 207
Aderholt, Morrie 188, 192
Ainsmith, Eddie 98
Aitchison, Raleigh 63–64
Albosta, Ed 172
Allen, Frank 65–66
Allen, Horace 91–92
Allen, Johnny 174, 181–84, 186–87
Almada, Mel 167–68, 172
Alpermann, Whitey 52
Alston, Walter 221–23, 226–28, 232
Amoros, Sandy 218–19
Anderson, Ferrell 182, 213
Anderson, John 16, 18, 22–23, 36–37
Anderson, Sparky 221
Andrews, Stan 192
Anson, Cap 9, 28
Antonello, Bill 195, 219
Archer, Jimmy 85
Aspromonte, Bob 233
Atwell, Toby 195, 214

Babb, Charlie 45–46, 53
Babich, Johnny 141–42, 148–49
Bailey, Gene 95, 99–100
Bailey, Sweetbread 94
Baird, Doug 89, 91
Baker, Tom 150, 155
Baker, William 125
Ballou, Win 118
Bancroft, Dave 107, 114–15, 118, 121
Bankhead, Dan 197–98
Banta, Jack 190

Barber, Turner 97
Barger, Cy 60
Barnes, Jesse 104, 107, 114
Barney, Rex 184, 188
Barnie, Billy 14–16, 19–22
Barrett, Bob 104, 114
Basinski, Eddie 194
Batch, Emil 44
Bavasi, Buzzie 210, 212, 215, 218, 228–29, 231, 233–34
Baxes, Jim 201
Beck, Erve 33
Beck, Walter "Boom-Boom" 135, 144
Becker, Joe 179
Behrman, Hank 179, 195–96, 207
Belardi, Wayne 208, 224
Bell, George 51
Bell, Sammy 179
Benge, Ray 134–35, 146–47
Benswanger, Bill 177
Berg, Moe 98, 108
Bergen, Bill 43, 46, 58
Berger, Boze 171
Berger, Wally 143
Berra, Yogi 228
Berres, Ray 141, 145, 158
Berry, Joe 194
Bessent, Don 217–218
Bevens, Bill 213
Beyers, Paul 88
Bigbee, Carson 110
Birkofer, Ralph 152–53, 158
Birrer, Babe 236
Bissonette, Del 105, 127, 132, 137–38
Black, Joe 214, 227
Bloodworth, Jimmy 209
Bohne, Sam 111
Bolling, Jack 195
Bonner, Frank 19
Boone, Ike 123–24

Index

Bordagaray, Stan "Frenchy" 143, 152, 180, 195
Borkowski, Bob 227
Borowy, Hank 173–74
Bottomley, Jim 97
Bowman, Bob 185
Boyle, Buzz 137–38, 150
Brack, Gibby 158, 164
Bragan, Bobby 183, 195–96
Branca, Ralph 184, 188, 220–21, 233
Brandt, Ed 146, 148, 152
Breadon, Sam 130, 171
Bresnahan, Roger 40, 78
Bressler, Rube 115, 116, 135
Bridges, Rocky 201, 205, 219–20
Briggs, Button 52–53
Brouthers, Dan 9, 12–14
Brown, Eddie 99–100, 106–7
Brown, Elmer 72
Brown, John 21
Brown, Lindsay 152, 158
Brown, Mace 175–76, 179
Brown, Tommy 190, 210
Brush, John T. 19, 38
Bucha, Johnny 224
Bucher, Jim 141, 157
Burch, Al 55
Burgess, Smoky 212
Burk, Sandy 65, 70
Burman, Jack 179
Burns, Thomas "Oyster" 5
Burns, Tom 28
Burright, Larry 236
Bush, Donie 166
Bushong, Doc 5
Butcher, Max 146, 150, 164
Butler, John 53
Butler, Johnny 108–9, 113
Butts, Warren 88
Byerly, Bud 215, 221
Byrne, Charles 6–10, 13, 15, 17–22, 29

Cadore, Leon 74, 98
Callahan, Leo 70, 79
Camilli, Dolph 158–59, 163, 171, 179, 186–87, 191
Camilli, Doug 236
Campanella, Roy 193–94, 212–13, 218, 223
Campanis, Al 172, 230
Campbell, Gilly 164
Cantrell, Guy 101, 115
Cantwell, Ben 158
Carey, Max 110, 119, 121, 130–35, 138–42, 177
Carleton, Tex 172

Carroll, Ownie 136–37
Caruthers, Bob 5, 10
Casey, Doc 30–32, 52–53, 56–57
Casey, Hugh 161–63, 171, 196, 205
Cassidy, Pete 30
Cavarretta, Phil 207
Chabek, Joe 80
Chadwick, Henry 43
Chambers, Johnnie 164, 167
Chance, Frank 62
Chandler, Ed 195
Chandler, Happy 207
Chapman, Ben 181, 190, 192
Chapman, Fred 158
Chapman, Glenn 141, 146
Chapman, Jack 6
Chase, Hal 87
Chauncey, George 22
Cheney, Larry 78–79, 89
Chervinko, Paul 158, 164
Chipman, Bob 179, 189
Cimoli, Gino 208, 219, 227
Clancy, Bud 141
Clark, Bob 5, 8
Clark, Watty 109, 138–39, 142, 149, 158
Clarke, Fred 20, 110
Clarke, Tom 73
Clement, Wally 58–59
Cochrane, Mickey 171
Cohen, Alta 127, 141
Cole, Dave 230, 234, 236
Collins, Bill 72
Collins, Hub 5
Collum, Jackie 230, 236
Combs, Earle 166
Comiskey, Charles 13, 41
Connery, Bob 140
Connors, Chuck 172, 210
Coombs, Jack 76
Cooney, Johnny 148, 154, 157–58, 188, 190
Cooper, Walker 171, 209
Corbitt, Claude 179, 195
Corcoran, Tommy 10, 19–20
Corkhill, John "Pop" 5–6
Coscarart, Pete 156, 177–79
Coulson, Bob 64
Cox, Billy 199–201, 210, 218–20, 222–23
Cox, Dick 99, 103
Crable, George 65
Craghead, Howard 144
Craig, Roger 210
Crane, Ed 12
Crane, Sam 95
Crisham, Pat 30, 36
Cristante, Leo 230

Cronin, Jack 19
Cronin, Joe 40, 45, 165
Cross, Lave 31, 36, 37
Crouch, Bill 70–71
Cuccinello, Tony 131–32, 146–48, 152
Cullenbine, Roy 171–72
Curtis, Cliff 69, 72
Cutshaw, George 68, 83–84
Cuyler, Kiki 113, 165

Dahlen, Bill 27–28, 31–32, 45–46, 58, 61–62, 65, 67, 69, 71, 73
Dahlgren, Babe 182, 188
Dalton, Jack 63
Daly, Tom 5, 37
Daniel, Jake 158
Dark, Alvin 202
Darnell, Bob 221
Daub, Dan 13, 21
Daubert, Jake 61, 63, 81–82, 86–87, 103
Davidson, Bill 62
Davis, Curt 141, 169–70, 195
Davis, George 13, 45
Davis, Lefty 39
Davis, Otis 195
Davis, Tommy 233
Day, Pea Ridge 127, 132–33
Dean, Dizzy 150, 182
Dean, Paul 150
DeBerry, Hank 93–94, 107, 112, 127–28
Decatur, Art 95, 103
Dedeaux, Rod 148
Dell, Wheezer 74
Demeter, Don 221
DeMontreville, Gene 27–29, 32–34, 37
Dent, Eddie 60
Derringer, Paul 170, 182
Dessau, Rube 61
DeVormer, Al 106
Dickerman, Leo 95, 100
Dillon, Frank 47
DiMaggio, Joe 196, 203
DiMaggio, Vince 184
Dittmer, Jack 220
Doak, Bill 100–1, 113
Dobbs, John 43
Dobens, Fred 193
Dockins, George 195
Dolan, Cozy, 38, 79
Donovan, Bill 30–31, 42
Donovan, Patsy 6, 52, 54, 58
Dooin, Red 43
Doolin, Mickey 85
Doscher, Herm 44
Doscher, Jack 44
Douglas, Phil 77

Dovey, George 58
Downey, Red 61
Downey, Tom 226
Downs, Red 68, 70
Doyle, Carl 168–70
Doyle, Jack 29, 41–42, 47, 236
Drake, Tom 179, 195
Dressen, Charlie 210–12, 215–16, 219–23, 226–27
Drews, Frank 189
Dreyfuss, Barney 56, 84, 110
Driscoll, Dave 129, 134, 136
Drysdale, Don 224
Dudley, Clise 117, 125
Duffy, Hugh 18
Duke, Willie 164
Dunn, Jack 37
Durham, Bull 49
Durocher, Leo 157, 162, 165–67, 169, 175, 177–78, 181, 183–87, 189, 191, 195, 197, 200–4, 206, 210, 213–14, 226
Dusak, Erv 203
Dykes, Jimmy 143

Earle, Billy 16
Earnshaw, George 146, 150
Eason, Mal 49
Eayrs, Eddie 94
Ebbets, Charles 22–23, 30, 41, 50–52, 54–60, 64–65, 68, 71–73, 75, 78–79, 84–86, 90, 93–96, 99, 102–3, 132, 136, 191
Eckhardt, Ox 148, 154
Edwards, Bruce 179, 193, 196, 211–14
Edwards, Hank 210, 214
Egan, Dick 72, 77
Ehret, Red 17
Ehrhardt, Rube 119
Eisenstat, Harry 158
Elberfeld, Kid 75
Elliott, Jumbo 104–5, 125–26
Elliott, Rowdy 89–90, 94
Elston, Don 229–30, 236
English, Gil 188
English, Woody 153–54, 164, 188
Enzmann, Johnny 75, 80
Epperly, Al 207
Erskine, Carl 195, 207
Erwin, Tex 59–60, 73
Evans, Red 165–66
Evans, Roy 39, 40, 46
Evers, Johnny 71, 77
Ewing, Buck 19, 36

Farrell, Duke 30–32
Faulkner, Jim 121

Feeney, Charles "Chub" 232
Felix, Gus 106–7, 114
Feller, Bob 184, 194
Ferguson, Alex 121
Fernandez, Chico 214, 234
Fernandez, Nanny 203, 205
Ferrell, Wes 172
Fette, Lou 172
Fewster, Chick 111
Finlayson, Pembroke 58, 61
Finn, Mickey, 123, 134–35
Fischer, William 69
Fisher, Bob 68–69
Fisher, Chauncey 19–20
Fitzsimmons, Fred 155, 175, 182, 186, 188, 191
Fletcher, Art 111
Fletcher, Elbie 163
Flowers, Ben 235
Flowers, Jake 112–13, 119–20, 123, 129, 136–37, 144
Flowers, Wes 172
Fohl, Lee 121
Fondy, Dee 195, 205, 210
Ford, Horace 108–9
Fournier, Jack 96–97, 111
Foutz, Dave 5, 11, 13–16, 19
Fox, Norman 221
Frankhouse, Fred 148–49, 164
Franks, Herman 171
Fraser, Chick 142, 151
Frederick, Johnny 117, 126–27, 130, 134, 138, 143–45
Freedman, Andrew 36, 40
Freeman, Freddie 143
Freigau, Howard 115, 118
French, Larry 175–76
French, Ray 98, 101
Frey, Lonny 134, 153–54
Fridley, Jim 235
Frisch, Frankie 118, 157, 177–79, 214
Fuchs, Charlie 190
Fuchs, Emil 104, 115
Furillo, Carl 172–73, 189, 200, 211, 214, 218

Galan, Augie 175–76, 194, 197
Gallagher, Jim 173–74, 189
Gallagher, Joe 171
Gallivan, Phil 127
Garcia, Chico 224
Garvin, Ned 40–41, 48
Gastright, Hank 15–16
Gatins, Frank 38–39
Geho, Melvin 234
Gehrig, Lou 150–51

Gentile, Jim 218
George, Greek 164
Geraghty, Ben 154, 158
Gerheauser, Al 194
Gessler, Harry "Doc" 43–44, 54
Getz, Gus 70, 74, 81, 83
Giallombardo, Bob 233
Gilbert, Charlie 168, 173
Gilbert, Pete 16
Gilbert, Wally 127, 131–32
Giles, Warren 209
Gillenwater, Carden 192
Gilliam, Jim 166, 214, 219
Gionfriddo, Al 195–96
Giuliani, Tony 172, 176–77
Glossop, Al 188
Gomez, Ruben
Gonzalez, Mike 98
Gooch, Johnny 116, 119
Gorman, John 152
Graham, Jack 171, 195
Gray, Dick 218
Greenberg, Hank 184
Greene, Nelson 101, 108, 113
Greenfield, Kent 121
Greenwade, Tom 192
Gregg, Hal 179, 199–200
Griffin, Mike 7, 18, 20, 22, 29–30
Griffith, Bert 91–92, 97
Griffith, Clark 41
Griffith, Tommy 86, 88, 102–3, 114
Grim, John 16–17, 31, 33
Grimes, Burleigh 83, 85, 107, 111–12, 130, 142, 149, 152–57, 159, 163, 165, 177, 233
Grimm, Charlie 145, 162, 189, 216
Grissom, Lee 172, 179
Gudat, Marv 133
Gumbert, Ad 17

Haas, Bert 154, 169–70
Hack, Stan 228
Haddock, George 10, 14
Hall, Bob 50
Hallman, Bill 21
Hamey, Roy 200
Hamilton, Jimmy 134
Hamlin, Luke 152, 156, 177–79
Hamric, Bert 210
Hanlon, Ned 10, 13–14, 21, 24, 26–28, 30–33, 35–40, 42–44, 46–48, 50–51, 54–55
Hargreaves, Charlie 95, 112–13, 116, 119
Harkness, Tim 234
Harper, George 111
Harris, Bill 214

Index 253

Harris, Bucky 141
Harris, Joe 116–17
Hartje, Chris 167
Hartnett, Gabby 145
Hartsfield, Roy 218
Hassett, Buddy 149–50, 163
Hatten, Joe 176–77, 211–14
Hatton, Grady 220
Haughton, Percy 80
Haugstad, Phil 195
Hawley, Pink 17
Hayworth, Ray 164, 167, 188, 192
Hechinger, Mike 72
Heilmann, Harry 124
Heimach, Fred 127, 141
Hemming, George 6–7
Hempstead, Harry 79
Hendrick, Harvey 110, 129
Henley, Weldon 54
Henline, Butch 111–12, 116
Henry, Dutch 97
Henshaw, Roy 153–54, 157
Herman, Babe 105–6, 126–27, 131, 159
Herman, Billy 166, 173–74, 176, 178, 189, 194
Hermanski, Gene 180, 200, 207, 211–14
Herr, Eddie 159
Herring, Art 140–41, 143–44, 195
Herrmann, Garry 42, 72–73
Heusser, Ed 194, 205
Herzog, Buck 71
Heydler, John 110
Heydon, Mike 30–31
Hickman, Jim 81
Higbe, Kirby 170–71, 191, 195–96, 217
Higgins, Bob 68
High, Andy 93, 104, 107, 165, 234
Hill, Bill 33
Hoak, Don 201, 222–23, 228–29
Hodges, Gil 184, 196, 206, 218, 233
Hofferth, Stew 174, 194
Holke, Walter 87
Hollingsworth, Al 168, 172
Hollingsworth, Bonnie 97, 101, 108–9
Holmes, Jim 57
Holmes, Tommy 207, 215
Hood, Wally 91, 216
Hopp, Johnny 175, 206, 216
Hornsby, Rogers 126, 130, 133, 220
Householder, Ed 43
Howell, Harry 23–24, 35
Howell, Homer "Dixie" 179, 195–96, 217
Hoyt, Waite 135, 158, 165, 236
Hubbell, Bill 103, 108–9
Hudson, Johnny 173
Hughes, Jay 26

Hughes, Jim 227, 231
Hughes, Mickey 5
Hummel, John 50–51
Hungling, Bernie 94, 98
Hunter, Billy 205
Hunter, George 57
Hunter, Willard 230
Hurst, Tim 23
Hutcheson, Joe 140
Hutchinson, Ira 163–64, 172
Hutchinson, Fred 221
Hutson, Roy 108

Irwin, Arthur 31–32
Irwin, Charlie 38–39

Jacklitsch, Fred 43, 53
Jackson, Randy 228–29
Jacobson, Merwin 111
Jancse, John 223–24
Janvrin, Hal 92
Jeffcoat, George 150
Jennings, Hughie 14, 27, 32–33, 38
Jethroe, Sam 205, 207
Johnson, Ban 39
Johnson, Walter 119, 125, 176
Johnston, Jimmy 80, 106–7
Jones, Binky 99–100
Jones, Fielder 18, 37–38
Jones, Willie 222
Jordan, Dutch 53
Jordan, Jimmy 152
Jordan, Tim 52, 86
Jorgensen, Spider 153, 179, 201, 209–10
Joyce, Bill 11
Judge, Joe 133, 138, 141

Kampouris, Alex 172, 188
Kay, Bill 68
Kazanski, Ted 222
Keeler, Willie 12–14, 24, 27, 38, 236
Kelleher, John 82
Kellert, Frank 226–28
Kelley, Joe 28–29, 46
Kelley, Mike 108
Kelly, George 132–33
Kennedy, Bill 9, 10, 42, 111
Kennedy, Bob 236
Kent, Maury 68
Kilduff, Pete 87–88
Killefer, Wade 106
Killen, Frank 23
Kimball, Newt 167, 172, 179, 188
King, Clyde 189–90, 217
Kinslow, Tom 6–8, 17

Kipp, Fred 221
Kirkpatrick, Enos 69
Kitson, Frank 34–35
Knabe, Otto 81
Knetzer, Elmer 61
Knolls, Hub 54
Konetchy, Ed 87, 94, 97
Kopf, Larry 86
Korwan, Jim 21
Koufax, Sandy 175, 224
Koupal, Lou 115, 121
Koy, Ernie 159, 167, 169–70
Kraus, Jack 183
Krausse, Lew 163
Kress, Chuck 224
Krueger, Ernie 82–83

Labine, Clem 190, 227, 231
LaChance, Candy 22, 24–25, 36
Lamar, Bill 91, 94
LaMaster, Wayne 160, 164, 172
Landis, Kenesaw 99, 110, 160
Landrum, Joe 201
Larsen, Don 236
Lary, Lyn 168
Lasorda, Tom 205, 233, 236
Latham, Arlie 8
Latimer, Tacks 43, 36
Lavagetto, Harry "Cookie" 152–53, 156, 177–78, 196, 205, 210–13
Lazzeri, Tony 165, 236
Leadley, Bob 9
Lee, Hal 115, 125–26
Lehman, Ken 195, 235
LeJohn, Don 224
Lembo, Steve 190, 205
Lennox, Ed 57, 67
Leonard, Emil "Dutch" 139, 152
Leslie, Sam 133, 138, 149–50
Lillis, Bob 214
Lindell, Johnny 210
Lindsey, Jim 158, 165
Lindstrom, Freddie 154, 158
Littlefield, Dick 232–33
Livingston, Mickey 170–71, 207, 214
Loes, Billy 205, 230–31, 235
Loftus, Dick 108–9
Loftus, Tom 8, 38
Lohrman, Bill 186–89
Lombardi, Ernie 127–28, 131–32
Lombardi, Vic 179, 199–200
Lopez, Al 113, 127–28, 132, 139, 144–48, 152, 179
Lovett, Tom 5
Lucas, Ray 141–42, 148
Lumley, Harry 45, 58–59, 62

Lund, Don 192, 205
Luque, Dolf 122–23, 135

Mack, Connie 17, 37, 64, 76, 115, 128, 146
Macon, Max 167
MacPhail, Larry 157–160, 163–65, 167, 169–78, 195
Magee, Lee 86–87
Maglie, Sal 231, 235–36
Magoon, George 30
Mails, Duster 83
Malay, Charlie 49
Malinosky, Tom 154
Mallette, Mal 208
Mallon, Les 134
Malone, Lew 95
Maloney, Billy 52–53
Mamaux, Al 83–85
Mancuso, Gus 167, 171
Mantle, Mickey 204
Manush, Heinie 154, 164
Maranville, Rabbit 104, 108, 111
Marquard, Rube 79, 90–91, 101, 121, 125
Marriott, William 108
Marrow, Buck 161, 164
Marshall, Doc 58
Martin, Pepper 143
Mathews, Wid 229
Mathewson, Christy 83
Mattingly, Earl 134
Mauch, Gene 188, 195–96, 199, 201, 205
Maul, Al 28, 33
Mauriello, Ralph 218
Mauro, Carmen 214, 219
Mays, Willie 204
McCabe, Bill 91
McCarthy, Jack 52–53, 57
McCarthy, Joe 126–27, 130, 180
McCarthy, Johnny 144, 150
McCarthy, Tommy 18–19
McCarty, Lew 81–82
McCloskey, John 55
McCormick, Mike 203–205, 208
McCreery, Tom 37–38, 41, 46
McDevitt, Danny 218, 235
McDonald, John 161
McElveen, Pryor 57
McFarlan, Dan 30–31
McFarland, Chappie 55
McGann, Dan 29, 31–32, 40
McGinnity, Joe 26, 34, 40, 109
McGraw, Bob 108, 112–13, 129
McGraw, John 9, 14, 24, 28–29, 34–35, 39–40, 42, 45–46, 50, 79–81, 115, 126, 155
McGrew, Ted 163, 165

Index

McGuire, Deacon 16, 31–32
McGunnigle, Bill 5–6, 20
McIntire, Harry 49, 56, 62
McJames, Doc 29, 39
McKain, Archie 184–85
McKechnie, Bill 110, 148
McKeever, Ed 68, 102–3, 188
McKeever, Steve 68, 103, 122, 134, 142, 168
McKenna, Kit 25, 36
McLish, Cal 190, 195–96
McMahon, Sadie 20–21
McManus, Frank 49
McMillan, Roy 220
McMillan, Tommy 56, 65
McPhee, Bid 8, 39
McWeeny, Doug 122
Medicus, Henry 50, 68, 70–71
Medwick, Joe 159, 169, 171, 185–86, 195
Melton, Rube 181–83, 187, 201
Merkle, Fred 81–83, 236
Meusel, Irish 115
Meyer, Benny 70
Meyer, Lee 61
Meyer, Russ 219–20, 229
Meyers, Chief 80, 82–83
Mickens, Glenn 210
Miksis, Eddie 190, 202, 207, 211, 213–14
Miles, Don 233
Miljus, Johnny 95
Miller, Fred 65
Miller, Otto 60, 82, 93
Miller, Ralph 21, 26
Miller, Rod 236
Millies, Wally 154
Milliken, Bob 201
Mills, Buster 148
Minner, Paul 179, 205–6
Mitchell, Clarence 83, 96
Mitchell, Dale 233
Mitchell, Fred 48, 53, 88
Mitchell, Johnny 97
Mize, Johnny 150, 159, 175, 177, 216
Mooers, Eddie 181
Moore, Cy 118, 134–35
Moore, Dee 182, 188
Moore, Eddie 119–20, 127–28
Moore, Gene 148–49, 163, 167, 172, 182
Moore, Randy 146, 148, 158
Moore, Ray 201, 224, 231, 235
Moran, Herbie 66, 72
Moran, Pat 91
Morgan, Bobby 190, 205, 222
Morgan, Eddie 150–51, 158–59
Morrison, Johnny 120, 127
Moryn, Walt 205, 219, 228–29

Moser, Arnie 179
Moss, Ray 108, 110, 129
Mossor, Earl 210
Moulder, Glen 210
Mowrey, Mike 80–81, 83
Muckenfuss, Benjamin 21
Mullen, Billy 95, 101
Mulvey, Dearie 158
Mulvey, James 158, 220
Mungo, Van Lingle 124–25, 139, 144, 176–77, 213
Munns, Les 140
Murch, Simmy 57
Murphy, Charles 52–53, 62
Murray, Billy 58
Musial, Stan 175, 204
Myers, Hi 60, 96–97

Nahem, Sam 158, 169–70
Naylor, Earl 195
Neal, Charlie 210
Negray, Ron 208, 230, 234–35
Neis, Bernie 88, 102
Nelson, Rocky 214, 221, 224, 233
Nevel, Ernie 224
Newcombe, Don 193, 221
Newsom, Bobo 129, 161, 180–81, 184–86, 236
Newton, Doc 39
Nixon, Al 80, 89
Noonan, Pete 58
Nops, Jerry 27, 32–33, 35
Northen, Hub 65, 70
Nugent, Gerald 134, 170

O'Brien, Darby 5–6
O'Doul, Lefty 124–27, 138–39, 149, 236
Oeschger, Joe 74, 108
Olmo Luis 181, 188–89, 206–7
Olson, Ivy 72, 77–78, 101
O'Malley, Walter 188, 191, 210, 223, 232–33
O'Mara, Ollie 70, 72
O'Neil, Mickey 106–7, 112, 114
Orengo, Joe 186–87
O'Rourke, Frank 83, 85
O'Rourke, Tim 11
Ortiz, Roberto 188
Osborne, Tiny 98–99, 108
Ostermueller, Fritz 184–85, 188–89
Ott, Mel 186
Outlaw, Jimmy 163
Owen, Mickey 162, 171, 189, 207

Padgett, Don 179, 195
Pafko, Andy 211–12, 216, 218–19

Index

Page, Phil 144
Palica, Erv 192, 226–27, 230
Palmquist, Ed 214
Parham, Bob 130
Parks, Art 164, 166
Parmelee, Roy 150
Partridge, Jay 108
Pasquel, Jorge 207
Pastorius, Jim 51
Peacock, Johnny 192
Peck, Hal 182, 188
Pendleton, Jim 219–20
Pennock, Herb 140
Perkins, Charlie 144
Petty, Jesse, 108, 118
Pfeffer, Jeff 64, 70, 71, 88, 92
Pfund, Lee 190
Phelps, Babe 145, 147, 177–79
Phelps, Ray 120–21, 140
Phillips, Dee 207
Picinich, Val 119, 141
Pick, Eddie 109
Pignatano, Joe 205, 235
Pinkney, George 5–6
Pintar, John 11
Plitt, Norman 83, 115
Podbielan, Bud 195, 215
Podres, Johnny 214
Poffenberger, Boots 167
Polly, Nick 165
Poole, Ed 46–47
Posedel, Bill 158, 167
Potter, Dykes 165
Powers, Pat 11
Pressnell, Tot 156, 172

Quinn, Bob (J.A. Robert Quinn) 140–43, 145–46, 149, 164
Quinn, Jack 128, 141
Quinn, John

Rachunok, Steve 172
Racine, Hector 192
Rackley, Marv 179, 206
Radtke, Jack 154, 158
Ragan, Pat 64, 80
Rakow, Ed 236
Ramazzotti, Bob 172, 207
Ramsdell, Willie 209
Ray, Johnnie 164
Redmond, Harry 61
Reese, Pee Wee 157, 165–66, 171, 178–79, 196, 198, 201, 218, 220, 222, 231, 233–34
Reidy, Bill 44
Reis, Bobby 146–47

Reiser, Pete 160, 191, 196, 203–4, 213
Reisling, Doc 49
Reulbach, Ed 62, 64, 71, 80
Rhem, Flint 182
Rhiel, Billy 127
Richards, Paul 111, 135
Richardson, Danny 11, 15
Richardson, Jim 127
Rickey, Branch 136, 141, 160, 171, 181–189, 191–93, 196–202, 205–6, 210, 213, 230
Rickey, Branch, Jr. 192, 199
Riconda, Harry 109, 118
Riggert, Joe 72, 75
Riggs, Lew 171, 195
Rigney, Bill 233
Ripple, Jimmy 167, 172
Ritter, Lew 40, 43
Rizzo, Johnny 179
Roberts, Jim 101
Robinson, Jackie 166, 192–93, 196–200, 202, 209, 218–20, 223, 228, 232–34
Robinson, Wilbert 24, 64, 71–74, 76–82, 85, 87–88, 91, 94, 96, 98–100, 102–4, 107, 109–14, 116–21, 122–26, 128–30, 140, 143–144, 162, 176–77, 180
Robison, Frank 36
Roche, Ray 179
Rodriguez, Hector 214
Roe, Preacher 199–201, 211, 223, 225
Roebuck, Ed 208, 227
Roettger, Oscar 111
Rogers, Lee 164
Rojek, Stan 168, 198
Romano, Jim 195
Rose, Pete 216
Roseboro, John 218, 235
Rosen, Goody 172, 188–89, 195
Rosenfeld, Max 141
Ross, Don 184
Rowe, Ken 230
Rowe, Schoolboy 182, 188
Rowell, Bama 202–3
Roy, Luther 121, 127
Rucker, Nap 54–55, 63, 88, 91, 93, 113, 117, 120, 124, 129
Ruether, Dutch 90, 101
Rufer, Rudy 215
Rush, Andy 101, 108
Rush, Bob 212
Rusie, Amos 74
Russell, Jim 206–7
Russo, Marius 155
Ruth, Babe 94, 151, 156
Rutherford, Johnny 201
Ryan, Connie 209

Index

Ryan, Jack (catcher) 21, 26
Ryan, Jack (pitcher) 65–67

Saffell, Tom 233
Saigh, Fred 214
Sain, Johnny 207, 216
Sanders, Ray 202–3
Sandlock, Mike 189
Sauer, Ed 206–7
Sawyer, Eddie 211
Sayles, Bill 186–87
Scanlan, Doc 47–48, 67, 71
Schardt, Bill 68
Schenz, Hank 207
Schliebner, Dutch 97
Schmandt, Ray 83, 87, 96–97
Schmitz, Andrew 188, 191
Schmitz, Johnny 211–12, 216
Schneiberg, Frank 63
Schott, Gene 168
Schreiber, Paul 95
Schultz, Howie 187, 197–98
Schultz, Joe 75, 79
Schupp, Ferdie 92, 94
Schwegman, Harry 223–24
Scott, Dick 221
Scott, Jack 111
Seats, Tom 190
Sebring, Jimmy 59
Selee, Frank 20, 44
Sewell, Luke 209
Sexauer, Elmer 207
Sharman, Bill 219
Shaute, Joe 129, 141
Shawkey, Bob 126
Shea, Merv 165
Sheckard, Jimmy 21, 25–26, 34, 38, 46, 52–53
Sheehan, Tom 74, 161, 191
Sheehan, Tommy 56–57, 61
Sherlock, Vince 147–48, 154
Sherry, Larry 221
Sherry, Norm 210
Shindle, Billy 13–14, 23
Shoch, George 11, 21
Shotton, Burt 125, 134, 195, 197, 201, 203–4, 210, 221, 226
Shuba, George 190, 200, 219
Siebert, Dick 135, 148, 154
Sington, Fred 164, 167–68
Sisler, George 192
Skaff, Frank 158
Slade, Gordon 123, 136–37
Slattery, Jack 115
Slaughter, Enos 175
Smith, Aleck 25, 30–32, 34–35

Smith, Charley 236
Smith, Dick 236
Smith, George 85, 96, 101
Smith, Germany 5, 8, 19–20
Smith, Happy 62–63
Smith, Jack 230
Smith, John 191, 233
Smith, Red 70, 73
Smith, Sherry 75, 94–95
Smith, Tony 62
Smyth, Red 80, 83
Smythe, Harry 144
Snider, Duke 184, 188, 200, 211, 214, 218
Snow, Graeme 79
Snyder, Jack 82–83
Solomon, George 68
Sothern, Denny 129, 135
Southworth, Billy 202, 204, 216
Speaker, Tris 29, 95
Spencer, Roy 158, 165
Spooner, Karl 214, 222
Stack, Eddie 67, 71
Stainback, Tuck 164, 167, 172
Staller, George 179
Stallings, George 5, 73, 95
Standaert, Jerry 101
Stanky, Eddie 166, 189, 197, 202–4
Stark, Dolly 68
Steele, Bill 75
Steele, Elmer 67
Steelman, Farmer 36, 39
Stein, Ed 9
Stengel, Casey 59, 65–66, 78, 83–84, 137, 141–43, 145–50, 152, 154, 163, 177, 216, 236
Stevens, Ed 179, 197–98
Stewart, Stuffy 95
Stock, Milt 98, 104, 111
Stoneham, Horace 186
Stovall, George 67
Stovey, Harry 12
Strang, Sammy 41, 49
Street, Gabby 129
Stricklett, Elmer, 49
Stripp, Joe 131–32, 157, 164, 168
Suhr, Gus 172, 179
Sukeforth, Clyde 131–32, 192, 197
Sullivan, Billy 182, 201
Sullivan, Ted 89
Summers, Bill 228
Sutton, Larry 59, 63, 67, 71, 73, 86, 93–94, 117, 124
Sweetland, Les 138
Swift, Bill 172

Index

Tamulis, Vito 160–61, 170–71, 179
Tatum, Tommy 172, 179, 201
Taylor, Danny 133, 154
Taylor, Zack 88–89, 106–7, 127, 147
Teed, Dick 201
Temple, Johnny 220
Tener, John 77
Tepsic, Joe 195
Terry, Adonis 5–6, 10
Terry, Bill 138–39, 142, 155
Terwilliger, Wayne 211–12, 218
Thielman, Henry 42–43, 46
Thomas, Fay 121, 135
Thomas, Ray 165
Thompson, Don 207, 219
Thompson, Fresco 111, 125–27, 217, 224
Thompson, Tim 201, 233
Thomson, Bobby 212, 221
Thurston, Sloppy 121, 140
Tierney, Cotton 102, 108–9
Tinker, Joe 72
Todd, Al 167
Tooley, Bert 69
Torgeson, Earl 219
Tracewski, Dick 221
Travis, Cecil 184
Traynor, Pie 152
Treadway, George 13–14
Tucker, Tommy 22–23
Tyson, Ty 114

Valentinetti, Vito 230, 236
Valo, Elmer 234
Van Buren, Deacon 47
Vance, Dazzy 10, 93–94, 111, 113, 118, 125, 127, 130, 136–37, 148
Van Cuyk, Chris 195
Van Cuyk, Johnny 195
Vaughan, Arky 177–79, 184–85, 205, 210
Veeck, Bill, Jr. 194
Vickers, Rube 42–43, 49
Von der Ahe, Chris 21
Von der Horst, Harry 24, 33
Vosmik, Joe 172, 180

Waddell, Rube 56
Wade, Ben 172, 210, 222–23
Wagner, Al 22–23
Wagner, Bull 70
Wagner, Honus 23, 45, 85
Wagner, J. Earl 32
Walker, Dixie 166–67, 196, 199–200
Walker, Rube 211–12
Wall, Joe 40
Walters, Bucky 170
Waner, Lloyd 188, 190
Waner, Paul 180, 188, 190
Ward, Chuck 83, 85
Ward, John 6–8, 11–13, 20, 29
Ward, Preston 190, 205–6
Warner, Jack 121, 134–35
Warwick, Carl 236
Wasdell, Jimmy 172, 177–79
Washburn, George 183–84
Watkins, George 154, 158
Webber, Les 180, 194
Weil, Sidney 131
Weyhing, Gus 36
Wheat, Lee 233
Wheat, Mack 79, 90
Wheat, Zack 59, 63, 73, 84, 90, 115
White, Bill 232
Whiting, Jesse 54
Whitman, Dick 182, 206, 210–11, 224
Whitted, Possum 95
Wicker, Kemp 167, 179
Wilhelm, Kaiser 55–56
Williams, Dick 201, 210–11, 219, 232
Williams, Stan 224
Williams, Ted 203
Williams, Woody 172
Wills, Maury 214
Wilson, Bob 210
Wilson, Hack 130–31, 138, 144
Wilson, Jimmie 111, 175
Wilson, Tex 101, 108, 113
Winford, Jim 161, 172
Winsett, Tom 151, 164
Witt, Whitey 108
Wojey, Pete 201, 230
Wood, Ken 221
Wright, Glenn 118, 120, 123, 127, 144
Wrigley, Zeke 36
Wyatt, Whit 161, 191, 195

Yarrison, Rube 99
Yawkey, Tom 165
Yeager, Joe 21
Yingling, Earl 67, 72
York, Frank 122–23, 125–26, 130, 132
Young, Dick 222
Young, Pep 171–72

Zachary, Tom 144, 154
Zimmer, Don 208, 234
Zimmerman, Bill 80
Zimmerman, Eddie 65

www.ingramcontent.com/pod-product-compliance
Lightning Source LLC
Chambersburg PA
CBHW032035300426
44117CB00009B/1068